William James Henderson

How Music Developed

William James Henderson

How Music Developed

ISBN/EAN: 9783337337643

Printed in Europe, USA, Canada, Australia, Japan

Cover: Foto ©Thomas Meinert / pixelio.de

More available books at **www.hansebooks.com**

HOW MUSIC DEVELOPED

A Critical and Explanatory Account of the Growth of Modern Music

By Wm J^{ames} HENDERSON

Author of "WHAT IS GOOD MUSIC?"

LONDON
JOHN MURRAY, Albemarle Street, W.
1899

TO

CHARLES BAMBURGH

Table of Contents

Chapter		Page
I.	The Beginning of Modern Music	1
II.	Harmony, Notation, and Measure	12
III.	The Birth of Counterpoint	23
IV.	The Golden Age of Church Counterpoint	38
V.	Progress of Popular Music	54
VI.	The Simplification of Music	66
VII.	The Evolution of the Piano	83
VIII.	The Evolution of Piano Playing	101
IX.	Climax of the Polyphonic Piano Style	116
X.	Monophonic Style and the Sonata	126
XI.	Evolution of the Orchestra	147
XII.	The Classic Orchestral Composers	158
XIII.	The Romantic Orchestral Composers	171
XIV.	The Development of Chamber Music	186
XV.	The Birth of Oratorio	199
XVI.	Work of Handel and Bach	208
XVII.	Haydn and Mendelssohn	220

CONTENTS

Chapter		Page
XVIII.	The Birth of Opera	234
XIX.	Italian Opera to Handel's Time	253
XX.	Italian Opera to Verdi	276
XXI.	Beginnings of French Opera	290
XXII.	Reforms of Gluck	312
XXIII.	Meyerbeer and his Influence	324
XXIV.	German Opera to Mozart	336
XXV.	Weber and Beethoven	348
XXVI.	Wagner and the Music Drama	357
XXVII.	The Lessons of Musical History	380
Index		395

How Music Developed

Chapter I

The Beginning of Modern Music

Descent of the Roman Chant from the kithara songs of the Romans and thence from those of the Greeks — First appearance of modern melody — Steps toward the formation of a musical system — Ambrosian and Gregorian chants — Their character — Nokter Balbulus and sequences — Spread of the Roman chant — Nature of music at this period.

IN reading any history of the development of music as an art one must ever bear in mind the fact that music was also developing at the same time as a popular mode of expression, and that the two processes were separate. The cultivation of modern music as an art was begun by the medieval priests of the Roman Catholic Church, who were endeavoring to arrange a liturgy for their service, and it is due to this fact that for several centuries the only artistic music was that of the Church, and that it was controlled by influences which barely touched the popular songs of the times. In the course of years the two kinds of music came together, and important changes were made. But any account of the development of modern music as an art is compelled to begin with the story of the medieval chant.

In the beginning the chants of the Christian Church, from which the medieval chant was developed, were without system. They were a heterogeneous mass of music derived wholly from sources which chanced to be near at hand. The early Christians in Judea must naturally have borrowed their music from the worship of their forefathers, who were mostly Jews. The Christians in Greece naturally adapted Greek music to their requirements, while those in Rome made use of the Roman kithara (lyre) songs, which in their turn were borrowed from the Greeks. Christ and the apostles at the Last Supper chanted one of the old Hebrew psalms. Saint Paul speaks also of "hymns and spiritual songs," by one of which designations he certainly means the hymns of the early Christians founded on Roman lyre songs. It is also on record that the Christian communities of Alexandria as early as 180 A. D. were in the habit of repeating the chant of the Last Supper with an accompaniment of flutes, and Pliny, the Younger (62–110 A. D.), describes the custom of singing hymns to the glory of Christ.

BEGINNING OF MODERN MUSIC 3

The psalms in the early Church were chanted antiphonally; that is, one verse was sung by one part of the congregation and answered by another with the next verse, or they were chanted by priest and congregation alternately. Of course there could not have been any high artistic endeavor in such music, because it must have been within the capacity of the least skilled performers. There could not have been any fixed system in the Church until its various branches in the vast Roman empire were unified under a Christian emperor, Constantine (306-337 A. D.). Under him art and architecture began to serve the Church, and it is about this time that we begin to discover attempts at the formation of a system in church music. Four distinct steps are traceable:—

First. A. D. 314.— Pope Sylvester founded singing-schools at Rome.

Second. A. D. 350. — Flavian and Diodorus made antiphonal chanting of the psalms a required part of the church service at Antioch.

Third. A. D. 367. — The Council of Laodicea forbade congregational singing, and confined the service to a trained choir.

Fourth. A. D. 384 (about). — St. Ambrose brought together the inharmonious elements in the church liturgy and formulated a general system of chanting known as the Ambrosian chant.

4   HOW MUSIC DEVELOPED

The foundation of singing-schools produced choristers who were able to meet the requirements of the improved music, for that was beyond the narrow powers of the early congregations. The reader will readily see how the first three steps toward the formation of a system were logical. But differences in practice naturally crept in, and the work of Ambrose appears to have been one of regulation. He founded his system on four of the ancient Greek scales, which were, of course, at the base of all the Greek and Roman tunes then used in the Church. It is unnecessary to go into any extended account of Greek music in order to get an idea of the character of the Ambrosian chant, but it is needful to give the subject some consideration, because Greek music influenced modern music for several centuries. All modern major scales are formed thus : two whole intervals followed by one-half interval (a semitone), then three whole intervals followed by a half. For example, take the scales of C and G : —

The Greek scales were formed on a wholly different principle. The foundation of the system was the tetrachord, which always contained, as its name implies, four notes. Between some two of these there was always a half-interval, and the scale was named according to the position of that semitone. The Doric scale had the semitone at the beginning of each tetrachord, the Phrygian in the middle, and the Lydian at the top, thus: —

The reader will understand that every scale was divided into two tetrachords, each having its semitone in the same position. There were, of course, several other scales, but these are sufficient to illustrate the subject.

The peculiarity of the sound of chants founded on these ancient scales to our modern ears is what we call the "lack of tonality." Our scales are all determined by the semitone between the seventh and eighth notes, called the leading note. The scale of G, for instance, cannot exist without the F sharp. Our ears have been trained to expect that progression, and so these old Greek scales do not seem to us to be in any key at all, and when we wish to describe a tune that has apparently no beginning, end, or rhythm, we say it sounds like a chant. For several centuries all modern music written by the scientific composers suffered from this lack of tonality, while much of the popular music of the people was written in the modern major and minor keys. Any musician will see that the old Lydian scale was our scale of C major. The ancient Æolian scale was almost the same as our scale of A minor. From these two our modern scales developed themselves among the people who were not busy trying to build church liturgies out of Greek music.

Not much is known about the musical character of the Ambrosian chant except that contemporary writers regarded it as very sweet and solemn. One important fact has come down to us, namely, that the Ambrosian

BEGINNING OF MODERN MUSIC 7

chant was metrical. This means that it followed the prosodial quantity of the syllables in the Latin text of the liturgy. A long syllable had a long note, and a short syllable a short note. From this peculiarity the chant obtained the name of *cantus firmus*, or fixed chant. It was, however, speedily merged in what is called the Gregorian chant. This has generally been attributed to Pope Gregory (590–604 A. D.); but recent investigations go to prove that he did little beyond issuing rules as to its use and for its regulation. The church chant, however, was changed in character in the time of Gregory, and one of the most fruitful alterations was the abandonment of its metrical character. The tones no longer had a determined length; and this abolished from the church music of the time the last vestige of rhythm. It furthermore left the singers free to do as they pleased, and so gave rise to abuses which seemed to be injurious to music, but which really led to good results, as we shall see. In form, the Gregorian chant was divided into five parts: the "intonation," which was the introductory phrase of the first half of the verse; the "recitation" of the principal part of that half on a single note; the "mediation," which finished the first half of the verse and formed the connecting link between it and the second half; the "recitation," which began the second half; and the "termination," which ended the verse.

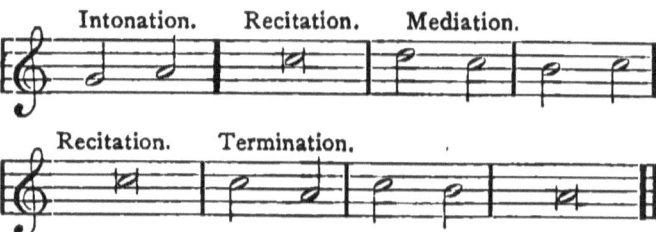

Gregory arranged the mass in its present form, and prescribed a special introit for each psalm, and probably one for each division of the mass. The famous old anonymous hymns, the Te Deum, Magnificat, Benedictus, etc., had taken their place in the church service in its very earliest days; and the mass had gradually been formed by selection and arrangement of these. Another form which gradually grew up in the Church was the Sequence. This had its origin in a desire to allow the congregation more opportunity to take part in the musical service. In their oldest and purest form these sequences consisted of ornamental passages intoned on a single vowel, — as the final " a " of " jubila." These sequences illustrate in a striking manner that freedom from control of text which came so conspicuously into music in Gregory's time. This freedom, while it led to abuses

BEGINNING OF MODERN MUSIC 9

of the church ritual, gave music a certain amount of independence as an art, and enabled it to develop more rapidly than it could have done had it been tied fast to the text. Nokter Balbulus, a monk of the famous convent of St. Gall, Switzerland, is said to have popularized the sequences in the ninth century by writing thirty-five special ones. Some of these are still used in the Roman Church. The convent of St. Gall, to which Nokter belonged, was a famous centre of musical culture in the eighth, ninth, and tenth centuries. The writing of special words for sequences was followed by others than Nokter; and in the end these reduced themselves to these five well-known texts: Dies Iræ, Stabat Mater, Victimæ Paschali, Veni Sancte Spiritus, and Lauda Sion.

The Roman chant soon spread through Europe. The successor of Gregory was acknowledged by the Western nations as the Supreme Head of the united Church, and this, of course, tended to a general use of the same ritual. In 604 Roman singers were sent to England, and in 660 monks went to teach the Gregorian chant in Brittany. Paris had become the capital of France not long before that, and the Gallic service was now remodelled on that of Rome. The Roman ritual was introduced into Germany by Saint

Boniface in 744, and it was probably made known at St. Gall about the same time. Charlemagne, in the eighth century, founded schools of music on Gregory's plan at Dijon, Cambray, Lyons, Orléans, and other French cities, and also at Regensburg, Würzburg, Mainz, and other German places.

The general introduction of the Gregorian chant established the melodic basis of modern music. It will be well for the reader to bear in mind that the three elementary constituents of music are melody, harmony, and rhythm. Melody is produced by the successive sounding of single tones of different pitch. Harmony is produced by the simultaneous sounding of single notes of different pitch. When those notes are united according to rule we call the result a chord. Rhythm is the regular recurrence of long and short beats. Now, if the reader has comprehended the account given of the early Roman chant, he will perceive that it embodied only one of the elements of music, namely, melody. There was no harmony, because everything was sung in one part. It was simply a plain chant; and when the organ first came into use to accompany it, the instrument played the same succession of single notes as the voices sang. This fact must be kept clearly in mind in order to understand the next steps in the development of modern music. In the beginning there was only melody; and that was like the earth before the creation, without form and void. There was no musical rhythm in either the Ambrosian chant, which followed the prosodial quantity of the words, nor in the Gregorian, which did not follow it. The text was prose; consequently it did not have a regular recurrence of long and short syllables, as poetry does, and therefore the music, following the text, could not have rhythm. All that existed in the beginning of the modern tone art was the raising and lowering of the voice through a certain number of intervals. How harmony and rhythm made their appearance in the early stages of the art, and what forms they took, must next be related.

Chapter II

Harmony, Notation, and Measure

The Organum of Hucbald — Use of combinations disagreeable to modern ears — Appearance of rhythm — Work of Franco, of Cologne — Establishment of Dual and Triple Measure — Introduction of notes to represent sounds of different duration.

IN the growth of modern music the second step was the introduction of harmony. The simultaneous sounding of notes of different pitch in combinations called chords is so essential a part of the music of to-day that even the uneducated mind has difficulty in conceiving a tune as wholly dissociated from the coloring influences of its harmony. Every schoolboy is accustomed to hearing melodies with what he calls a " bass " (an accompaniment founded on chords), and in the commonest music-hall songs the familiar harmonies are the results of centuries of experiment among the ecclesiastical fathers of modern music. It is difficult for us to understand that there was a time when harmony was unknown to musicians, but such is the case;

and the first experiments resulted in the use of combinations which sound intolerable to our ears, while some of those which we regard as the most familiar and useful were deemed unbearable by some of the early authorities. For example, no modern chord can be formed without the third, *i.e.*, the third whole note above the key-note. In the key of C that is E; in G it is B, thus: Yet for several centuries after harmony began to be employed that particular combination was forbidden, so that it was impossible to write the common chord of C major or of G major or of any other modern major key. The result was that for several hundred years music developed along lines not those of chord harmony, the first rude experiments at which early gave way to what is called counterpoint. What that system was we shall see in good time, but we must now give our attention to the early attempts at harmony.

The origin of modern harmony is wrapped in obscurity. It is believed that the Greeks knew something about chords and perhaps used a few simple ones in playing accompaniments on the lyre. But they made no extended study of them, and the early fathers, who founded their system on Greek music, had nothing to learn in this matter from the Greeks. All steps in the development of modern music have been the result of long processes of growth, and it cannot be doubted that many experiments in harmony were made before the first treatise on the subject was written. The first records of harmony are found in an old work called "Enchiridion Musicæ," and they speak of a system called Organum or Diaphony, attributed to Hucbald, a Benedictine monk of St. Armand, in Flanders, near the close of the tenth century. Hucbald appears to have studied Pythagoras's musical system, in which intervals between notes were measured according to the laws of acoustics by the number of vibrations made by each note in a second. Hucbald, finding that certain intervals had a mathematical ratio, decided that they must make concords, and he founded his system of harmony on that theory. He used the intervals of the fourth, the fifth, and the octave. The fourth is the fourth note of the major scale in ascending, the fifth the fifth note, and the octave the eighth, or the recurrence of the key-note. To make this matter clearer, let me state that modern scientists have decided that the C below the staff, in the treble clef, has 256 vibrations a minute. The next C

HARMONY, NOTATION, MEASURE 15

above has 512, just double. The F of this scale, which is the fourth, has 384. This is the sum of the first C increased by one-half of itself. Consequently C and F make a scientific concord and a musical one, too. But there is hardly anything more disagreeable to the modern ear than a series of consecutive fourths. Yet Hucbald thought that such a series must be scientifically correct, and that it ought, therefore, to make good music. So he wrote such harmonies as these:—

Sit glo - - ri - a Do - mi - ni in sæ - cu - la.

This is very unpleasant to modern ears, yet it is not quite so bad as a series of fifths. When Hucbald wished to write in four parts he simply repeated the two treble parts in the bass an octave lower. And when he wrote in three parts he simply "doubled" the lower note of his fourth or fifth in the octave above, which is a process also forbidden in modern part-writing because it makes two parts the same in melodic progression. Hucbald also employed a form of harmony in which the lowest note always remained the same. This was what we now call a "drone bass," such as is heard in the bagpipe, and it was certainly more flexible than the other kind because it admitted of the use of other intervals than the fourth and fifth. But the idea of writing in more than one part, once having appeared in music, developed itself gradually. All the earliest harmonic combinations sound ugly to our ears because of the difference in the character of the old scales adapted from Greek music for the Church and that of our scale. If the harmonists of those early days had been using our scale, no doubt they would have discovered how to write fine chords. They did, in the course of time, hit upon some of the combinations now used, and so the foundations of modern harmony were laid. But the modern style of writing did not come into use for several centuries after Hucbald's time.

The next element of music which made its appearance was rhythm. This came about through the improvements in notation and the practice of singers. It seems that after learning to add a second part to the *cantus firmus*, or chant, the singers, who were acquiring considerable dexterity in their art, began to ornament the additional part. This addition of ornaments was called the art of descant, because it was descanting upon a given theme. The singers all took to it with de-

HARMONY, NOTATION, MEASURE 17

light because it gave them fine opportunities for the display of their voices and of their musical skill. In some parts of France and the Netherlands this practice became a sort of mania. The voice which carried the chant was called the tenor, from the Latin *teneo*, "I hold." The other voice added an ornamental part *above* the chant, and as there was no measure in music, the two parts seldom came out together at the end. As long as the voices had moved in parallel fourths or fifths it was not difficult for them to keep together, but with the descanter singing two or more notes to every one of the *cantus firmus* it was quite impossible for them to do so. No one knows just when this art of descant entered into music, but it is certain that it was known some time before the close of the twelfth century, for it was about then that Franco, of Cologne, made successful attempts to systematize notation, and in doing so regulated the measure of music.

The earliest form of notation of which we have any knowledge is called the Neume notation. These Neumes were much like Greek accents in some respects, and in others resembled a sort of shorthand. All that could be accomplished by them was an indication of the direction in which the voice was to move, whether up or down, and of the number of notes which it was to pass. In Hucbald's day a series of horizontal lines, like our musical staff (but containing many more lines) was used. The names of the notes were written opposite the ends of the spaces between the lines, and then each syllable of the text was written in the space belonging to the note to which it was to be sung. Short lines were drawn upward or downward, as the case might be, between each syllable of one part so that that part could be followed. Another system in use in Hucbald's time, and even later, was arranged this way, the letters representing the tones: —

C—D   F—E—D   G—F   E—D
Lau - de dig - num   ca - nat sanc - tum.

As time passed on it became evident that there ought to be some way of indicating a fixed pitch from which the notes were to start. So a line was employed and the Neumes were written in a definite manner with relation to it. If the line was red, the chant was in the key of F, and all melodies ended on F. If the line was yellow, the key was C. In the eleventh century both lines were used at the same time, and the certainty of the meaning of the Neumes became greater. Afterward

Guido, of Arezzo, a famous teacher and theorist, who died in 1050, added two more lines, and thus came into existence a four-line staff. The character of the Neumes themselves had undergone many alterations, until, in Guido's time, they began to look a little like modern notes. But still there was no rhythm in the ecclesiastical music, and no way of representing it in notation. Franco advocated the introduction of measure into church music. He did not, of course, invent it, for it already existed in the popular songs and dances of the people, and had existed in them from the earliest times.

Franco was the first theorist to record the distinction between dual and triple time. The reader who is unacquainted with musical science should learn that the rhythms of music are like those of poetry. Instead of poetic feet, music has " measures " separated by vertical lines drawn through the staff, and called " bars." Measures are often called bars. The musical measure corresponds to the poetic foot. A bar with two beats in it is like a foot of two syllables, except that in music the accent is normally always on the first beat. A bar with three beats is like a dactyl, one accented and two unaccented syllables, or beats. Dual time, or measure, corresponds to a poetic rhythm made up of two-syllable feet; triple time to one of three-syllable feet. A polka is in dual time; a waltz, in triple time. Franco first explained these points, and insisted that triple ought to be used in church music for the naïve reason that its three beats in one bar made it resemble the perfection of the Holy Trinity, three persons in one God. He made many improvements in harmony, among others recognizing the third, already described, as a concord, though not a perfect one. Another important feature of Franco's teaching was his advocacy of contrary motion of parts. The manner of writing practised by Hucbald prescribed what is called parallel motion; that is, the melody of the *cantus firmus* and that of the descant always rose or fell together. If the one ascended one interval the other did so, too. Contrary motion permits the parts to move in opposite directions, and this makes it possible to avoid such disagreeable arrangements as consecutive fourths or fifths, and so leads the way to a richer and more beautiful harmony. Others had already practised what Franco preached in regard to this matter, so the most significant part of his work was that which dealt with measure. In order to write the measured music it was necessary to have notes representing sounds of different duration, and these notes Franco either invented or adopted. Here are the four notes which he used:—

Longa.   Brevis.   Maxima or   Semibrevis.
                  Duplex Longa.

These names mean "long," "short," "double long," and "half short." The short note had half the duration of the long, and the duplex longa double it, while the semibrevis was half the length of the short note. We still have notes called breve and semibreve.

We have now seen how melody, harmony, and rhythm entered the process of development of modern music. But I have already called attention to the fact that the early medieval composers had no conception of a tune founded on subservient harmony, such as is now familiar to every one. They got their ideas as to the plan of composition from the art of descant, which consisted, as I have tried to explain, in adding an ornamental part to a selected chant. It became an essential of music in those early days that this second part should be melodious in itself. When the early composers began to write in more than two parts, they still preferred the style in which every part was a melody in itself. In our modern music the parts which constitute the harmonic accompaniment of a melody are not necessarily melodious in themselves, as any one can easily see who listens to the accompaniment of a popular song. The early church composers knew nothing about that kind of writing. They did not have instrumental accompaniment at all. Even after the organ began to be used, it simply played the same notes that the voices sang. The compositions were written wholly for voices, and each voice-part was a melody in itself, and all sounding together produced harmonious results. This kind of writing is still employed at times. For instance, in the finale of "Die Meistersinger" overture, five different melodies are heard at the same time. This method of composition is called "polyphonic;" and we have now reached the period at which the art of descant developed into the art of counterpoint, upon which polyphonic writing rests.

Chapter III

The Birth of Counterpoint

The great French school of contrapuntists — What counterpoint is, and how it began — Canons and the famous "Sumer is icumen in" — Character of the French music — The masses of Machaut and Tournay — The Gallo-Belgic school and Dufay's improvements.

THERE is one peculiarity of the early attempts at writing in several melodious parts which must now be brought to the attention of the reader, and which is very difficult to explain to a person not versed in musical laws. Instead of writing free melodies to accompany the fixed chants, the early composers took up the practice of making the tune serve as its own accompaniment by the employment of a number of ingenious devices, all included in the art of counterpoint. I shall presently endeavor to explain the nature of this style of writing; but as it began in France, we must first note the historical facts in connection with the development of musical art in that country. The reader will remember that Charlemagne established schools for the cultivation of the Roman chant in many French towns. History shows us that the connection between France and the Roman Church grew closer and closer until, under Philip the Fair, the State dominated; and in the beginning of the fourteenth century the papal court was removed by the king to Avignon. In the twelfth century the University of Paris became the centre of study in Europe. It was natural in these circumstances that the cultivation of Roman Catholic church music should have flourished in Paris, and that, about 1100 A. D., a distinct school of French composers should have developed. This school flourished until 1370, and there has descended to us a knowledge of nearly five hundred composers who belonged to it. It would be impossible and useless to attempt to tell the reader all about these composers. What I desire to do is to point out what this school accomplished in the development of music.

Counterpoint is to-day the art of constructing two or more melodies which can be sung or played simultaneously without breaking the rules of harmony. Originally, however, it was the art of adding parts above or below a part already selected. It originated, as we have seen, in the practice of the descanters.

A part improvised by a descanter came to be called *contrapunctus a mente* (a counterpoint out of the head), while an additional part written by a composer was called *contrapunctus a penna* (a counterpoint from the pen). As musicians acquired skill in the construction of these additional parts, they began to introduce new devices, and to write with greater and greater freedom. The more free their writing was, the further it tended to depart from parallel motion. In the course of time some one hit upon the musical device called "imitation," which means the repetition in a secondary part (say the bass) of some passage already heard in the principal part (the treble) while that principal part is still going on. The result of this device is that one portion of a melody is made to serve as the second voice to another portion of it. Who first hit upon this device, no one knows; but the earliest example of it which has been preserved is found in the " Posui adjutorum " of Perotin, one of the first of the French school of writers. Here is the passage; and by giving it careful study the reader will be able to understand the fundamental principle of canon, fugue, and all the polyphonic forms:

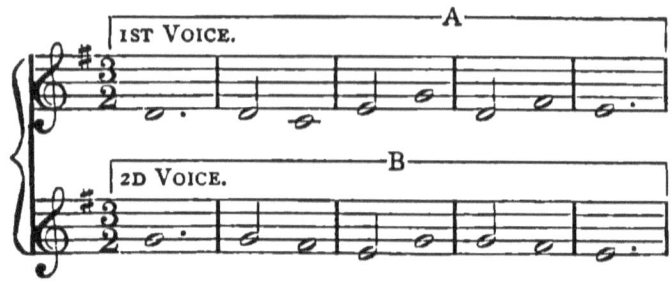

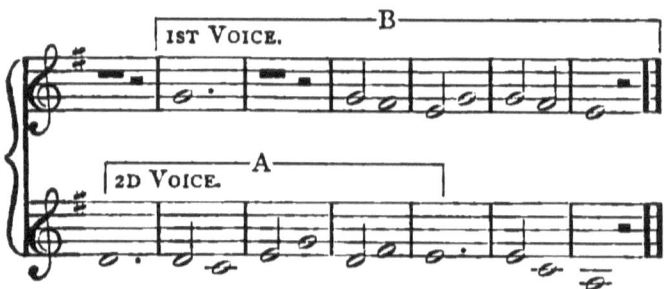

I think that even a reader who is not a musician can understand this. A is the first half of a melody, and B is the second half. While the first voice is singing the first half, the second voice sings the second half as the alto part of the first half. In order to make the first half act as alto in the second half, the composer had to push the second voice one bar ahead of the first voice, and then to add three extra notes to A in order to make a conclusion to his alto part. There are two imitations in this bit: the second half of the part sung by the first voice imitates the

THE BIRTH OF COUNTERPOINT 27

first half of the second-voice part, and the second half of the second-voice part imitates the first half of the first-voice part.

By extending and developing such imitation as this, composers came to write in "double counterpoint," which means the construction of two parts in such a way that their different portions can be transferred from one to the other just as they are in the selection from Perotin. The reader will see at once that composing in this manner required a great deal of calculation, and was a constant tax on the ingenuity of the musician. In its early stages it prevented any attempt at making music expressive, and reduced composition to a mere exercise of scientific skill. But it forced the composers to a close study of the materials of their art, and they acquired a great mastery over them and constantly learned more and more about the possibilities of music. Double counterpoint, which is at the foundation of the most rigid forms of polyphonic writing, was generally known in the French school at least as early as the thirteenth century, but the example from Perotin seems to show that at least some of the composers knew it much earlier. This might account for the existence of the celebrated example of early English polyphony, a "canon" called "Sumer is icumen in."

This was discovered by Sir John Hawkins, who wrote a history of music in 1776. Its manuscript was copied by a monk of Reading, John of Forneste, in 1228, and it must have been composed shortly before that time. The fact that Walter Odington, an Englishman, wrote a treatise on music in 1230, when the only famous school was that of Paris, leads me to believe that these early English composers were disciples of the French. But it is certain that the composer of "Sumer is icumen in" was a greater master of counterpoint than his teachers, because this "canon" is the finest specimen of polyphonic writing that has come down to us from those early times. Here is its beginning:—

THE BIRTH OF COUNTERPOINT

THE BIRTH OF COUNTERPOINT

THE BIRTH OF COUNTERPOINT 33

I urge the reader to give careful attention to the remarkable interweaving of the first four voice parts. At the fifth bar of the melody, in the first voice, the second voice enters with the beginning of the air. When the second voice reaches the fifth bar of the air, the third voice comes in, and at the same time the first voice begins the second half of the melody. When the third voice reaches the fifth bar of the first half of the air, the fourth voice comes in, and the second voice begins the second half. And so it goes on, the entrances always being made according to the rule established at the start, and each voice singing the tune without the alteration of a single interval to make it fit into the scheme. Rigid imitation of this kind is called "canon." In this particular canon the two lowest voices have a bass in two parts, written in double counterpoint, which they sing over and over again all the way through. A constantly repeated bass is called a "basso ostinato," and this is the first example of it.

This kind of writing possessed the merit of high organization, without which there can be no work of art. One might search in vain for evidences of artistic design in the early Gregorian chant, while in such works as those of the early Frenchmen and their English disciples they confront one in every measure.

The result was that these writers developed several kinds of contrapuntal writing. But it must be admitted that their work was cold and mathematical, being wholly the result of ingenious calculation. Furthermore it must be borne in mind that they had no conception whatever of music as a means of expression. In a vague way they felt its suitability to the worship of their churches, and its Gothic complexity did indeed harmonize well with ecclesiastical architecture. But it never occurred to the composers of the French school to try to make music beautiful for its own sake. They were too busy exploring the resources of their art, and their *materia musica* was as yet too scanty to allow them to treat their art with the command of mastership. But they served well the cause of music by discovering many of its essential rules, and by formulating in their treatises much of its fundamental theory. It is not at all surprising that in the last period of this school we meet with a large work. The last important master of the school was William of Machaut, who flourished between 1284 and 1369, and wrote the mass for the coronation of Charles V. of France.

The teachings of the French spread into Belgium, and there arose a school called the Gallo-Belgic. The first evidence of its existence is found in the mass of Tournay, sung by the choristers of the Tournay cathedral. Its composer is unknown, but it was written about 1330. It is in three parts, the tenor (voice carrying the fixed chant) in the middle, the descant (or counterpoint) above, and a bass below. It is not nearly so well developed in its polyphony as "Sumer is icumen in" or the works of the Frenchmen. Two of its voices move always in parallel fourths or fifths (as in Hucbald's "organum") and the other has a contrary motion. The most famous composer of the Gallo-Belgic school was William Dufay, born 1400, died 1474. He almost wholly abandoned the use of parallel fourths and fifths, which did so much to restrict composition, and he also adopted the open-note notation, which had made its appearance in France in the closing years of the French school. Dufay used the following notes : —

I have placed under Dufay's notes their present equivalents, with the names. Dufay is the first composer of whom it is known that he made earnest efforts toward a more plastic style of composition than that previously in vogue. This was undoubtedly due to the considerable development of the art of composition. In his search after a freer style, he abandoned the strict "canon," and used "imitation" only here and there in his works. Furthermore, he discerned the musical worth of the songs of the people, and in doing so paved the way for the exertion of a large influence by folk-song upon artistic composition. His method of using the popular songs, however, was as bad as it was remarkable. In composing a mass he would substitute in place of the fixed chant of the liturgy some popular air; and he put the words in along with it, probably because the words of the liturgy could not be sung to the tune. Hence, in three masses by Dufay, still extant, the melodies and texts of three songs of his day are found. One of these songs, " L'Omme Armée," became such a favorite that for more than a century nearly every prominent composer wrote a contrapuntal mass around it. This abuse had finally to be checked by the authorities of the Church. Dufay did another thing, of more benefit to music. He wrote some music in a very simple style, in which there were passages of

THE BIRTH OF COUNTERPOINT 37

pure chord harmony, such as we use in our music to-day. As an example of this, I quote the beginning of a fragment of one of his masses, reproduced in Naumann's "History of Music":—

Before Dufay's death the Gallo-Belgic school began to be overshadowed by that of the Netherlands, with which the art of writing unaccompanied church counterpoint reached its climax. To this school we must now turn our attention.

Chapter IV

The Golden Age of Church Counterpoint

The great Netherlands school — Okeghem and the mechanics of music — Riddles in tone — The advent of pure beauty — Work of Josquin des Prés — Attempts at expression by Willaert and others — Secular music — Orlando Lasso and his beautiful works.

AT the period of musical history which we have now reached, the Dutch, as I have had occasion to say in another work, "led the world in painting, in liberal arts, and in commercial enterprise. Their skill in mechanics was unequalled, and we naturally expect to see their musicians further the development of musical technic." The Dutch musicians at first revelled in the exercise of mechanical ingenuity in the construction of intricate contrapuntal music. In the first period of their great school they acquired by such exercise so great a mastery of the materials of their art that in the second period they began to make serious attempts at writing beautiful music for beauty's sake. In the

CHURCH COUNTERPOINT 39

third period the possibilities of writing something different from church music began to be developed, and we find the Dutch masters attempting the description in tones of external phenomena by the process called tone-painting. This period also saw secular music taken into the fold of art, and began the production of madrigals and other secular songs. In the fourth period the dry old science of counterpoint was so completely conquered that the composers of the time were able to make it the vehicle of the purest expression of religious devotion the world has yet found, and church music passed through its golden age. On account of these facts let us consider this great school, which had more influence on the development of music than any other school in the history of music, under the following heads : —

NETHERLANDS SCHOOL (1425–1625 A. D.).

First Period (1425–1512). — Perfection of contrapuntal technics. Chief masters: Okeghem, Hobrecht, Brumel.

Second Period (1455–1526). — Attempts at pure beauty. Chief master, Josquin des Prés.

Third Period (1495–1572). — Development of tone-painting and secular music. Chief masters: Gombert, Willaert, Goudimel, Di Rore, Jannequin, Arcadelt.

Fourth Period (1520–1625). — Counterpoint made subservient to expression of religious feeling. Chief masters: Orlando Lasso, Swelinck, De Monte.

The reader will note that the division of these periods is not based on chronological, but artistic grounds; and hence, in respect of years, they overlap. The most famous writer of the first period was Johannes Okeghem, born between 1415 and 1430, in East Flanders. He studied under Binchois, a contemporary of Dufay, at Antwerp, was a singer in the service of Charles VII. of France in 1444, was made by Louis XI. Treasurer of the Cathedral of St. Martin's at Tours, and died there about 1513. A considerable quantity of his music has been preserved. It is notable chiefly for its technical skill; and during his life Okeghem was the most famous teacher of his day. His most noted pupil was Antoine Brumel (1460–1520), whose personal history is lost, though many of his masses and motets are preserved. Jacob Hobrecht (1430–) achieved great celebrity. Eight of his masses are extant. As I have said in another account of the Netherlands school, " It is the prevailing influence of one or two masters in each period that marks its extent. Its character was formed by that influence, and salient features of the style of each period may be fairly distinguished. The first period was marked by the extreme development of the 'canon.'" I have already endeavored to explain the nature of canonic writing. If the reader will bear in mind that it is the most rigid form of imitation, requiring the original melody to be imitated throughout in the subsidiary parts, he will not go astray. Okeghem and his contemporaries completely explored the resources of canonic writing. They invented all kinds of canons. They originated the "crab" canon, in which the part sung by the second voice was the first-voice part written backwards. Here is an example taken from a text-book by Dr. Bridge:—

"CRAB" CANON, OR CANON RECTE ET RETRO.

Begin at either end; play either forward or backward.

You can sing or play this through forward and then backward, and its counterpoint remains correct. They had also the inverted canon, in which the second part consisted of the first part turned upside down. The canon by augmentation makes the melody appear in a subsidiary part in notes longer than those in which it appeared in the principal part; and the canon by diminution is formed on the opposite principle. These old musical puzzle-workers had other forms far more complicated, and they took great delight in writing "riddle" canons. In these only the subject was given, with the motto, "Ex una, plures," meaning that the musician must work out the other parts from the one; and then some hint as to the manner of working them out would be given, as, "Ad medium referas, pauses relinque priores." The working out of these riddle canons became a mania with Okeghem and his immediate successors; and the result was that they acquired an immense command over the technics of contrapuntal writing. But "the highest praise that can be awarded to their works is that they are profound in their scholarship, not without evidences of taste in the selection of the formulas to be employed, and certainly imbued with a good deal of the dignity which would inevitably result from a skilful contrapuntal treat-

CHURCH COUNTERPOINT 43

ment of the church chant." It is, however, of singular significance in the history of this period that some of the works of both Hobrecht and Brumel show a tendency toward some conception of chord harmonies. Here is an example, which looks modern: —

BEGINNING OF A MOTET BY BRUMEL.

(From Naumann's " History of Music.")

On the whole, however, the first period of the Netherlands school was characterized by a devotion to the mechanics of music. The second period was illuminated and dominated by the famous Josquin des Prés, whose music is still heard at times, and is still ravishing to the ear. Josquin was born at Condé in or about 1450, and was a pupil of Okeghem. He was a singer in the Sistine Chapel at Rome, and on the death of Sixtus IV., in 1484, went to the court of Hercules d'Est, Duke of Ferrara. He was afterward a short time in the service of Louis XII. of France, and finally of Maximilian I., Emperor of the

Netherlands, who made him provost of the Cathedral of Condé. In that town he died, on August 27, 1521. A large number of his works exists. There are in print nineteen masses, fifty secular pieces, and over one hundred and fifty motets. Josquin is the first genius in the development of music who had sufficient musical material already formulated to enable him to write freely. His works are notable for their elegance of style, and for the firm mastery of the difficult counterpoint of his time. Martin Luther, noting how he moulded seemingly inflexible material to his purpose, said, "Josquin is a master of the notes; they have to do as he wills; other composers must do as the notes will." Baini, the biographer of Palestrina, in describing the immense popularity of Josquin's compositions, says that there was "only Josquin in Italy, only Josquin in France, only Josquin in Germany; in Flanders, in Bohemia, in Hungary, in Spain, only Josquin." In its technical aspect Josquin's music presents for consideration no special feature, except that he wrote always in more than two parts. His music is notable chiefly for its pure beauty, and he was the first composer to make a determined effort to secure that. He was able to do this because his predecessors had so fully developed the technics of polyphonic writing. Josquin, however, was not without grave faults. He continued the practice of using secular airs in the mass, and wrote a mass on " L'Omme Armée." He also had the bad taste twice to set to music the genealogy of Christ, a mere catalogue of names.

The third period was very rich in masters of ability. Of Gombert little is known save that he was a pupil of Josquin. Adrian Willaert, the most brilliant light of his period, was born at Bruges in 1480, and was a pupil of either Josquin or Jean Mouton. After many changes he settled in Venice, where on Dec. 12, 1527, the doge, Andrea Gritti, appointed him chapel-master of St. Mark's. He carried the teachings of the Netherlands school into Italy, became the head of a great music school, was the teacher of many noted organists, and had a profound and wide influence on musical art. Claude Goudimel was born in 1510, founded a music school in Rome, and was the teacher of the great Palestrina. He subsequently went to Paris, became a Protestant, and was killed in the massacre on St. Bartholomew's eve, Aug. 24, 1572. Cyprian di Rore was born in Brabant in 1516, and succeeded Willaert as chapel-master of St. Mark's in Venice. He died in 1565. Clement Jannequin was a native of Flanders. Little is known of his life, but some of his compositions are extant. Willaert's work must first claim our attention. Finding two organs in St. Mark's he introduced antiphonal writing into the music of his time. He wrote some of his grand works for two choruses of four parts each, so that each chorus could answer the other across the church. He paid much less attention to rigid canonic style than his predecessors had done, because it was not suited to the kind of music which he felt was fitting for his church. He sought for grand, broad mass effects, which he learned could be obtained only by the employment of frequent passages in chords. So he began trying to write his counterpoint in such a way that the voice-parts should often come together in successions of chords. In order to do this he was compelled to adopt the kind of chord formations still in use and the fundamental chord relations of modern music, — the tonic, dominant, and subdominant. The tonic is the chord of the key in which one is writing; the subdominant is that of the fourth note of the scale of that key; and the dominant that of the fifth, thus:—

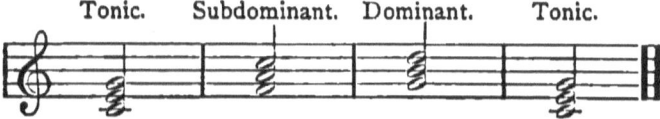

This is the succession of chords which children strum when they try to play accompaniments on the piano. It is the simplest progression of harmony we have, and lies at the basis of all our common tunes. It is called diatonic harmony because it is formed of chords on the whole tones of the scale, in contradistinction to chromatic harmony, founded on the chords of the semitones. It is necessary to speak of chromatic harmony here, because Cyprian di Rore made a special study of it, and his "Chromatic Madrigals," published in 1544, had a great influence upon the progress of music. The old church scales were essentially diatonic, and chromatic harmonies were not practicable in music written in those scales. Di Rore's madrigals were influential in showing composers how they could write more flexibly and more beautifully by breaking the shackles of the old Gregorian scales. Still, most of the music of that time continued to be essentially diatonic, for the composers had just begun to explore the possibilities of chord modulation. These possibilities do not seem to have been exhausted even by the music of Wagner.

The development of secular music at this time was remarkable. The scientific composers began to make a practice of writing music to be used outside of the church. They wrote madrigals and other part-songs of real merit, and in them they made attempts at expression. Of course these first attempts were purely imitative. The composers tried to imitate natural sounds and movements in music. Gombert wrote a clever and humorous " Bird Cantata." Jannequin, in his " Cris de Paris," tried to paint the street life of the French capital, while his " La Bataille " is a military picture in music. These remarkable descriptive pieces were written for four voices, unaccompanied, and in polyphonic style. After trying to tell some kind of a story in secular music they tried it in religious music. One of Willaert's motets, at any rate, tells the story of Susannah, and is plainly a forerunner of the oratorio. We have seen now how the first period of the Netherlands school brought contrapuntal technics to a high state of development, how the second period produced a genius and a desire for pure beauty, and how the third period introduced a broader, simpler, and more imposing style into church music and made definite attempts at expression. We now come to the fourth period, which was destined to bring ecclesiastical counterpoint to its perfection. This period also produced a master of splendid genius, whose works live yet and ought to live as long as there is a place in the Roman

CHURCH COUNTERPOINT 49

Church for pure and lofty music. This man was Roland Delattre, usually known by the Italian form of his name, Orlando Lasso, or di Lasso.

Lasso was born in Mons, between 1520 and 1530. He studied at home, at Milan, Naples, and Rome, and at an early age became chapel master of the Church of St. John Lateran. In 1557 he went to Munich as director of the ducal choir. There he passed most of the remainder of his life, dying there on June 14, 1594. He was a contemporary of the great Palestrina, whose fame his far outshone. Lasso was celebrated all over Europe, was employed and honored by monarchs, and was called the " Prince of Music." He was one of the most prolific composers that ever lived. He is said to have written 2,500 works. Many of his compositions are in print to-day, and his quaintly beautiful madrigal, " Matona, mia cara," is often heard in concert. Other composers of this period were Jan Peters Swelinck, pupil of Cyprian di Rore, born at Deventer, 1540, died at Amsterdam, 1621, and Philip de Monte (1521–). Their work was by no means without merit, but it was overshadowed by that of their great contemporary.

Lasso was a complete master of the counterpoint of his time, but he aimed at making it a vehicle of expression for religious feeling, and succeeded. He adapted his style to his purposes. Sometimes he wrote pure hymn-tunes in four-part chords, much like our modern hymns. If he was writing for grand and imposing effects, he could handle the most complicated polyphony with ease. He wrote works for two and three choirs, and other works for only two voices. His famous " Penitential Psalms" are for two voices, and are marvellously beautiful and pathetic. Yet some of Lasso's music is as old-fashioned and stiff as Okeghem's. Again he becomes almost modern in his employment of chromatics. But there is one notable feature of Lasso's work: it contains no parade of contrapuntal difficulties for their own sake. On the contrary, it is admirable for the skill with which it conceals its own mechanical ingenuity and presents an appearance of spontaneity and fluency. It abounds in the highest and purest expression of religious feeling, and it is always beautiful as music per se. In fine we always know, when listening to the works of Lasso, that we are in the presence of a genius.

We have now reached the period at which Italy became the home of modern music. Willaert and Di Rore in Venice, Goudimel and Lasso in Rome sowed seed which was to produce beautiful fruit. At the same time influences were at work which introduced a simpler style into music and which made it an art more popular with the masses. One of these influences was the music of those very masses. The popular songs of the day had, as we have seen, long ago forced themselves upon the attention of the artistic composers. The time was now approaching when those composers turned to the popular music for suggestions as to the future development of their art. Before entering upon an account of the birth of a new style in music, the reader must go back with me and take a rapid view of the growth of the folk-song.

FIRST STANZA OF "MATONA MIA CARA."

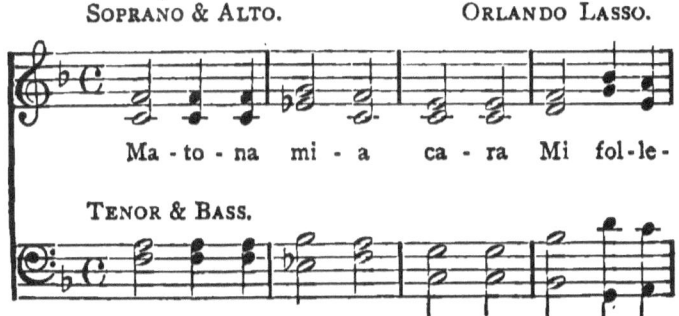

Chapter V

Progress of Popular Music

Troubadours, jongleurs, minnesingers, and meistersingers — Wagner's "Tannhäuser" and "Die Meistersinger" as historical pictures — The German volkslied — The musical guilds — The waits and the minstrels.

WE saw that as far back as Dufay's time composers began to introduce secular melodies into the mass. This was an evidence that the ecclesiastical composers had been forced to make attempts to popularize their works by a rude adoption of the melodies of the people. The question, therefore, naturally arises: Who were the composers of the secular music? Of course that is a question that cannot be answered very definitely, but we do know who were the secular musicians of the time, and we know that they were nearer the fundamental principles of modern music than the churchmen were. The enormous mass of ecclesiastical music produced in the middle ages was fit only for the worship of cathedrals. It could never have been made to utter the notes of human passion, and until some other style was found, the modern symphony, song, and opera must have remained impossible. Church counterpoint survives to-day only in church music and in the German fugue, a form of music which is conspicuous for its intellectual rather than its emotional qualities. The early secular musicians had no science at all, and very little art. Their music was, therefore, simple and unpretentious, but it contained the germs of our modern art forms, and it was bound in time to force its way into the studies of the fathers.

The secular musicians of the early time were wanderers on the face of Europe. They were the troubadours, jongleurs, minnesingers, meistersingers, and minstrels.

The whole race of strolling musicians in the middle ages almost certainly descended from the Roman comedians who were driven out of the seven-hilled city when Alaric swept down upon it with fire and the sword. They wandered into foreign lands to sing and pipe before the Frankish chiefs, now their lords and masters. In the earliest days they were simple vagabonds, whom the law did not allow redress for bodily injury wantonly inflicted. In the latter half of the twelfth and the early part of the thirteenth centuries these strolling musicians began to be employed in the mysteries and miracle plays, and thus gradually arose in the public estimation. Even before that time they had begun to be taken into the service of the knightly troubadours and minnesingers as accompanists, their French title being jongleurs.

Subsequently it became their business to go about singing the songs of their masters, in short, to become their publishers. The troubadours themselves were nobles, originally those of southeastern France. They got their first inspiration from the folk songs, but their own songs were distinguished by refinement and improved melody. These knightly singers existed simultaneously with the jongleurs, who sang and played for money. The most celebrated troubadours were King Thibaut, of Navarre (1201–1253), and Adam de la Halle (1240–1286). It is a notable and significant fact that the songs of the troubadours, like most of the folk songs, ignored the church modes and moved in the modern major and minor keys.

The last of the German minnesingers, Heinrich von Meissen, died in 1318, but the celebrated Confrèrie de St. Julien des Ménestriers, of Paris, lasted at any rate till

PROGRESS OF POPULAR MUSIC   57

1741, for it is recorded that in that year Louis XV. made Jean Pierre Guignon "le Roy des Violons." The songs of the troubadours and wandering minstrels were the popular songs of the day of Columbus, and in Spain the troubadours still survived. The character of the music sung by these persons is well described by Fanny Raymond Ritter in her "Essay on the Troubadours." She says : —

"The merit of the troubadours in furthering the progress of music as an art was that they liberated melody from the fetters of calculation, gave it the stamp of individuality, and bore it on the wings of fancy into the domains of sentiment. They had the further merit of introducing new and peculiar changes of time, which, apparently irregular, were really forcible, symmetrical, and original. It is also more than probable that the troubadours received new ideas in regard to melody from the East; as they found among the Arabs not only a different system of tones, but many fanciful vocal ornaments then unknown in Europe, and which they introduced in their own songs on their return from the Crusades. But as harmony was in that day yet undeveloped, the flowing vine of melody received little support from it, and therefore often appears weak. The rules of composition were then highly complicated and ill classified, yet they were well understood by the best educated troubadours; and though their earlier songs were stiff, closely resembling the Gregorian chant in form and style, in some of the latter ones we find graceful melodies that leave little to be desired, and that possess more real variety and individuality of character than do the words attached to them."

It is not a far cry from France to Germany across the Rhine, and the chanson of the troubadour soon found its counterpart in the minnesong of the fatherland. The era of the minnesinger has been divided into three periods. The first, whose beginning is not definitely fixed, ended near the close of the twelfth century. The second period comprised the last decade of the twelfth century and the first half of the thirteenth. It was the golden age of the minnesong, the age of Wagner's "Tannhäuser" and the great Sängerkrieg at the Wartburg Castle, the age of the Landgrave Hermann, Wolfram von Eschenbach, and Walther von der Vogelweide. This time has been made alive for us by the genius of Wagner, whose contest in "Tannhäuser" introduces the actual personages of the real story. The third period was that of decline. The fourteenth century saw the gradual decrease of feudal power, and the burghers and artisans dared to do what had hitherto been reserved for their lordly masters. Thus the minnesong was supplanted by the meistersong, and the meistersinger became the musical lawgiver of Germany. The songs of the meistersingers were somewhat stiff and formal, yet not lacking in melody, as that used by Wagner as the theme of his march goes to show. Perhaps no better description of a meistersong could be given here than that sung by " Kothner " in expounding the " Leges Tabulaturæ " to " Walther von Stolzing ": —

> Each mastersinger-created stave
> Its regular measurement must have,
> By sundry regulations stated
> And never violated.
> What we call a section is two stanzas ;
> For each the self-same melody answers:
> A stanza several lines doth blend,
> And each line with a rhyme must end.
> Then come we to the "After Song,"
> Which must be also some lines long,
> And have its especial melody,
> Which from the other diff'rent must be.
> So staves and sections of such measure
> A mastersong may have at pleasure.
> He who a new song can outpour
> Which in four syllables — not more —
> Another strain doth plagiarize,
> He may obtain the master prize.

In Germany, too, flourished the folk song. Who wrote the old volkslieder no one knows, but many of them have been preserved to us. The " Limburg Chronicle " contains a number in use between 1347 and 1380, and the "Locheimer Liederbuch" is a collection dated 1452. H. de Zeelandia, in his "Lehrcompendium," gives many in vogue in the first half of the fifteenth century. The essential features of the volkslieder are clearness and symmetry of melody and firmness of rhythm. The early ones also display a constant tendency to escape from the fetters of the ecclesiastical modes. In fact to them is due the final development of modern tonality.

The German church music of the time, from which developed the chorale, was founded on the volkslied. The familiar example of "Isbruck, ich muss dich lassen," set in four parts by Heinrich Isaak in 1475, and adapted after the Reformation by Dr. Hesse as "O Welt, ich muss dich lassen," was but the continuation of the practice of Heinrich von Laufenberg, who in the fifteenth century set sacred words to secular tunes continually. This brief review of the state of music in Germany in the time of the Netherlands school shows us that the volkslied and the meistersong were the ruling powers, and that there was as yet no foreshadowing of the mighty art which has since developed in the land of the Teutons.

In these days existed also the musical guilds which were the forerunners of the continental town orchestras. As far back as the thirteenth century the strolling musicians began to gather in towns, and there they formed societies for the protection of their common interests. Some of them became town pipers, and in the fifteenth century some were made town and corporation trumpeters. One result of the work of the guilds at this time was that musicians began to acquire some of the rights of citizenship. The guilds were accustomed to place themselves under the patronage of some noble, who selected from the guild a " piper king." It was his business to see that " no player, whether he be piper, drummer, fiddler, trumpeter, or performer on any instrument, be allowed to accept engagements of any kind, whether in towns, villages, or hamlets, unless he had previously enrolled himself a member of the guild." At irregular intervals a court was assembled, consisting of a mayor, four masters, twelve ordinary members, and a beadle, whose business it was to mete out punishment to guild offenders. These guilds were simply the musical protective unions of the day. Outside of the German nations, where these guilds did not exist, the ordinary musician was a stroller, with hardly any legal rights and no consideration. His occupation was regarded as menial, and the servants of the knights treated him with contempt. The jongleur who played the accompaniments for the troubadour, or even sang his songs when the master had no voice, was regarded as a servant and nothing more. The idea of any musician being entitled to the consideration of an artist, except the great church composers, would have been scouted.

In England the strolling musician was represented by the minstrel and the waits, and his status was about the same as it was on the Continent. In a somewhat better case were those who were under the protection of some prince or noble. For instance, the children of the chapel ate in the chapel hall with the yeomen of the vestry and were well cared for. They were the young students of choir singing, instructed by a master of song, who was appointed by the dean of the chapel. These children we find as a part of the household establishment of Edward IV., who died in 1483.

The musicians of the Church were in much better circumstances. As far back as the time of William the Conqueror we find that Hereford Cathedral had endowments which included support for seven choristers. We find similar endowments granted to St. Gregory's in 1363; to Wells in 1347; to

PROGRESS OF POPULAR MUSIC 63

the collegiate churches of Southwell, in Nottinghamshire; to Beverley, in Yorkshire, and Westminster. At Oxford, New College had an endowment for sixteen choristers, and Magdalen, All Souls', and St. John's had similar funds. Nearer to Okeghem's day the famous Dick Whittington, Lord Mayor of London, in 1424 founded an endowment for choristers in the Church of St. Michael Royal, which he built. Nevertheless, the first recorded case of a salaried organist is that of Leonard Fitz Simon, organist of Trinity College, Oxford, about 1580, at 20s. per year.

Here are two examples of the popular music of the early times,—the first a song by King Thibaut of Navarre, and the second the first part of the old meistersong used by Wagner in " Die Meistersinger " : —

By THIBAUT OF NAVARRE.

L'au-trier per la   ma - ti - née   ent'r un bos et
Une pas - to - re   ai tro - vé - e   chant-ant pour son

un   ver - gier   et di - sait un son pre-mier
en - voi - sier

HOW MUSIC DEVELOPED

chi mi tient - li mais d'a - mour
Tan - tost cel - le par - en - tor
Ka je loi de frai-nier si li dis sans
de - lai - er Belle, diex vous doint bon jour.

Ge - ne - sis am neun und zwan - zig-
sten uns be - richt wie Ja - cob floh
vor sein bru - der E - sau ent - wicht.

The reader will note that in the first of these there is a clearly marked rhythmic movement of the simplest kind. The tune is distinctly in the modern key of G major, and it is not polyphonic. The second tune is in F major and while its rhythm is not clearly indicated, it is plainly not a polyphonic composition. The directness of this kind of music and its suitability to the expression of simple feelings were bound to make themselves felt sooner or later in music. We are now to examine into the causes which led to the simplification of church music and forced composers to turn their attention more and more to the music of the people.

Chapter VI

The Simplification of Music

Causes which led composers toward a less complex style — The Renaissance and the Reformation — The Council of Trent — Palestrina and his music — Last days of the Roman and Venetian schools — The English cathedral composers — Characteristics of the period.

IT is hardly necessary to tell the reader that the methods employed in writing church music prior to the dawn of the seventeenth century were not always judicious. The use of secular tunes together with their texts prevailed for more than two centuries, and led to great laxity in the treatment of the liturgy. In the course of time too many composers came to regard the words of the mass as mere pegs to hang tunes on, and the tremendous complexity of the huge polyphonic works was such that the words could not be distinguished. One part would be singing "gloria in excelsis" while another was thundering "et in terra pax," and there was such a jumble of words and music that,

SIMPLIFICATION OF MUSIC 67

while it was all very imposing, it was not comprehensible to the congregation. As long as the congregation knew very little Latin, and less music, this condition did not have serious effects ; but the time had now come when the people began to ask questions. It becomes our duty, then, to inquire what influences led to reforms in church music. I shall first enumerate the influences and afterward discuss them in detail.

1. The revival of Greek learning in Italy after a lapse of seven hundred years.
2. The invention of printing.
3. The Renaissance.
4. Popular music.
5. The diffusion of musical learning among the people.
6. The Lutheran choral hymn and congregational singing.

In 1453 the Turks, under Mohammed II., slew Constantine, last of the Roman emperors, and overthrew Rome's eastern empire, whose capital was Constantinople. The Christian scholars of Turkey fled toward the home capital of their fallen empire, and took up their residence in Italy. These scholars were all masters of the Greek tongue, and they awakened a new interest in it and its literature. The field had been untouched for about seven centuries, and the whole treasury of Greek history, oratory, and poetry was reopened to the Italian mind. Its effects were wide and general. One of them was to lead to the study of the New Testament in the original tongue, and this study very speedily demonstrated the unworthiness of the Latin Vulgate used by the Church. Any blow at Latin was a blow at the authority of Rome. The whole Italian system of worship had been built upon the Vulgate, which was in the language authorized in the Roman Church throughout western Europe, and used as the sole means of intercommunication between its branches in various nations. Doctrines and edicts alike proceeded from Rome in the ancient language of the city, and to throw discredit upon the veracity of that tongue in the Vulgate was to subject it to general doubt and suspicion. Such doubt did certainly spread among the people, who began to demand a clearer comprehension of the liturgy. To this end they desired a less complex setting of the musical part of the church service.

This demand was powerfully backed by the introduction of printing in 1444. This introduction resulted in lowering the price of books, and a plentiful supply of cheap reading attracted readers. Hence the mass of the Roman Catholic laity became readers as well as listeners. The whole system of worship had been based on the existence of a non-reading public. But now the age of popular inquiry began, and it became necessary for church music to abandon its complexity and address itself to meet the demands of awakening intelligence.

The dawn of the Renaissance in art was caused by the revival of Greek learning, which reintroduced Greek models. The enormous effect of a new contemplation by the Italian mind of Doric architecture and Greek sculpture can hardly be comprehended by us to whom these things are so familiar. The force and beauty of simplicity were brought home to the people by the very examples which awoke in them a desire for imaginative life and personal expression. The Renaissance led to a clearer, stronger, more eloquent style in all art, and in time it was bound to make itself felt in music. The fact that Leonardo da Vinci worked before Josquin des Prés proves nothing except that music was behind the other arts in the development of her technic, and had to work out her own laws of existence before she could feel the influence of reformatory thought.

The popular music of the time naturally appealed to composers as their feeling for distinctly outlined form increased, and this feeling was directly influenced by the artistic teachings of the Renaissance. As art remodelled itself on Greek patterns, and architecture found in the Doric lines a relief to the endless details of the Gothic, so music inclined toward the simple contours of the song-forms. The elementary attraction of pure rhythm grew in potency as composers realized more clearly that it was one of the fundamental components of music; and with a recognition of this fact came that of the deeper significance of chord harmony. The folk-song itself had always clung to the major and minor scales, and had not often employed the purely ecclesiastical modes. The mode known as the Ionic — the old Greek Lydian mode, condemned by the ancients as lascivious — was nothing more nor less than our major scale of G, and as such the church composers knew it. Its possibilities made themselves more and more clear as the artistic musicians of the day studied the popular tunes, and so in time it came to its true seat of honor in music.

A knowledge of music had begun to spread among the people. Not only did the constant hearing of the noble masterpieces of their time tend to cultivate their taste, but they began to practise music themselves. Conservatories had been founded in Venice, Rome, and other cities, and as far back as Willaert's day it was fashionable for young ladies of good family to learn to play the monochord, one of the precursors of the piano. The music written for the instrument was precisely like that for the organ, polyphonic in style and learned in treatment. The study of such music was naturally very difficult for beginners, and it became necessary to supply them with something simpler.

The music of the Roman Church was brought into strong contrast with that employed by Luther in his work of the Reformation. Luther insisted on the exercise of individuality in worship. He held, contrary to the Church, that every man had a right to study the Bible for himself. He even gave communion to the laity. In direct line with such work was his revival of congregational singing, which had been generally unpractised since the days of Ambrose. The first Lutheran hymn-book was published in 1524. Luther employed many extant folk-songs and caused new tunes like them to be written. He is said to have written "A stronghold sure." These Lutheran hymns were broad and simple chorals, like those of the Protestant Church of to-day. The spread of their use among the Protestant congregations of the time was an attraction toward that form of worship which the authorities of the Roman Church could not ignore, and hence the Catholic composers moved toward a simpler style.

The story of what followed the recognition of these influences by the fathers of the Church has been very prettily told, but unfortunately it has been of late discredited. The story is that two parties arose in the Church, one of them demanding the abolition of all the extant church music and a return to the plain chant of Gregory, and the other that the music of the time be preserved, but its style simplified. The Council of Trent (1562) discussed the matter, and in 1563 Pope Pius IX. appointed a commission of eight cardinals to take measures of reform. Cardinals Borromeo and Vitellozzi, appointed as a sub-committee, went to Palestrina, whose music had already attracted attention, and asked him to write a mass demonstrating that the church music of the time could be preserved. He entered upon his task with such enthusiasm that he wrote three masses, of which that called the Marcellus mass was performed with enormous success.

This story has been proved to be a myth. The Council of Trent did pass a resolution that a complete reform of church music was necessary, but the demand was based, not on the character of the music, but on the fact that it made the text of the liturgy unintelligible. The Council furthermore issued a mandate, to bishops to banish improper music from their churches. This was, of course, aimed at the secular airs, or those which resembled them. The mass of Marcellus was not written to order, and there was nothing new in its style. The mass is simply a model of all that was best in Palestrina's day. It embodied all that was noblest in the polyphonic style developed by the Netherlands school. Its melody is pure, sweet, and fluent, and its expressive capacity perfectly adapted to the devotional spirit of the text. Palestrina's contemporaries, such as Lasso, and some of his predecessors, wrote in the same style. Lasso's "Penitential Psalms" are much simpler in style than this mass. Its apparent simplicity lies in the fact that its profound mastery of technical resources conceals its superb art. The polyphonic writing is matchless in its evenness; every part is as good as every other part. The harmonies are beautiful, yet there is apparently no direct attempt to produce them. They seem just to happen. But above all other qualities stands the innate power of expression in this music. It is, as Ambros has hinted, as if the composer had brought the angelic host to earth.

With Palestrina church polyphony reached its highest and its final development. The search after simplicity led composers in a path diverging widely from the old contrapuntal highway. New developments in secular music were soon to come about, and still more powerfully to influence church composition. The harvest and the glory of vocal counterpoint had come, and thenceforth musical art was to develop along new and hitherto unexpected lines. A few words should be written here concerning the career of so great a man as Palestrina, who has been universally accorded a seat among the Titans of music. His full name was Giovanni Pierluigi Sante, and he was called Palestrina from the place of his nativity. The date of his birth is uncertain, but it was probably 1514. The portrait of him in the pontifical chapel at Rome has an inscription to the effect that he died in 1594, aged eighty. He was the son of poor peasants and got his first musical instruction as a choir singer. In 1540 he went to Rome and became a student in Claude Goudimel's conservatory. At the age of thirty he published his first compositions, and some of them are still

SIMPLIFICATION OF MUSIC 75

heard in the Sistine Chapel occasionally.[1] He had previously served a short period as organist and choir master in his native town, and in 1548 he married. In 1551 he succeeded Arcadelt as choir master of St. Peter's, Rome, and the Pope made him one of the singers of the Papal Chapel. In 1571 he was made chapel master of St. Peter's, and later, in conjunction with his younger contemporary Nanini, he founded a music school in Rome. The influence of this school was very great, and it kept the "Palestrina style" alive in Europe for nearly a century. Palestrina died on Feb. 2, 1594, and the Supreme Council of the Church had his body laid in the basilica of the Vatican with the honors usually shown to a cardinal.

Before leaving the subject of Palestrina, let me endeavor to make clear to the reader wherein his style is so fine. Composers before him had begun to aim at the simplification of church music. They sought to accomplish their purpose by breaking the shackles of canonic law. The canon had demanded the most exact imitation in the

[1] At the time of writing (October, 1897) Palestrina's works are not performed as often as they used to be in the Papal Chapel, and there is a determined movement on the part of some of the clergy for their restoration and a more frequent use of the Gregorian chant. The movement is a healthful one, and I wish it success.

different voice-parts. The new style allowed the greatest freedom. The result was that free polyphony took the place of rigid canon. Consequently, composers were able to devote more attention to the development of fluent, beautiful, and expressive melody. The merit of Palestrina's work was that it carried this style to perfection. His compositions became the models for succeeding composers, and indeed they remain to this day unequalled as examples of pure church music. In Palestrina's music one must note the absence of rhythmic effects, of modern tonality, and of the note of passion. Palestrina paid little attention to folk-music, but sought to attain simplicity of style by preserving the old church scales, avoiding chromatic harmonies, and by generally preserving purity and contemplative feeling. His writing is marvellous in its contrapuntal skill, which makes the apparently independent melodies of the different voice-parts constantly combine in simple and lovely chords. The lack of contrast in his music has often been quoted as a fault; but it was in accordance with Palestrina's own theory that church music should always be dignified, and should never contain anything exciting.

As we have now reached the period at which artistic music began to develop in all

SIMPLIFICATION OF MUSIC 77

its branches, it will be most convenient to narrate the progress of Roman Catholic church music subsequent to Palestrina's time before passing to other topics. The reader must bear in mind that this music was still designed to be sung without accompaniment, in order that the tone-quality of pure vocal sound might be untainted. When the organ was first used it simply doubled the voice-parts, and when independent accompaniments began to be written they considerably altered the character of church music. There were now two distinct schools of Catholic composition, — that of Rome, and that of Venice. The former followed the pure diatonic style of Palestrina; the latter was influenced by the style of Willaert and the chromatic music of Di Rore. The chief masters of the Roman school were Nanini, Vittoria, Anerio, and Allegri. Giovanni Maria Nanini was born in 1540 and died in 1607. He was a co-worker with Palestrina, and was the teacher of many of the succeeding composers. His "Hodie nobis cœlorum Rex" is still sung at Christmas in the Papal Chapel. Tommaso Ludovico da Vittoria was born about 1540, and died about 1604. He is regarded as one of the greatest of Palestrina's successors. A goodly number of his works has been preserved. His Requiem, written for the funeral of the Empress Maria (1603), is conceded to be his greatest production, and is one of the most notable compositions of that period. "Technically considered, it is a marvellous blending of old independent movement of parts with modern dissonances and progressions. Spiritually considered, it is a wonderful expression of poignant personal sorrow, chastened by religious contemplation and devotion." The marks of change here are the use of the dissonance and the expression of personal feeling. The dissonance in music embraces all those harmonies which sound harsh to persons accustomed only to elementary chords like the tonic, dominant, and subdominant. They are used most freely in modern operatic music, especially that of Wagner, and have always been employed to express passion of some kind. Palestrina avoided them. Felice Anerio (1560–1630) wrote many admirable masses. Gregorio Allegri (1586–1652) is best known as the composer of very fine "Misere" now sung in Holy Week in the Sistine Chapel. This work is regarded as equal to some of Palestrina's.

The Venetian school, after its earliest period produced two great composers from one family. These were Andrea Gabrieli (1510–1586) and his nephew Giovanni Gabrieli

SIMPLIFICATION OF MUSIC 79

(1557–1613). The former followed Willaert's plan of writing for antiphonal choruses, but he employed most frequently three instead of two. The latter was more of an instrumental composer than his uncle, and hence conceived the idea of writing instrumental accompaniments. In his "Surrexit Christus" he used an orchestral accompaniment of first and second violins, two cornets, and four trombones. This work of Giovanni Gabrieli's fairly marks the termination of the era of *a capella* (unaccompanied) polyphonic church music. The opera had been born, and so had the oratorio, and church music began to borrow ideas from them. Giovanni Legrenzi (1625–1690) increased Gabrieli's orchestra to nineteen violins, two violas, three viole da gamba, four theorboes (lutes of large size), two cornets, one bassoon, and three trombones. Antonio Lotti (1667–1740) was an opera writer as well as a church composer, and he wrote masses full of passionate feeling. His later works are full of passages in which the voices alternate with the instruments and there are accompanied solos and choruses. With Lotti, who used unaccompanied choruses occasionally, we bid a final farewell to the great period of *a capella* church music, and enter upon the era in which music for the church was made in the same way as other kinds. The masses of Mozart, Beethoven, Cherubini, and other modern writers are all richly instrumented.

England had fairly kept pace with the Continent in her mastery of polyphony, which so early produced the remarkable canon " Sumer is icumen in." Thomas Tallys (born about 1520, died Nov. 23, 1585) was one of the greatest of the English masters, and is regarded as the father of English cathedral music. His works do not equal those of his contemporaries in inspiration, — he was neither a Lasso nor a Palestrina, — but he had a large command of polyphonic technic. One of his notable works was a motet, entitled " Spem in alium non habui," written for eight choirs of five voices each, in antiphonal style. His best known work, however, is a Litany and Responses. His pupil, William Byrd (born about 1538, died July 4, 1623), wrote many admirable church works notable for the majesty of their style. Orlando Gibbons (died 1625, at the end of the Netherlands period) was the last great light of the English school.

During the whole period of church counterpoint, which never lost the radical elements of its character until after Legrenzi's day, music felt the influence of the old chant and the early study of the canonic style. In concluding the account of this period, I cannot do better than to quote a few luminous sentences from the admirable " Evolution of the Art of Music " by Dr. C. H. H. Parry : "Of definite principles of design beyond this elementary device [the canon] these composers had but few. Their treatment of musical figures and melodic material is singularly vague. The familiar modern practice of using a definite subject [part of a distinct tune] throughout a considerable portion of a movement, or at certain definite points which have a structural importance, was hardly employed at all. The voices, which entered one after another, naturally commenced singing the same words to phrases of melody which resembled each other. But composers' ideas of identity of subject matter were singularly elastic, and even if the first half-dozen notes presented similar contours in each voice-part successively, the melodic forms soon melted into something else, and from that point the movement wandered on its devious way without further reference to its initial phrases." This points to one of the fundamental differences between the music of the polyphonic era and that of the monophonic, in which one voice or instrumental part (as the treble of a piano) uttered a melody full of periodical repetitions of the germinal tune-thought, and the other parts supplied an accompaniment of chords. This style of composition was developed first in the opera and afterward by instruments. It will be more convenient to take up the progress of instrumental music first, and at the outset let us review the evolution of the piano.

Chapter VII

The Evolution of the Piano

Plucking and striking strings — The dulcimer — Invention of the keyboard — The clavichord and its action — Manner of playing the clavichord — The harpsichord family — Invention of hammer action — Claims of Cristofori — Modern improvements — Equal temperament.

THE piano, like all our contemporaneous musical instruments, is the result of a long development. Its fundamental principle is the setting of a stretched string in vibration by a blow, the vibrations acting upon the air so as to produce sound. A subsidiary principle (subsidiary because common to all stringed instruments, such as violins, harps, or guitars) is the shortening or lengthening of a string in order to obtain a higher or a lower note. In the piano, the application of this principle gives us a number of strings of different lengths. In the violin we have only four strings, but the length of the vibrating part is altered by pressing down the strings at different points with the fingers of the left hand. Before the idea of setting strings in vibration with a bow was conceived, they were plucked with the fingers, as in the case of the harp and the guitar, and it is probable that this is the oldest method of causing strings to sound. The Hebrew *kinnor*, the first musical instrument mentioned in the Bible (called "harp," Genesis iv. 21), was either a lyre or a small harp, and, according to Josephus, it was played with a plectrum, a small piece of ivory or steel, used to pluck the strings. Egyptian pictures of great antiquity show players using their fingers upon harp strings. At the same time the Egyptians were well acquainted with the principle of dividing a string by pressing upon it with the fingers of the left hand, as is proved by their pictures of lute players.

But the use of a blow to set a string in vibration was also known in very early times. The instrument called a dulcimer, which is always seen now in Hungarian orchestras, is almost as old as the harp. It consists of a number of strings stretched across a shallow box, which acts as a resonator, and set in vibration by two little hammers in the hands of the player. It was this instrument which suggested the hammer action, and it is this action which makes the

EVOLUTION OF THE PIANO 85

fundamental difference between the piano and its immediate precursors. An instrument similar to the dulcimer was the citole, the chief difference being that the strings were plucked with the fingers. Add the principle of stopping the strings with the fingers of the left hand, and the citole becomes the zither. In Lydgate's "Reson and Sensualité (circa 1430) "cytolys" are enumerated among other instruments.

The first important step toward the evolution of the pianoforte was the invention of the keyboard. The origin of this important part of the instrument is uncertain. It is probable that it was first applied to the organ. At any rate, it is said that a keyboard of sixteen keys was attached to an organ built in the Cathedral of Magdeburg at the close of the eleventh century, while most historians date the clavichord or the clavicytherium two centuries later. It is possible, however, that some sort of rude arrangement of keys was employed in the monochord, an instrument used for measuring the scientific intervals between notes of different pitch. It is said to have been invented by Pythagoras in the sixth century before Christ. It consisted of an oblong box with one string stretched across it, and a movable bridge for dividing (or stopping) the string at different points. The continual shifting of the bridge was very troublesome, and as early as the second century (according to Claudius Ptolomæus and Aristides Quintilianus) there was a four-stringed instrument called a helicon. It is surmised that the famous teacher Guido d'Arezzo (born about 995) was the first to use the monochord in teaching singing, and that he devised some kind of a keyboard, because in one of his writings he advises his pupils "to practise the hand in the use of the monochord."

The keyboard having been invented, whether for monochord or organ, its application to stringed instruments of the dulcimer or citole family naturally followed. It is impossible to tell whether the first action was a plucking or a striking one, for there are no records, and it is easily conceivable that both may have been used simultaneously in different places. Guido's action is supposed to have consisted of a straight lever with a bridge on the inner end. When the outer end, the key, was struck the bridge arose, gave the string a blow which set it in vibration, and remaining pressed against the string, divided it and determined its pitch. This subsequently became the action of the German clavichord. Another

EVOLUTION OF THE PIANO

action consisted of a similar straight lever with a piece of quill protruding from the inner end. When the outer end was pressed down the inner end moved past the string and the quill plucked it, causing it to vibrate. This became the action of the clavicytherium, which some writers, without good ground, say was antecedent to the clavichord, and subsequently of the Italian spinet, the harpsichord, and the virginal.

The first mention of the clavichord and harpsichord is found in the " Rules of the Minnesingers," by Eberhard Cersne, A. D. 1404. The celebrated musical theorist, Jean de Muris, of the University of Paris, writing in 1323, and enumerating musical instruments, mentions the four-stringed monochord, but says nothing of the clavichord or harpsichord. This gives reasonable ground for the inference that those instruments were either not invented at that time or had so recently appeared that they were not yet known in Paris, then the centre of musical culture. We are quite safe in assuming that both instruments date from the thirteenth century, and as they were the immediate ancestors of the piano, we must give them especial attention. The famous collection of Mr. Morris Steinert, of New Haven, contains examples in good working order of all the different kinds of clavichords, harpsichords, spinets, and early pianos, and it has been my privilege to examine and play upon all these instruments, thus obtaining a singularly effective object lesson in the history of the piano. The clavichord was always built in oblong shape, like our square piano. The keyboard was precisely like that now used, except that some builders made the naturals black and the sharps and flats white. The principle of the action remained that of the old monochord. The key was pivoted just inside of the front board of the case, and consisted of a single straight shaft of wood. On the inner end was a thin, slablike upright of brass, called a "tangent." When the player struck the outer end of the key, the tangent was driven upward against the string, causing it to vibrate. The tangent also acted as a bridge, and divided the string into two unequal parts, the longer of which gave out the tone. The shorter section was prevented from sounding by a narrow band of cloth interlaced with the strings at that end of the instrument. This band also acted as a damper, and caused the whole string to cease vibrating the moment the tangent was lowered. Clavichords made before 1725 (or about that year) had fewer strings than keys. One string had to produce two and sometimes three tones. This was accomplished by the use of the tangents, which divided the string at different lengths, as the violinist does with the fingers of his left hand. These instruments were known as "gebunden," or bound.

About 1725 Daniel Faber of Crailsheim made instruments with one string for each tone, and such clavichords were called "bundfrei" (bound free) or "ungebunden" (unbound). In the latest clavichords each note had two strings tuned in unison, — a contrivance which gained power at the expense of some of the lovely expressiveness of the instrument.

The reader will understand that, as the clavichord string ceased sounding as soon as the tangent was permitted to drop by lifting the finger from the key, the method of playing it was different from that employed for the piano. A hard blow was of no use; it only twanged the string disagreeably. Pressure, with its direct communication of the finger-touch to the string, was the secret of clavichord playing, and it was this which made the instrument so beautifully responsive to the thought of the performer. By forcing the pressure a little a sort of *portamento* effect could be obtained, and by causing the finger to shake up and down on the pressed key one could get a faint and pathetic tremolo from the vibrating string. This effect the Germans called "bebung," and it was one of the most familiar graces of clavichord playing. No one who has played upon a clavichord can fail to see how thoroughly the instrument works its way into the confidence and love of an artist, and there is no room for wonder that it was the intimate friend of the great Bach.

It is difficult to arrive at satisfactory conclusions from the statements of early writers in regard to instruments of the harpsichord family. Scaliger, born in 1484, says that Simius, who lived in the last period of Greek music, invented the Simicon. In this the tone was produced by tangents, which were subsequently armed with crow quills to pluck the strings. Adriano Banchieri, in his "Conclusioni nel suono dell' organo" (Boulogne, 1608), said that the spinet, one form of harpsichord, was invented by Giovanni Spinetti, and took its name from him. Banchieri had seen such an instrument with the inscription, "Joannes Spinetus Venetus fecit, A. D. 1503." But the fact that De Muris enumerated the instruments of his time without naming the harpsichord or any of its kindred, while Cersne distinctly mentioned it in 1404, shows that it was certainly much older than

EVOLUTION OF THE PIANO 91

either Spinetti or Scaliger. Ottomarus Luscinius, a Benedictine monk, in his " Musurgia" (Strasburg, 1536), describes the virginal, a square instrument, of which the strings were plucked by plectra. Marin Mersenne, born at Oise, in 1588, in his "De Instrumentis Harmonicis," describes the clavicymbalum, which, according to his figure, is the same instrument as the spinet of Banchieri and the virginal of Luscinius.

There were, indeed, several varieties of shapes and many names for what were essentially the same instrument. Some were square, some were trapezoid, like our grand piano, and some were upright, but they all had the same plectral action and produced the same kind of tone. It will be readily understood that these instruments were incapable of gradations of power. No matter how forcibly or how gently the key was pressed, the elasticity of the plucking quill remained constant, and so produced just the same amount of twang from the string. Wooden uprights, called jacks, were placed at the inner ends of the key levers, where the tangents were in clavichords, and the quills ran through them. In some instruments pieces of hard leather were used instead of quills. Bach was acquainted with the harpsichord, though he always preferred the clavichord. Handel, Scarlatti, and Mozart were all great harpsichord performers. The instrument held its favor among musicians for a considerable time after the introduction of the piano, to which it finally had to yield the supremacy.

The first famous harpsichord builder was Johannes Baffo, Venice, 1574, but the most celebrated makers were: Hans Ruckers, Antwerp, 1575; Andreas Ruckers, his son, 1614, Tschudi and Kirkman, the English builders of Handel's day. Kirkman built harpsichords with two banks of keys and several sets of strings, which were controlled by stops similar to those of an organ. This was an attempt to overcome the dynamic monotony of the instrument, but I can testify from careful trial of the fine Kirkman harpsichords in the Steinert collection that the attempt was not a brilliant success. You can get an approximate idea of the sound of a harpsichord by plucking the strings of a modern piano with the plectrum of a mandolin, or with a common quill toothpick.

The invention which overthrew the clavichord and the harpsichord and brought into existence the piano was the hammer action. For years the problem of applying the keyboard to the principle of the dulcimer, already

EVOLUTION OF THE PIANO 93

explained, had occupied the minds of instrument builders. The solution was the work of Bartolomeo Cristofori, born at Padua, May 4, 1653, and it was made public in 1711. Two others claimed the honor: Gottfried Silbermann and Christopher G. Schröter. In 1726 Silbermann made two pianos and showed them to Bach, who condemned them because of their heavy touch and the weakness of their trebles. Silbermann was discouraged, but according to Agricola, a contemporary writer, he worked at improvements upon his instruments, and sold one of them to Frederick the Great, in whose music room it stood till 1880. It was then examined by Bechstein, the leading German piano maker of to-day, who found that it contained the Cristofori action. The priority of Cristofori's claims is established by an article written by Scipione Maffei and printed in the "Giornale dei Litterati d'Italia," in 1711, with a diagram of the inventor's hammer action. A translation of Maffei's article will be found in Rimbault's "The Pianoforte." (London, 1860.) It was also published in German in Matheson's "Musikalische Kritik," in Hamburg, 1725, so that the contemporaries of Silbermann and Schröter ought to have known of Cristofori's work. Indeed, Schröter's claim was made by himself in a letter written in 1738, which appears to have been evoked by irritation at Cristofori's glory.

It should be noted here that in the letters of an instrument maker named Paliarino, written in 1598, the instrument "piano e forte" is twice mentioned. It has been conjectured, and probably rightly, that this was a harpsichord with contrivances for loud and soft effects, for it is unlikely that even a rude hammer action could have been in existence more than a century before Cristofori's invention. It is, however, probable that some attempts were made before his, for his was altogether too satisfactory to have been anything but the result of a development. Nevertheless it was the first hammer action of permanent value, and its essential principles are employed in the finest actions of to-day. Therefore Cristofori fairly deserves the honor of inventing the piano. The instrument, however, did not gain great favor in Italy, owing to the inability of the harpsichord players to acquire the right touch, and it soon fell into disuse. Silbermann, however, following the details of Maffei's letter before-mentioned, built pianos, and other German makers, notably Friederici of Gera, who is said to have made the first square piano, followed his lead. At least as early as 1766 Johannes Zumpe built square pianos in England.

It would fill a volume to narrate the history of the successive steps in the development of the piano since the days of Zumpe. It is possible, however, to point out a few of the important steps. The famous maker, John Andrew Stein, Augsburg, was a pupil of Silbermann, and was born in 1728. He left a son, Andrew, also a maker, and a daughter, Nanette, who became Mrs. Streicher, and was the head of a great piano house in Vienna. The elder Stein's pianos were admired by Mozart, while Nanette Streicher's pianos were used by Beethoven. Before the time of the elder Stein the forte and piano effects, which gave the instrument its name, and which were then as now, produced by the action of the dampers, were obtained by operating " two iron springs, ornamented with copper knobs, in that part of the chest nearest the bass. In order to move these springs it was necessary that the player should use his left hand, and consequently he was obliged for a moment to quit the keyboard. Stein improved these springs by making them act by means of knobs placed against the knees." The modern pedals are first found in John Broadwood's patent of 1783. The pedals have been much improved since that time, and have played a very conspicuous part in the development of piano playing and of piano music. The "loud" pedal, as it is commonly called, is less used by pianists to gain force than to prolong sound, which before its invention could only be done by keeping the keys pressed down. With the dampers raised by the "loud" pedal, the strings struck continue to vibrate, while the fingers are free to go on striking other keys. This enables pianists to do far more than they could in early times in the way of producing sustained tones and modulations of harmony, and hence composers for the instrument are able to write passages which would formerly have been impossible.

Double, and even triple, stringing had been introduced in clavichords, and was continued in pianos. The elder Stein invented the shifting of the keyboard which causes the hammer to strike only one string instead of three. This contrivance is used by some of the best makers of the present day. Stein also improved the "escapement," the arrangement by which the hammer falls back the instant it has struck the string, and this, with other features of the action, was further developed by Streicher, so that the Viennese pianos became famous for the

EVOLUTION OF THE PIANO 97

extreme lightness of their touch, and music written by composers in that part of the world was designed to meet this quality. The English pianos, meanwhile, were built with heavier strings and a deeper fall of the hammer, so that greater sonority was attainable, and composers wrote for them bold passages in successions of heavy chords, which would have gone for nothing on a Viennese piano. At the very outset Cristofori had to shift the pins to which the wires were attached, from the soundboard, which would not stand the strain, to a separate rail. It became necessary to brace the whole interior with steel arches, of whose inventor there is no record, but Broadwood was the first to introduce the method now employed. Sebastien Érard, a celebrated French maker, introduced many improvements in the action and devised what was called then the "celeste" pedal, by which the hammers struck a strip of leather interposed between them and the strings. The leather is now replaced by felt. The iron frame, now replaced by steel and found in all fine pianos, was invented by Alpheus Babcock of Boston in 1825. Frederick W. C. Bechstein, of Berlin, in 1855 combined iron frames and the powerful English action in his instruments, and took a commanding position. The upright piano was patented Feb. 12, 1800, by John Isaac Hawkins of Philadelphia. Subsequent developments in the piano have been of too wide a range to be mentioned in the space at my command, and at any rate have all been in the nature of improvements, — highly important, indeed, but without radical departure from the fundamental features of the instruments.

A few words, however, must be said on the subject of equal temperament. Previous to the time of Bach and Jean Philippe Rameau, the scale of the piano was arranged according to the laws of acoustics. It is impossible to enter into this fully, but the result was that a piano could not be tuned to play in all the twenty-four keys. This is difficult to explain, but I shall endeavor to make it clear. The pitch of a tone is determined by the number of vibrations it makes in a second, and it follows that there must be a regular ratio of increase in the number of vibrations of the notes of a scale as we proceed upward. This establishes the scientific basis of the scale. Now, any one who is at all acquainted with the piano knows that the same black key is struck to produce either C sharp or D flat. But this has been true only since Bach's day. Previous to that time instruments were tuned according to the scientific laws, and by these we find that the C of the third octave has 256 vibrations, the C sharp 266.66, and the D flat 276.48. Thus D flat is a higher note than C sharp, and scientifically requires a differently tuned string and a separate key. The same trouble confronts us with most other notes, so that " theory requires no less than seventy-two keys to the octave in order that the musician may have complete command over all the keys employed in modern music."

In order to reduce the octave to twelve semi-tones with twelve keys and to make the sharps and flats agree, as they do now, the system of equal temperament deliberately puts out of tune every interval except the octave. By slightly lowering some and raising others, the present scale was obtained. Its advantage is that it makes it practicable to play in all twenty-four keys, and because of the identity of the sharps and flats it becomes easy to modulate from one key to another. For instance, C sharp, which is the distinguishing note of the scale of D major, is also D flat, and thus it becomes easy to modulate from D to D flat, which leads to G flat, a very remote key. This gives the modern composer immense freedom of style, and adds greatly to the key complexity of music, whereas, before the adoption of the system of equal temperament, composers had to confine themselves to a few closely related keys.

Who invented the system of equal temperament, no one knows. It is mentioned in the "Harmonie Universelle" of Marin Mersenne, the French writer before quoted, but it is quite certain that it was not extensively employed before the time of Bach, who brought the system to practical perfection, and demonstrated it in his "Well-Tempered Clavichord," a set of twenty-four preludes and fugues going through all the keys. The science of equal temperament was first set forth in a satisfactory manner by Jean Philippe Rameau, the French opera composer, in his "Traité de l'Harmonie," Paris, 1722.

Chapter VIII

The Evolution of Piano Playing

Work of the organ schools of Venice and Rome — Polyphonic playing and the advent of the singing style — Scale playing and the use of the thumb — Bach's fingering and Mozart's vocal playing — Development of tone-color — Pedalling and variety of touch — Chopin, Schumann, and Liszt technics.

THE origin of piano music, and, indeed, of much of the entire mass of modern instrumental music, was the organ compositions of the early masters. The early clavichords were used almost exclusively for the home practice of organists; and even after it became fashionable for young ladies to learn the art of playing, there was no difference whatever between the style of music written for the organ and of that composed for the clavichord, nor in the manner of playing either instrument. Every musician knows that in our time the kind of touch used for the organ is essentially different from that used for the piano, and that music suitable for one instrument is not suitable for the other. But it was not thus in the earliest days; for the only professional pianists (or clavichordists, to be more precise) were the organists, and instrumental music had not yet reached a state of development high enough to produce a divergence of styles. The fact that the same keyboard was used in both instruments was sufficient to suggest to the early organists that one style of playing was practicable for both. It naturally did not occur to them to write different sorts of music; and it is necessary, therefore, for us to inquire what was the nature of the early organ music.

We have already seen that when the organ was first introduced into the church it was employed simply to play the same notes as the voices sang. This practice naturally suggested to composers a style for their organ music when they began to write for the organ independently of the voices. Just when they began to do that it is not possible to say, because the early compositions have not been preserved as the great masterpieces of church counterpoint have. The first organist of repute whose name has come down to us was Francesco Landini, of Venice. He flourished about 1364. But we do not meet with any definite school of organists in Venice until the third period of the Netherlands school, when the great Adrian Willaert was the leading master. In 1547 was published a collection of music entitled "Ricercari da cantare e sonare," by Jacob Buus. These "ricercari" were compositions in the old ecclesiastical keys and the polyphonic style. "Da cantare e sonare" means that they were to be sung or played. Anything "cantata" was vocal, anything "sonata" was instrumental; and so after a time they began to call a composition for instruments alone a sonata, though it was a very different sort of work from a sonata by Mozart. In 1549 fantasies for three voices, vocal or instrumental, by Willaert were printed. Willaert used original themes in his fantasies, and his style shows a gradual approach to the modern manner. In 1551 was issued a collection by various authors, entitled "A New Collection of Various Kinds of Dances to be Played on the Harpsichord, Clavicimbal, Spinet, or Monochord." The word "dances" is very significant, because it shows the first recorded effort to write instrumental music in purely instrumental form. In this collection there was no polyphony, but the melody of the dance was in the treble, and the bass was a simple chord accompaniment. This is an evidence of the manner in which the music of the people began at that early date to influence compositions for instruments.

But the dominion of church counterpoint was not to be overthrown at once; and so we find that the first clearly defined instrumental form was the "toccata." Those of Claudio Merulo, a Venetian organist, printed in 1598, were the first to be published. They were written for the organ, and resembled Willaert's church vocal music in that they consisted of running or polyphonic passages, followed by successions of broad chords. Giovanni Gabrieli did more, perhaps, than any other of the Venetians to lead instrumental music toward the modern style. He wrote what he called "canzone;" and in these compositions the melody assumed a position of importance. Furthermore, he showed a tendency to make his melodic themes recur at regular intervals, although he had no well-defined system. Still, he made important advances. The Roman school of organists made valuable contributions to the development of instrumental music. Girolamo Frescobaldi (1591–1640) wrote ricercari in which there was something like a systematic employment of clear melodic themes. He wrote canzone in which there were passages slightly resembling the choral hymns of the Reformation; and in his "Capriccio Chromatico" he made a bold use of chromatic harmonies. Indeed, his music shows a general tendency toward the modern major and minor keys. We are not surprised, then, to find in the works of Bernardo Pasquine (1637–1710) arpeggios (running passages composed of the notes of chords, much used in modern piano music), flowing passages for both hands, and repetitions of the thematic ideas. But the manner of composing for the clavichord and harpsichord had been so greatly influenced at this time by the evolution of a distinct method of playing the instruments that we must, before advancing any further, go back and briefly review that topic.

The first systematic method of playing the organ and harpsichord was set forth in 1593 in a book by Girolamo di Ruta, a Venetian, and it contained rules for fingering which were in use for more than a century. A work by Lorenzo Penna, published at Bologna in 1656, shows very clearly what the general principles of clavichord and harpsichord technic were in that day. " In ascending the fingers of the right hand move one after the other, — first the middle, then the ring finger, again the middle, and so on in alternation. Care must be taken that the fingers do not strike against one another. In descending, the middle, followed by the index finger, is used. The left hand simply reverses this process. The rule for the position of the hands is that they shall never lie lower than the fingers, but shall be held high, with the fingers stretched out." This style of fingering held its own until Bach's time. It was in existence as late as 1741, though more fingers were employed. But the fingers were still held straight, and the thumb was not used.

It is difficult to separate the purely musical and the purely technical causes which led to the abandonment of the polyphonic style for the monophonic in piano music, and for that reason I must state them together. The first influence was the introduction of solo singing in vocal music. We shall review the history of that when we take up opera. It is sufficient at present to say that before 1600 all vocal music written by the art composers was in the ecclesiastical polyphonic style, and that the single-voiced song with accompaniment entered vocal music at the end of the sixteenth century. The influence of this new element made itself felt in instrumental music at once. We have noticed already that in Giovanni Gabrieli's works the melody assumed a new importance, and this importance constantly increased. The second cause was the full establishment of the difference between piano and organ technic. This was chiefly due to Domenico Scarlatti (1683–1757). It was in his day that the system of equal temperament was made known, though it may be doubted whether he lived long enough after its publication in those times of slow communication to profit by it. But he certainly did profit by the high state of excellence to which the manufacture of harpsichords had advanced. And he was greatly influenced by the operatic works of his father, Alessandro, in which the simple aria was the chief element of attraction. Domenico naturally endeavored to imitate the general form and melodic fluency of the aria in his sonatas, and in doing this he developed a harpsichord style of much beauty. He introduced many technical features which are purely modern, such as the execution of runs in double notes (thirds and sixths), the rapid repetition of the same note by striking it with different fingers in succession, and running arpeggios with both hands in opposite directions. Such feats were not called for by the polyphonic music, but the new style of writing made a great use of passages built on the successive notes of the scale, and to execute these a new manner of playing had to be evolved. In evolving it the musicians discovered new feats, and these in turn took their place in the compositions of the time.

In fact the development of the instrument itself affected the development of the technics of playing, and these affected the evolution of piano music. Then the music itself reacted on the technic, and this made new demands of the instrument makers. We have seen that when the early pianists set about the formulation of rules for playing their instruments they made poor work of it. Their rules were arbitrary and were not evolved from a study of the natural action of the hand. Smooth running of scale passages with such rules as those of Lorenzo Penna could be accomplished only at a very moderate pace. The old polyphonic compositions for the clavichord and harpsichord demanded of the player a technic which would enable him to bring out clearly the three or four voice-parts. The new style, which borrowed so much from vocal music, naturally sought for a smooth, flowing, even performance, in which the instrument should, as nearly as possible, sing like a solo voice with accompaniment. Emmanuel Bach, who wrote an important book on clavichord playing, proclaimed his belief that the singing style was the only true one for the instrument. These early musicians had, indeed, arrived at the heart of the matter, for the highest achievement of piano technic to-day is the preservation of a pure singing tone throughout the intricacies of modern music.

The discovery of the value of the thumb revolutionized clavichord and harpsichord playing. George Frederick Handel (1685–1759) and François Couperin (1668–1733) both made free use of the thumb, but it was Johann Sebastian Bach (1685–1750) who systematized its employment. He decided that the old position of the hand with the back flat and the fingers stretched to their full extent was unnatural. He saw that the whole strength of the fingers could not be brought to bear while they were in this position, and that the thumb could not be placed upon the keyboard at all. When he attempted to use his thumb, he had to raise the back of his hand and bend his fingers, and this he saw at once placed the whole hand in a position of command over the keyboard which it had never before possessed. He therefore rearranged the fingering of all the scales, introducing the system which still continues in use. Bach himself discovered that with his new system of fingering he could play polyphonic or monophonic music with equal ease, and hence we find that his compositions abound in both kinds of writing. He himself, being a church composer, naturally clung to the ecclesiastic style, and in his great organ and piano fugues transferred the whole contrapuntal science of the fifteenth and sixteenth centuries to instrumental music. But we shall see that better when we come to a consideration of the music apart from the technic and the style.

The singing style of playing was further developed by the immortal Wolfgang Amadeus Mozart (1756–1791). The instrument on which he played was the harpsichord, and the evenness of its tone encouraged his natural predilection for a vocal style. Mozart was a master of writing for singers, as is shown by his operas, and he readily saw his way to preserving the vocal manner in his playing of the harpsichord and his compositions for it. He held that a good pianist should have a perfect legato style (legato means "bound," and legato style is that in which the notes flow smoothly one into the other) a singing touch and a manner without affectation. Mozart did not live long enough to benefit much from the growing acquaintance with the newly invented piano, but one of his contemporaries, who outlived him by more than two-score years did so. This was Muzio Clementi (1752–1832), a man of no genius in composition, but of exceptional capacity for the reception of suggestions from his instrument. Clementi's mind appears to have been largely occupied with the problem of the possibilities of the piano. Yet he was not wholly devoted to the development of power and rapidity, for after a memorable meeting with Mozart he cultivated the singing style more assiduously than he had previously. He lived through a period of vital growth in music, for he was a contemporary of Haydn, Mozart, Weber and Beethoven. It would have been strange had he been insensible to the productions of such an era. In his youth, and indeed through most of his life he lived in England, and there he formed his early style on the English piano, which had thick strings, a heavy touch and a deep hammer fall. The result was that his music abounded in bold and brilliant passages of octaves, thirds, and sixths. He aimed at a sonorous and imposing musical diction, and he demanded of a pianist great physical power. Clementi's piano technic was the first which was clearly differentiated from that of the harpsichord and his "Gradus ad Parnassum" (1817) a series of 100 studies, remains to this day the foundation of solid piano playing. Many things have since been added to piano technic, but Clementi's rules lie at the base of it.

The works of Beethoven, to which more extended attention will be given hereafter, introduced nothing strictly new in the technic of piano playing, but they did compel certain changes in style. Beethoven wrote often in a new kind of polyphony, more free and striking than that of the early composers for the clavichord and harpsichord, and very much more difficult. This new polyphony was made practicable by the technics of Clementi, but it required an attention on the part of the pianist to the enunciation of the several voice-parts not required by Clementi's music. Again Beethoven displayed great originality in the treatment of musical rhythms, and the proper accentuation of notes having unexpected emphases required unusual independence of finger. This independence was highly developed by Beethoven's successors, and at the present day is absolutely indispensable to piano playing. But the most important demand of Beethoven's piano music was dramatic style. His music, as we shall see later, was the first outside of opera in which the expression of passion was sought, and this expression required that the pianist should have at his command a great range of force, from the gentlest pianissimo to the most imposing fortissimo, and a wide variety of what is called tone-color. This tone-color means quality of instrumental tone, and in a piano it is capable of many changes,

EVOLUTION OF PIANO PLAYING 113

hard or soft, sweet or harsh, melting or icy, as the necessities of the music require.

Beethoven, having departed by reason of the dramatic nature of his music, from the continually smooth legato of Mozart, paved the way for Weber, Chopin, Schumann, and Liszt to develop the highest powers of expression in the piano. To do this they had to carry variety of touch to its present state of progress and to evolve the modern use of the pedals, for tone-color is produced by different combinations of touch and pedalling. Weber imparted a new and joyous brilliancy to piano music, and much of his music requires a luxuriant richness of color. Beethoven had begun to make use of the pedals and in his last piano sonatas explicit directions are given for their use. Weber's music requires still more extended employment of them, but it was Chopin who systematized their use and showed how to get varieties of tone-color by employing them separately or in combination. Again, Chopin remodelled the Bach system of fingering by adapting some of the early methods to modern music. It is quite common now in certain kinds of passages to pass the third finger over the little one of the right hand or the little one under the third. Chopin wrote new kinds of passages of great beauty which cannot be played without resorting to this expedient and to others introduced by him.

Schumann added more to piano playing by writing in a very original style. His rhythms are very much involved, he treats accompaniments in an unusual manner, and he writes "interlocking" passages, in which both hands have to participate. To play Schumann's music well, a pianist must go through a special series of exercises to fit his hands for the work. Finally Liszt, who felt that the piano was as capable an instrument as the orchestra, if rightly treated, gave us the present development of the varieties of touch. He wrote studies designed to give pianists the most complete independence of finger, — a very necessary thing in modern piano music, in which very often two fingers of one hand may be engaged in enunciating a melody while the other three are assisting in the accompaniment. Liszt showed us the immense value of the loose wrist, without which the velvety quality of tone produced, when required, by such pianists as himself, Rubinstein, and Paderewski, is quite unattainable. Liszt taught his pupils to hold the wrist high, but more recent players use either a high or a low position accordingly as they desire sonority and brilliancy or mellowness and gentleness.

The whole development of piano playing has, of course, gone hand in hand with that of piano music, and that has followed the course of music in general. It becomes necessary, then, for us now to review the evolution of piano music. We have seen how it grew out of organ playing and was at first polyphonic. We have seen how the monophonic style — the melody with accompaniment — came in. We must now try to see how the polyphonic style worked itself out in the great compositions of Bach, and how the monophonic style developed itself in a new and highly organized form, the sonata, whose fundamental principles lie at the basis of all modern composition.

Chapter IX

Climax of the Polyphonic Piano Style

The development of the instrumental fugue — What is a fugue? — Its combination of polyphony with development of a theme — Johann Sebastian Bach and his organ and clavichord fugues — Fundamental traits of this music.

WHEN instrumental music began to develop independently it naturally followed the lines already followed by vocal music. That had been wholly contrapuntal, and instrumental music was at first entirely polyphonic. In its development the art of music inevitably fashioned certain forms, for no art can exist without form, which is the external demonstration of design. Without design there is no art. Musicians very soon learned that the first principle of form in music was repetition. A phrase of melody once heard and never repeated is quickly forgotten. A dozen different phrases in succession would not make a recognizable tune. The germinal part of the tune has to be heard often, and there must be a beginning, a middle and an end. For example:—

Now this is a melody in the pure song form, such as the earliest popular music contained. But the church composers, the only scientific musicians of the early day, in ignoring that form, as we have seen, developed a scheme of repetition of the identifying parts of their tunes by making the different voices sing them at different times. And this scheme evolved the art of polyphonic writing, which we have seen developed so beautifully by the Netherlands masters and the early Italian church composers. The reader will remember that the principle which lies at the foundation of polyphonic writing is "imitation." After instrumental music began to develop independently it clung for a time to the forms based on imitation, but when the vocal style became dominant in Italy, owing to the enormous popularity of the opera, imitation and its forms fled into Germany, where they found their highest embodiment in instrumental music in the North German fugue. The fugue is the most complex and highly organized polyphonic form we have, and it is necessary that the reader should know something of its construction.

A fugue has been defined as "a musical composition developed, according to certain rules of imitation, from a short theme or phrase called the subject. This subject is from time to time reproduced by each of the two, three, four, or more parts or voices for which the fugue is written." The subject, then, is a definite theme, of from four to eight measures, from which the fugue is developed. The next essential part is the answer. This is the first appearance of the subject in one of the subsidiary voices. This appearance is always in the dominant key, and usually has its last notes changed so as to make an ending. The counter-subject is that part of the theme of the first voice which forms the accompaniment to the answer. The announcement of these parts of the fugue is called the exposition. After the exposition the composer works up the melodic ideas of his material in passages of double counterpoint, free imitation, and various other polyphonic devices, all distributed so as to give interest and variety to the fugue, until he

THE POLYPHONIC PIANO STYLE 119

reaches the stretto, a portion in which by ingenious changes he brings out a climax, after which he may add a coda (tail-piece) and come to an end. Here is an example by Sir Frederic A. Gore-Ouseley:—

The reader will see at once that the exposition part of a fugue is built on the principles of double counterpoint, and that it is in its essentials the same kind of music as that written by the Netherlands masters for voices to sing in church. The distinguishing part of the fugue is the working-out of the thematic ideas by devices suitable solely to instrumental music with its freedom from text, the development of a climax, and the restatement of the original ideas before closing. It is in this well ordered discussion of musical ideas which have been laid down as primary propositions, that we find the immense advance of the fugue as an intellectual form over the polyphonic works of Lasso or Palestrina. I have already quoted Dr. Parry's statement that those writers rarely employed the "modern practice of using a definite subject throughout a considerable portion of a movement." This practice is at the foundation of all modern instrumental music, and its first complete systematization was reached in the fugues of Bach. Scarlatti and others were developing the principle in its application to monophonic music, but Bach, clinging to the polyphonic style, which was already far more advanced than the monophonic, and having a singularly deep insight into the soul of his art, attained perfection in the application of the new and vital principle to contrapuntal composition while the monophonic sonata was yet in its infancy.

The authoritative biography of the father of modern music is "The Life of Bach," by Dr. Philip Spitta, of Berlin. An excellent English translation is published. Johann

Sebastian Bach, a member of a family devoted to music through several generations, was born at Eisenach, in March, 1685. He received his early instruction from one of his brothers. His life was almost devoid of incident. He served as organist and concert-master in Arnstadt, Mülhausen, Weimar, and Anhalt-Koethen. He became cantor of the Thomas School in Leipsic in 1723, and retained that post till his death, July 28, 1750. In every department of music known to his time Bach demonstrated that he was a genius of the highest order. He is regarded as the most excellent of all models for students of composition because his works combine, in the highest beauty, originality of melodic ideas with profundity of design. His mastery of the formal material of his art enabled him to imbue the severest form, such as the fugue, with grace, beauty, and expressiveness. His melodic diction is not of the kind popular with the masses, and his music to-day is enjoyed only by those who truly love the best. But it is always played by artists and orchestras of high rank, and will continue to be heard probably for centuries.

Bach was a master of composition for the organ, for the clavichord, for the orchestra, for the solo voice, and for chorus. It is not possible in a book like this to give detailed consideration to his works. His famous settings of "The Passion" will be noticed in their proper place, and so will the influence of his orchestral compositions. At present we are to review briefly his piano compositions, which were written for the clavichord. This, perhaps, is one of the most remarkable features of these great works. Played on a modern piano, with all its power and brilliancy, they seem to be perfectly suited to it. The clavier compositions of Bach consist of "inventions," suites, preludes, fugues, sonatas, concertos, and fantasias. In his " Well-Tempered Clavichord," already mentioned, Bach left us a set of preludes and fugues which have never been surpassed. He also left us a treatise, "The Art of Fugue," in which the laws of the form are illustrated by sixteen fugues and four canons for one piano, and two fugues for two pianos all on the same theme.

Bach's organ toccatas and fugues grew directly out of the old style introduced by Merulo and the Venetian masters. They sought to bring out the power and variety of their instrument by contrasting chord passages of breadth and majesty with scale passages of brilliant character. Bach systematized this style of composition by showing

THE POLYPHONIC PIANO STYLE 123

how to produce contrast and variety while developing logically by the devices of counterpoint a definite subject and working up to a climax of great eloquence. In his works for the clavichord he demonstrated the same principle of subject and development, but in a style adapted to the nature of the instrument. His preludes and fugues are amazing not only in the extent of their mastery of the technics of composition, but also in their almost prophetic insight into the possibilities of the piano as a means of expression. All these preludes and fugues have a note of personal intimacy. Some are playful, some are bold, some are sad, some are full of celestial calm, some are passionately pathetic. The higher qualities of these compositions are their consistency, their sense of fitness, their apparent inevitableness. The subject of a Bach piano fugue not only suggests the answer and the logical development, but it fixes the character of the musical mood of the composition. The harmonies, the changes of key, the action and reaction of the imitative passages in double counterpoint, all are not only marvellous in their exhibition of technical skill, but all are of such a nature that they sustain and expound the feeling contained in the subject. It is this mastership of artistic organization that places the music of Sebastian Bach above that of all his contemporaries, all of his predecessors, and most of his successors. He moulded the rigid materials of canonic art, which held earlier composers in its grasp, to his own ends and left us instrumental polyphonic works which have never been equalled and which are still the fountainheads of our musical learning.

It ought to be noted that his own perfection of the system of equal temperament enabled him to do much that his predecessors could not have done, even had they possessed his genius. By making it possible to play in all twenty-four keys, and to modulate from the tonic of a composition into very remote keys, Bach introduced into instrumental polyphony an elasticity, a pliancy, a freedom, which it had never before possessed. He was able to fill his polyphonic writing with the passionate utterance of chromatic harmony; and in his "Chromatic Fantasia and Fugue" he produced a work which was actually a bridge between the style that went before him and the style that followed him. With Bach the development of instrumental polyphony came to an end. Nothing has been added to its technic except the application of the most recent laws of harmony. Bach was ahead of his time, and music was working out simpler problems than his when his work was completed. They were problems in monophonic style, and to these we must now turn our attention.

Chapter X

Monophonic Style and the Sonata

Corelli and his violin style — C. P. E. Bach and his departures from polyphony — General plan and purpose of the early sonata — Haydn and his two principal themes — Mozart and song-melody — Clementi and the influence of his style — Beethoven's improvements in sonata form — His employment of instrumental music for emotional expression.

THE fundamental difference between the sonata and the polyphonic forms is that the sonata is written in the monophonic style. Polyphony is, indeed, occasionally employed, but the reigning style is that in which a melody, song-like in character and sung by a single part, is accompanied by other parts written in chord harmonies. The necessary repetition of the melodic ideas is made, not by the process of imitation, as in the fugue, but by what is called the cyclical method. In this a tune or a composition always returns to a restatement of the original theme from which it started. We have seen how this melodic style entered instrumental music in the days of Giovanni Gabrieli, and how Domenico Scarlatti transferred to the harpsichord the aria of the opera. From this time forward the monophonic style developed gradually from the initial impulse of the vocal solo. Composers who had not Bach's peculiar insight into polyphonic writing and profound genius for it naturally sought a form which would give their melodies coherence and intelligibility. The rapid development of the violin as a solo instrument was one of the influences in directing them along certain lines of construction. The violin naturally lent itself to a flowing, song-like style, yet it is easy to see how easily such a style would fall into monotony. The early violin composers, in their search after a form which would embrace coherency, variety, and contrast, did much toward assisting piano writers to reach the true method of composing.

Arcangelo Corelli (1653–1713) was the most influential of these early violin composers. He endeavored to unite in his works the attractive and popular features of church music, song, and the dances of his time. The attractiveness of making compositions out of different kinds of dance movements in alternation had presented itself to composers at an early date. Morley, in his "Plain and Easy Introduction to Practical Music" (1597), says: "It is effective to alternate pavanes with galliards, because the former are a kind of staid music ordained for grave dancing, and the latter for a lighter and more stirring kind of dancing." This alternation of dances is what first suggested to composers the plan of following a slow movement with a lively one, or *vice versa*. As these different kinds of dances differed in rhythm,— the pavanes, for instance, being in common and the galliard in triple measure,— composers grasped the idea that changes in rhythm would heighten the contrast between movements. The one thing that did not seem to be settled at the outset— and that was due to the newness of harmonic as opposed to polyphonic style— was the matter of key contrasts. Sometimes these early writers put all their dance movements in one key, making what we now call a "suite," and sometimes they did not.

Corelli wrote his sonatas most frequently in four movements. The composers who immediately succeeded him wrote more often in three movements, but preserved the alternation of rhythm and tempo. Corelli used only one subject in each movement, and the development of it was of a simple nature compared to the developments found in subsequent works. Later composers found that in order to secure the necessary amount of contrast and variety, together with those points of repose which are essential to artistic form in music, it was necessary to have two principal themes of contrasting nature. The development of these themes was confined to the first movement, while the other movements were less complex in design. The Germans were not wholly idle in advancing the sonata, but it is extremely difficult to ascertain how their work and that of the Italians affected one another. We know that a violin sonata by H. J. F. Biber, published in 1681, shows a well-ordered sequence of contrasting movements. The first was a very slow one (largo), in contrapuntal style; the second, a passacaglia (theme and variations); the third, rhapsodical and declamatory; and the fourth, a gavotte. Dr. Parry has pointed out that Biber received his suggestions for the first movement from church polyphony, for the second and fourth from dances, and for the third from operatic declamation. This sonata, however, shows nothing of that methodic repetition of subjects and definite distribution of keys now regarded as indispensable; and in some respects Corelli's sonatas were of a distinctly higher type. Following the admirable analysis of Dr. Parry, I may state here that as early composers gradually perceived the possibilities of the sonata form, they evolved this scheme for their alternation of movement: —

1. Summons to attention, followed by appeal to intelligence through display of design.
2. Slow movement — appeal to the emotions.
3. Finale — lively reaction after emotion.

This treatment of the character of the movements grew out of the crude attempts of the earliest writers and was formulated in the concertos of Sebastian Bach, but more clearly in the piano sonatas of his son Carl Philip Emmanuel Bach. Previous to that, however, something had been done toward a definite arrangement of the distribution of keys. To this Domenico Scarlatti, who has already been mentioned, made some important contributions. His compositions called sonatas have a distinct melodic subject, and this is preserved throughout. His first movements foreshadow the shape which the first movements of the classical sonatas subsequently assumed. These movements are divided plainly into two parts, and each part is repeated. Each of them opens with an announcement of the melodic subject in the tonic key of the sonata. After stating his subject Scarlatti passes into a key closely related to that of the sonata, and gives a bit of what is called "passage work;" that is, florid or ornamental piano writing without a complete tune. The second part embarks upon a brief musical development of the subject by means of simple musical changes in its original shape, then modulates back into the original key, restates the beginning of the movement and comes to an end. One of the peculiarities of his works is that sometimes in the musical development ("working-out," as it is called) of his theme he introduces a new melody, different from the first. Later writers caught at this idea and raised this second melody to an importance equal to that of the first.

Scarlatti's great contemporary, Johann Sebastian Bach, did not stand in the direct line of development of the piano sonata. As I have tried to show in writing of clavichord works, his sympathies when composing for a keyboard instrument were governed largely by his immense genius for the organ and his profound insight into the nature and scope of polyphonic composition. Nevertheless, his violin sonatas, the result of a close and admiring study of those of Corelli and Vivaldi, show a leaning toward the modern form. He followed the lines laid down by Corelli. All but one of his violin sonatas are in four movements, the first and third slow, and the second and fourth lively. The slow movements, as one would naturally expect from Bach, are intense in their emotional eloquence. But Bach's manner of development was almost always polyphonic, and this was hostile to the sonata method, which was radically monophonic.

Carl Philip Emmanuel Bach (born, Weimar, March 14, 1714; died, Hamburg, Dec. 14, 1788), the third son of Sebastian Bach, was by nature and artistic taste fitted for the work which his father did not attempt. We have already noticed his theory that one should play the clavichord and write for it in the singing style. It was his feeling for this style and his keen insight into the capabilities of his instrument which made him, though not a composer of genius, a powerful agent in the establishment of the modern sonata form, — so powerful, indeed, that he has been called the father of the sonata. We owe something, however, to the demands of public taste. Music-lovers have usually, with the exception of the few, preferred the purely sensuous beauty of music to its intellectual qualities. They grew weary in those days of the severity of the fugue form; and the composers of the time naturally endeavored to

MONOPHONIC STYLE 133

supply them with what they desired, something easily, rhythmically pleasing. For years after Emmanuel Bach's day it continued to be the aim of composers to write with elegance and taste.

Emmanuel Bach excluded polyphonic writing from his sonatas, and adopted a style entirely monophonic. He contributed toward the development of the sonata in the direction of clearness and symmetry, and he insisted upon a well-regulated contrast of keys and of the characters of the different movements. In short, he established the outline of the sonata, with the exception of duality of themes, determined the direction in which it was to develop, and gave it a powerful impulse. The first sonatas in which Emmanuel Bach showed his ability were six published in 1742, and dedicated to Frederick the Great.[1] The opening movement of each is in the sonata form, as it existed then. The principal theme is properly announced, there is a short section of "working-out," and a conclusion with the principal theme in the tonic key. In the working out the composer does not use the principal key, and thus in returning to it in his conclusion gets

---

[1] The author desires to acknowledge his indebtedness at this particular point to "The Pianoforte Sonata," by J. S. Shedlock.

the effect of repose. In at least one of these sonatas, the second, there is a clearly marked second theme in the first part. There are touches of humor here and there in these sonatas, and some of the slow movements are full of feeling. The finales are all light and lively.

Emmanuel Bach is best known by six collections of sonatas and other compositions published at Leipsic between 1779 and 1787. In these sonatas the composer's resolute and final departure from the old polyphonic style is fully demonstrated. To enter wholly into the monophonic method of writing was no small undertaking, and we meet with many evidences of effort in these works. But the "working-out" part of the sonata is always monophonic. The composer takes passages or phrases from his original melody, and treating them with changes of pitch, harmonic modulation, and bits of passage-writing, founded on figures previously used in the statement of the theme, he makes a musical exposition of his original idea. This is precisely what later composers did, but they had better command of the monophonic style, and hence produced better music than Emmanuel Bach.

MONOPHONIC STYLE

OPENING OF A MOVEMENT BY E. BACH, SHOWING
CHANGE FROM POLYPHONIC STYLE.

The reader should now be in a position to understand that it is expected that at least one of the three or four contrasting movements of a sonata should be in what is called sonata form. This is almost always the first movement, in accordance with the general design of movements already given. This movement consists of three parts, which may be called proposition, discussion, and conclusion. The propositional part proposes a theme or themes; the discussion subjects the theme or themes to every device of musical treatment; and the conclusion restates the themes in their original form and brings the movement to a restful finish. Up to the point at which we have now arrived composers proposed, as a rule, only one theme for discussion. Occasionally a second was introduced, but it seems to have been merely episodal. We now come to the time when two themes were employed systematically, and from that time dates the establishment of the complete outline of the present sonata form. All the changes since made are in details. The composer by whom this important work was done was Haydn.

Josef Haydn was born April 1, 1732, in Rohrau, Austria. He studied first at home and afterward at Vienna. In 1759 he became conductor of a small orchestra maintained by Count Morzin, and in 1760 he married a wigmaker's daughter, who had been his pupil. In 1761 Haydn became conductor of the orchestra of Prince Esterhazy at Eisenstadt, where he remained thirty years industriously

MONOPHONIC STYLE 137

composing. He became acquainted with Mozart, for whom he entertained the highest admiration. In 1790 he visited London and was received with great enthusiasm, so that he made a second visit in 1794. He died May 31, 1809, eighteen years before the death of Beethoven, and four years before the birth of Wagner. His music, therefore, brings us into close connection with the present period. His music is accessible to players of the piano, and there are good editions of his sonatas.

Haydn has been called the father of the symphony and the string quartet, and his most important compositions are in these departments. But a symphony is simply a sonata for orchestra, and a quartet is one for four instruments. Hence we shall find that Haydn's piano sonatas show the same advances in form as his symphonies and quartets. In the first movements of three of his earliest sonatas (op. 22, 24, and 29) he uses in the propositional part two principal themes, wholly different from one another. He did not, however, in the works of his middle life follow this plan, but in his English symphonies he used second themes invariably and in a manner which allows no room for doubt as to his definite purpose. The form of his first movements is clear and symmetrical. It is in three parts, the proposition, discussion, and conclusion being plainly distinguished. The working-out part is shorter and simpler than those found in later sonatas, such as Beethoven's. But Haydn's first movements convince the hearer of their claims to consideration as works of art on lines of design carefully planned. The systematic use of the second theme was adopted by all subsequent composers, and was the means of raising the sonata from an experiment to the most satisfactory and convincing of all musical forms.

In Haydn's three-movement sonatas the appeal to the intelligence by the opening allegro is always followed by an appeal to the emotions in a slow movement, with broad melody and harmony and much sentiment. His finales are always bright and lively, and frequently sparkle with gayety. In form the finale is usually a rondo, an early cyclical form in which a single melodic subject is periodically repeated, the repetitions being separated by passages of new matter. When Haydn wrote a sonata in four movements, he introduced as the third the minuet, a piece of music in dance rhythm. Emmanuel Bach had used this form in one or two of his sonatas, but it is easy to see that the idea was originally suggested by the

MONOPHONIC STYLE

alternation of different kinds of dances in the archaic sonatas of Biber and Corelli. The minuet, being a graceful and elegant dance in triple rhythm, formed a most excellent bridge between an emotional slow movement and a jocund finale. The minuet movement consists, as a rule, of two parts, called minuet and trio. In the old dance it was customary to give relief to the first melody by a second, always written in three-part harmony and hence called "trio." This plan, except the adherence to three-part harmony, was followed by the artistic composers when they adopted the minuet as part of the sonata. In addition to what has been said, two important facts must be noted. Haydn was intimately acquainted with the simple, fluent melody of Italian music, and he was not acquainted with Bach's "Well-Tempered Clavichord." The result was that his themes are all essentially song-like in character. They are more extended and more definite in shape than Emmanuel Bach's, and they helped to fix more firmly the distinctive character of monophonic composition.

After Haydn was born, and before he died, Mozart lived. Wolfgang Amadeus Mozart was born at Salzburg, Jan. 27, 1756. He received his early tuition from his father, an excellent musician, and speedily developed into a "wonder child." He made several tours through Europe as a pianist, but finally settled in Vienna, where he married and spent the remainder of his brief life in pouring out operas, quartets, songs, sonatas, and other compositions, some of which were certainly made to sell, but all of which display something of his marvellous genius. It cannot fairly be said of Mozart that he contributed a great deal that was new to the mere technics of sonata writing. Mozart had little of the spirit of the explorer, and less of that of the reformer. He was content to take musical forms as he found them and instil into them a vitality which was inseparable from serious attempts at composition. Some of his works, indeed, show the evil results of that fatal facility which is a menace to art; but nearly all of them display a fecundity of invention, a grace and freedom of style, and a sense of artistic elegance which did much to influence subsequent writers.

Mozart's piano sonatas are worthy of the pianist's attention, but they cannot be said to have done anything toward the advancement of the form which Haydn's did not. Mozart learned the sonata form from Haydn's works. He gave something back

MONOPHONIC STYLE 141

to his teacher, but it was chiefly in the shape of suggestions as to instrumental treatment, for Mozart was a master pianist, and Haydn was only a respectable performer. Mozart's sonatas show wonderful cleverness in adapting to the idiom of the piano the vocal style of the contemporaneous Italian opera, of which Mozart was the finest composer. His C minor sonata, written in 1784, is his greatest piano work. It is so fine that, except for the comparative baldness of its instrumental style, it ranks with the works of Beethoven's middle period.

The reader must bear in mind the important fact that instrumental music, pure and simple, was still young, and that composers were chiefly engaged in developing musical beauty. The technics of instrumental writing were not sufficiently advanced to admit of high emotional expression. The reader will remember that in the old schools of church counterpoint the technics of the art were developed by Okeghem, after which Josquin des Prés showed how to write beautifully, and the masters of the last period discovered how to make beauty go hand in hand with expression. So the early writers of the sonata were chiefly engaged in experimenting with the technics of their new form and the instruments for which they wrote, and this paved the way for Haydn and Mozart, when once the former had established the sonata form, to seek for pure beauty. This they found, and Mozart's works in particular abound with it. The time was now at hand when the sonata form was to be made the vehicle for the expression of the most profound human emotion. But before it could achieve that end, something had to be added to its technic and its organization. Part of this addition was made by Clementi.

Muzio Clementi (1752–1832) was born before Beethoven and died after him. His works show that he at first influenced Beethoven but was afterward influenced by him. Clementi's masculine treatment of the piano, which we have already noticed, went far toward leading Beethoven away from the thin style of Haydn and Mozart. There are many passages in Clementi's early sonatas which are similar in construction to passages afterward written by Beethoven. Again, Clementi extended and elaborated the "working-out" part, and sometimes introduced into the body of a movement phrases from its introduction. But the works of Beethoven speedily superseded those of Clementi, and it is to these we must now turn our attention. Fortunately they call for only brief discussion, for

MONOPHONIC STYLE 143

Beethoven's sonatas are more remarkable for their content than for their form.

Ludwig van Beethoven was born at Bonn, Dec. 16, 1770. He studied music in his native city and in Vienna, receiving a few lessons and much encouragement there from Mozart. He was for a time in the service of the Elector of Cologne, but in 1792 he went to Vienna to study under Haydn, and there he finished his life, dying March 26, 1827. In Beethoven's youth the technics of sonata composition had reached the point of complete beauty, and the young man soon set about making the sonata the vehicle of personal expression. In doing so he introduced some improvements into the form. First of all he leaped to a greater freedom in the use of keys. He not only wandered into more remote keys than his predecessors within the limits of a movement, but he made wider changes of key in passing from one movement to another. He elaborated the slow introduction which preceded many of his first movements (by no means all) and made it of high significance. He constructed the passage-work leading from the first theme to the second out of material taken from the first theme, thus making a logical connection. He sometimes introduced in the "working-out" part new thoughts, derived from the original matter. He made intentional and highly expressive use of the practice of running one movement into another without a pause, a device which had been employed by Emmanuel Bach for purely musical effect. Beethoven used it for purposes of emotional expression. The complete first-movement form, as developed by Beethoven, is as follows:—

FIRST PART.

Slow introduction (not always used): first theme, in the tonic: connecting passage: second theme, in a related key: concluding passage. [Repeat first part.]

MIDDLE PART.

"Working-out"—a free fantasia on both themes, developing all their musical possibilities and dramatic expression by devices of instrumental color, harmony, counterpoint, etc.

THIRD PART: RECAPITULATION.

First theme, in the tonic: connecting passage: second theme, in the tonic: coda.

In place of the old minuet movement Beethoven introduced the scherzo.

Scherzo means joke, and the scherzo was originally a light, genial composition not to be taken seriously. Haydn in writing his minuets took the stateliness out of their movement and imbued them with humor. Beethoven, preserving the form and rhythm of the minuet, so changed its tempo and its melodic style that it became a new kind of writing, which he called scherzo. But from a merely jocular movement this grew in his hands to be one of grim humor, and even, as in the C minor symphony, of mystery and awe.

The slow movement usually follows the first movement. If there are four movements, the scherzo is generally third, and the finale, instead of being merely bright and lively, is raised to an emotional importance nearly as great as that of the first movement, which it frequently follows in form. Beethoven's music has been divided into three styles, that of his earliest works showing distinctly the influence of Haydn and Mozart. Then comes a transition, to which the "Kreuzer" sonata and the "Eroica" symphony belong, and after that comes the second period, containing the works of the master's maturity, such as the piano sonata in D minor, the "Appassionata," and the fifth and seventh symphonies. The third style embodies the sorrow and bitterness of Beethoven's unhappy last years, and includes the ninth symphony and the last five piano sonatas.

In the presence of Beethoven's music I always feel the helplessness of analysis or critical study. It is useless to try to reveal the why and wherefore, but it cannot be denied that Beethoven's sonatas convey to the hearer not only the presence of an imposing personality, but the conviction that the expression of the music is not simply individual, but general. There is a breadth and a depth to the utterance of these works which belong not to one man but to humanity. Beethoven succeeded in introducing into instrumental music that direct, sweeping, overwhelming proclamation of emotion which had previously been regarded as the exclusive property of the singer's voice. Beethoven's music is essentially the dramatization of pure tones. His intense expression was not the result of accident. He hungered for it and studied the means of imparting it to his music. In doing so he solidified the structure of the sonata in such a way that he made it the most symmetrical, highly organized, and yet elastic of all musical forms, and paved the way for the whole school of romantic composers who followed him, and who tried not only to make music express the great elementary emotions, as he did, but also to make it tell complete stories. Their purposes are best exemplified in their orchestral works, and I must defer discussion of them till after the reader has accompanied me in a review of the development of the orchestra and orchestral music.

Chapter XI

Evolution of the Orchestra

Early groupings of instruments without definite plan — Significance of the work of Monteverde — Scarlatti's use of the string quartet — Handel and the foundation of the modern style — The symphonic orchestra of Beethoven — Berlicz, Wagner, and special instrumental coloring — Plan of the contemporaneous orchestra.

THE modern orchestra is about two hundred years old. That is to say, the first skeleton of our present arrangement of instruments is found near the close of the seventeenth century. Earlier than that the distribution of instruments and the manner of writing for them contained none of the essential elements of the present style. Three centuries ago lutes and viols were employed in combination with drums and trumpets in a very confused manner, and even for this assembly of instruments there were no special compositions. An orchestra as such can hardly be said to have made its appearance until the time when the development of music as a part of dramatic entertainments compelled the preparation of some sort of substantial accompaniment to the choruses and dances. In the "Ballet Comique de la Royne" (1581) of Beaujoyeux there was an array of oboes, flutes, cornets, trombones, violas di gamba (precursor of the violoncello), lutes, harps, flageolet, and ten violins. This looks like a tolerable orchestra, but the manner of writing for it prevented it from being one. The performers were separated into ten bands, each designed to accompany some particular character or set of characters. Neptune and his followers, for example, used harps and flutes. The ten violins were employed only in one scene. In those days, as we have already seen, compositions were written " da cantare e sonare," and a canzone for strings was simply a piece of vocal polyphony played instead of sung.

The advent of Italian opera and oratorio ushered in the first organized use of the orchestra. Cavaliere's "Anima e Corpo," an oratorio, had an orchestra consisting of a viola di gamba, a harpsichord, a bass lute, and two flutes. This orchestra, like that of the Bayreuth theatre, was concealed. But it was not used like a modern orchestra. For instance, the composer recommended that a violin be employed to accompany the soprano voice throughout the work. This oratorio was produced in February, 1600, and in December of the same year at the first performance of Peri's opera, "Eurydice," the orchestra consisted of a harpsichord, a viola di gamba, a large guitar, a theorbo (large lute), and three flutes. These last instruments were used only to imitate the sounds of a Pandæan pipe, played by a shepherd in the opera.

A decided advance in the development of the orchestra was made by Claudio Monteverde, whose "Orfeo" (1608) had an accompaniment of two harpsichords, two bass viols, ten tenor viols, two "little French violins," one harp, two large guitars, two organs (small ones), two violas di gamba, four trombones, one regal (a little reed organ), two cornets, one piccolo, one clarion (an instrument of the trumpet family), and three trumpets. But even in this opera Monteverde showed that he had not discovered the true relations of the instruments. The "little French violins" seem to be the first modern violins used in the orchestra, yet they may have been somewhat crude instruments, for the first maker of real violins of whom we know anything was Gasparo di Salo (1542–1610). He was a much better maker of violas than of violins, and it was Giovanni Paolo Maggini (1581–1631) who left us the violin as we have it to-day. Monteverde may have regarded violins from Salo's Lombardy home, Brescia, as French, because the French and Italians were continually at war there. The violin, having once entered the orchestra, however, speedily began to move toward its proper position as the principal voice, and as soon as composers recognized its sphere, they began to employ the other instruments with due regard for their relative capacities. Monteverde was the first composer who took advantage of the contrasting qualities of tone in the orchestra. His position in regard to the treatment of orchestral music shows a remarkable advance, and had a direct and wide influence upon the development of the orchestra.

Monteverde's operas contain many bits of independent orchestral music, but it was in attempting to illustrate the incidents of his dramas by means of the orchestral part that he divorced the accompaniment from the voice parts and discovered the relative values of some of his instruments. In one of his operas he uses a string quartet, composed of three violas and a bass, and while the voices sing the text to a recitative, these instru-

EVOLUTION OF THE ORCHESTRA 151

ments depict the rushing together of horses in combat, the struggle of the opponents, and other actions not described by the text, but performed by the actors. In writing this passage Monteverde invented two well-known effects: the tremolo (a rapid tremulous repetition of a single note), and the pizzicato (plucking the strings with the fingers). The feeling for instrumental description displayed in this score led Monteverde to emphasize the essential utility of the strings, and at the same time it led him to use the other instruments to produce contrasts.

In the opera "Giasone" (1649) of Cavalli we find a song accompanied by two violins and a bass in a style which lasted till Handel's day. Alessandro Stradella in 1676 used a double orchestra in which violins were the principal instruments. About the same time we find Alessandro Scarlatti writing for first and second violins, violas, and basses, distributing the parts in quartet form, in the same way as composers do to-day. He used his first violin as the soprano of his string quartet, his second violin as the alto, his viola as the tenor, and his bass as the fundamental bass. Wind instruments continued to be used to add color and contrast to the foundation of strings and in tutti passages

(passages enlisting all the instruments of an orchestra at once) to strengthen them.

It is hardly necessary to stop to consider the orchestra employed by Sebastian Bach, because his system of writing for orchestra was not in the direct line of development, though modern composers have learned much from it. In his string writing he is an excellent master for the present, but his wood wind parts (flute, oboe, or bassoon) are written usually in such a way that they become separate solo voices. In short, his instrumental scores lean toward the polyphonic, rather than the monophonic style. Handel (1685-1759) employed an orchestra much like that of to-day, and methods not unlike those of the present in writing for it. In fact Handel's orchestra may be regarded as the foundation of the modern symphonic band. In his big oratorio choruses Handel used a number of oboes to strengthen the violin parts, and a number of bassoons to strengthen the basses, but in other parts of the same works he used the wind instruments to enrich the general score with independent parts. Again, he employed the wind and strings separately, contrasting one with the other just as modern composers do.

In the Hallelujah Chorus of Handel's "Messiah" the orchestra consists of two trumpets, kettle-drums, violins, violas, and basses. In the chorus, " How Excellent," in " Saul," the composer uses three trombones, two trumpets, kettle-drums, three oboes, violins, violas, and basses. For the purpose of comparison, it may be stated that in his mass in B minor Sebastian Bach used three trumpets, tympani (kettle-drums), two flutes, two oboes, two bassoons, violins, violas, basses, and organ. The use of the wooden wind instruments in pairs is noteworthy because subsequent composers followed that practice. Haydn's earlier works are written for two horns, two oboes, two flutes, and the usual array of strings. In his later works Haydn employs nearly the full modern orchestra. In " The Creation " he uses two trumpets, tympani, three trombones, two clarinets, two horns, two oboes, two flutes, two bassoons, a contra-bassoon, violins, violas, and basses. Haydn introduced the violoncello into the orchestra, thus completing the modern list of bowed string instruments; and Mozart demonstrated the value of the clarinet, thus completing the wood wind.

Beethoven's full orchestra consisted of two flutes, two oboes, two clarinets, two bassoons, four horns, two trumpets, three trombones, tympani, and the usual array of strings. These instruments stand in this order in Beethoven's scores, reading from the top of the page downward, and subsequent composers have followed this arrangement. When voices appear in the score, they are placed between the violin and violoncello parts. Contemporaneous composers incline to abandon that custom, and to place the voices just above the first-violin part. This will keep the string parts, the foundation of the accompaniment, together below the voices, thus making the score easier for the conductor to read. Beethoven's orchestra was substantially that of Schubert, Spohr, Mendelssohn, Weber, and Schumann.

Later composers began to use various characteristic instruments in their scores in order to obtain special effects of what is called instrumental color. Hector Berlioz (1803–1869) did very much to advance this line of development, and Richard Wagner (1813–1883) carried on the work. Not only are special instruments, such as the English horn (a wooden wind instrument with a pastoral tone, heard, for instance, as the shepherd's pipe in "Tannhäuser" and "Tristan and Isolde"), introduced, but the general mass of instruments is enlarged or diminished according to the composer's design. For instance, in the first scene of Act III., "Die Walküre," in which is the famous "Ride

EVOLUTION OF THE ORCHESTRA 155

of the Valkyrs," Wagner uses two piccolos (small, high-pitched flutes, with a fife-like tone), two flutes, three oboes, one English horn, three clarinets, one bass clarinet, eight French horns, three bassoons, four trumpets, one bass trumpet, four trombones, one contrabass tuba (a very deep-toned brass instrument), four tympani, cymbals, snare-drums, two harps, and the usual body of strings. Wagner specifies thirty-two violins (sixteen first and sixteen second) as necessary to produce the proper balance of tone. Older composers were content to take their chances in such matters. In "Götterdämmerung" the funeral march is scored for three clarinets, one bass clarinet, four horns, three bassoons, two tenor tubas, two bass tubas, one contrabass tuba, one bass trumpet, four trombones, tympani, and strings. The absence of flutes, oboes and trumpets shows that Wagner was aiming at a gloomy color, to be obtained only by the omission of such instruments and the use of an increased number of those of low pitch.

The orchestra of to-day consists of four groups of instruments, which can be enlarged or curtailed according to the design of the composer. These are, in the order in which they usually stand in the score, wind instruments of wood (the "wood wind"), wind instruments of brass (called simply "the brass"), instruments of percussion (drums, cymbals, etc.), and strings. The general plan of the orchestra, which has developed from the earliest attempts at instrumental contrast, contemplates such a distribution of instruments in each department as to make that department capable either of independent employment, or of combination with the whole or part of some other department, or of incorporation in the mass of tone produced by the whole orchestra. The wood wind, for example, consists of flutes and oboes, which are purely soprano instruments, clarinets, which extended from upper bass to moderately high soprano, English horn, which has a tenor range, bass clarinet, which runs from deep bass up into treble, and bassoons, which comprise bass, baritone, and tenor registers. That organization of instruments is capable of independent performance, possessing, as it does, all the components of full and extended harmony and a wide variety of color.

The brass choir consists of trumpets, which are soprano instruments, French horns (bass to alto), trombones (bass, baritone, and tenor), and tubas (bass). This band is capable of independent performance, or of being joined in a body with the wood,

EVOLUTION OF THE ORCHESTRA 157

as in military music, or of combining with the strings on the plan seen in its infancy in Handel's "Hallelujah" chorus. The strings, of course, contain all the elements necessary to independence or combination. The modern orchestra, however, has gained enormously in power from the development of methods of using parts of the separate choirs independently or in combination. For instance, flutes, clarinets, and bass clarinet can produce rich four-part harmony, and so can play alone. Flutes, oboes, and bassoons can do the same thing and produce a wholly different instrumental color. Bassoons and French horns make fine deep-toned harmonies; and four French horns can play alone in full harmony. Any of these little groups can be joined with strings to get a new quality of tone. Thus it is not difficult to see that the modern orchestra offers to the composer a great variety of instrumental combinations, giving him a remarkable range of coloring, and it is equally plain that these conditions have been gradually developed by successive composers since the days of Monteverde.

Chapter XII

The Classic Orchestral Composers

"Sinfonia avanti l'Opera" — Its development into the overture — Effect of this on orchestral composition — The classical symphony — Haydn and his achievements — Exploring the secrets of orchestral writing — Mozart and his notable system — Condition of the symphony when Beethoven began writing.

THE classic orchestral composers are those who wrote the classic piano sonatas, and they developed their orchestral works on the same lines as those of their piano works. The symphony, as I have already said, is nothing more nor less than a sonata for orchestra; but it has its special characteristics, and these deserve some attention. The word "symphony" was first applied to separate instrumental portions of operas. For instance, an extended introduction to an aria was called "sinfonia." As ballet movements were introduced into operas, and instrumental preludes came to be employed, these separate pieces were more and more extended, and the term "sinfonia" came to be of considerable significance. The early composers were compelled to seek for some coherent design for their symphonies and as that played before the opera was the most independent of all, it was that in which a definite form first made its appearance. It was at first called "Sinfonia avanti l' Opera" — "symphony before the opera." As such it was written by Alessandro Scarlatti (1659-1725), and the French composer, Giovanni Battista Lulli (1633-1687). Lulli's overtures, as they came to be called, were divided into three movements, slow, lively, and slow, without pauses between them. A diametrically opposite form to this came to be known as the "Italian Overture." Its movements were lively, slow, lively — like those of the three-movement sonata — except that there was no pause between movements. The origin of this form is the same as that of the alternating movements of the sonata. It took firm hold as soon as it appeared, and from the beginning of the eighteenth century was the acknowledged form.

The symphony now moved forward on much the same lines as those of the piano sonata, and what has been said about the early steps in the development of that form will apply to this one. It should be noted, however, that the introduction of playing opera overtures at concerts greatly aided the development of the symphony. The introduction of this custom was due to the time-honored habit of going late to the opera. The bustle of arrivals prevented the overtures from being heard, and so it became the custom to play them separately. The early instrumental concertos had very great influence on the development of the symphony, because they showed composers the essential differences between piano and orchestral composition. These were not like our modern concertos, written to display the resources of some solo instrument, but were literally concerts of instruments. In the earliest forms contrasts of tone and power were obtained by using a single trio or quartet of strings for the principal passages, and bringing in additional strings (called "ripieno" instruments) to enforce the tone in the tuttis. Alessandro Scarlatti wrote concertos of this sort. Sebastian Bach wrote a number of concertos for instruments, and all of them are in the three-movement form based on the Italian overture. Handel also wrote concertos. But these concertos of Handel and Bach were in the contrapuntal style, and the genius of the sonata form was tending always toward the monophonic style.

CLASSIC ORCHESTRAL COMPOSERS 161

For that reason these concertos did not have so direct an influence on the symphony as did the overture, which naturally followed the vocal style of the opera.

The symphony in the early stages of the classical period, which began with Emmanuel Bach, followed pretty closely the lines of the piano sonata in form. E. Bach was at work writing symphonies when Haydn was a little boy. It must be confessed, however, that his symphonies are less distinct in form than his piano sonatas. It is because of the decided clearness of the orchestral works of Haydn that he is celebrated as the father of the symphony. He established the sonata form and it is not at all surprising that he applied it successfully to his orchestral compositions. Haydn wrote (or is said to have written) one hundred and eighteen symphonies, beginning in 1759 and continuing to his later years. His earliest works are so irregular and uncertain that they do not throw much light on anything except his instrumentation. His position as conductor of Prince Esterhazy's orchestra gave him abundant opportunity to experiment with instrumental forms and effects, and his symphonies written during his long service in the Esterhazy household show steady advance in style. The Esterhazy orchestra contained in

1766, six violins and violas, one 'cello, one double bass, one flute, two oboes, two bassoons, and four horns. It was afterward enlarged to twenty-two, including trumpets and kettle-drums. In 1776, after Haydn had learned from Mozart how to use clarinets, two of these instruments were added, making twenty-four in all. It was a pretty small orchestra according to our present ideas, but it sufficed for the establishment of the symphony.

Haydn improved not only in his method of developing the subjects of his movements, but in his knowledge of the kinds of themes best fitted for orchestral treatment, which are organically different from those suited to the piano. His experiments in instrumentation went far towards assisting composers to a true knowledge of the art of orchestration (writing for orchestra). He himself learned rapidly from the trials of his own combinations by the Esterhazy band. In his early days, for instance, he frequently wrote the same part for his first and second violins and the same part for his violas and basses, so that his strings were playing in only two real parts, and his harmony was very thin. His treatment of the wood wind was crude at first, but his experiments rapidly improved this, and by 1770 he had introduced the now

CLASSIC ORCHESTRAL COMPOSERS 163

familiar style of making the wind instruments intone long chords, while the strings played figured passages, or *vice versa*. The movements of all his symphonies are very short, and one who looks for great breadth or depth in them will be disappointed. They are bright and genial, except in their slow movements, which are generally tender without being pathetic. In the first movements the working-out is usually short, and not at all involved, as if Haydn were timid about presenting too much for intellectual consideration at one time. The finale is generally in rondo form, so that there is only one real working-out in the whole symphony.

It must be borne in mind that the public taste of that time would hardly have been prepared for such advanced works as those of Beethoven, even if Haydn's technic of composition had been equal to the task of writing them. The composer was thoroughly in accord with the spirit of his time, and his influence in popularizing good music cannot be over-estimated. Haydn's later works show a marked advance over his earlier ones, which must be attributed to the influence of Mozart. The reader will remember that Mozart's life began after and ended before Haydn's. Mozart also had opportunities to learn something about the possibilities of orchestral music while he was at Mannheim in 1777. The band there was one of the finest in Europe at the time, and its excellent achievements in light and shade no doubt gave Mozart many valuable suggestions. Mozart wrote forty-nine symphonies, but only three of them are heard often to-day: that in E-flat major, op. 543, that in G minor, op. 550, and that in C major, op. 551, commonly called the "Jupiter" symphony. These were his last three symphonies, written in 1788, and it is notable that in none of the three is the full Beethoven orchestra employed. All three use only one flute. The E-flat symphony has clarinets, but no oboes. The other two have oboes, but no clarinets. The G minor has no drums nor trumpets, and none has trombones. Nevertheless, by the pure beauty of their melodic subjects, the clearness of their discussion, and their general grace and symmetry, these works have succeeded in maintaining a place among living music. They are most satisfactory examples of the kind of composition produced in the classic period, the period of pure beauty in music. It is difficult to discuss the work of Mozart with judicial calm, even at this distance from the time of its performance. Contemporaneous records all bear such enthusiastic testimony as to the extraordinary genius of the wonderful boy that it is difficult to avoid injustice to his works. We must remember that in Mozart's boyhood, when he wrote his first symphonies, the form of the sonata was still uncertain, and we must, therefore, be satisfied with finding in his precocious compositions a keen perception of the value of balance and continuity.

It was after writing his first three symphonies that Mozart began to hear operas, and this greatly improved his style. His Parisian symphony, opus 297, produced in 1778, shows the results of his operatic study as well as his attention to the Mannheim band. The first movement is decidedly irregular in form, abounding in different melodies and striking harmonies. The subjects are dramatic in feeling, but in construction are essentially orchestral. In his last three symphonies he shows a complete mastery of the organization of the orchestral sonata in its then stage of development, which was chiefly his work. A peculiarity of Mozart's style was its generous employment of free counterpoint,— that is, polyphonic writing in which the different voices occasionally intone different melodies (or parts of them) at the same time, without adherence to canonic law. This kind of counterpoint is common in modern orchestral composition. Otto Jahn, the authoritative biographer of Mozart, says : —

"The perfection of the art of counterpoint is not the distinguishing characteristic of this symphony [C major] alone, but of them all [the last three]. The enthralling interest of the development of each movement in its necessary connection and continuity consists chiefly in the free and liberal use of the manifold resources of counterpoint. The ease and certainty of this mode of expression make it seem fittest for what the composer has to say. Freedom of treatment penetrates every component part of the whole, producing an independent, natural motion of each. The then novel art of employing the wind instruments in separate and combined effects was especially admired by Mozart's contemporaries. His treatment of the stringed instruments showed a progress not less advanced, as, for instance, in the free treatment of the basses, as characteristic as it was melodious. The highest quality of the symphonies, however, is their harmony of tone-color, the healthy combination of orchestral sound, which is not to be replaced by any separate effects, however charming. In this combination consists the art of making the orchestra as a living organism express the artistic idea which gives the creative impulse to the work, and controls the forces which are always ready to be set in motion. An unerring conception of the capacities for the development contained in each subject, of the relations of contrasting and conflicting elements, of the proportions of the parts composing the different movements, and of the proportions of the movements to the whole work; finally, of the proper division and blending of the tone-colors,—such are the essential conditions for the production of a work of art which is to be effective in all its parts. Few persons will wish to dispute the fact that Mozart's great symphonies display the happiest union of invention and knowledge, of feeling and taste."

Haydn's later works gained much from their composer's study of the clear form, the pure orchestral idiom, and the musical beauty of Mozart's. Furthermore the orchestral descriptions of chaos, the birth of light, spring, summer, etc., in "The Creation" and "The Seasons" were made possible to Haydn by Mozart's experiments in instrumental tone-coloring. But this is aside from the present subject. It will be well for the reader now to grasp a few defined facts as to the state of the symphony when Beethoven took it up. Here I must again appeal to a master of the subject, Dr. Parry, who says:—

"By the end of their time [Haydn's and Mozart's] instrumental art had branched out into a very large number of distinct and complete forms, such as symphonies, concertos, quartets, trios, and sonatas for violin and clavier. The style appropriate to each had been more or less ascertained, and the schemes of design had been perfectly organized for all self-dependent instrumental music. Both Haydn and Mozart had immensely improved in the power of finding characteristic subjects, and in deciding the type of subject which is best fitted for instrumental music. The difference in that respect between their early and later works is very marked. They improved the range of the symphonic cycle of movements by adding the minuet and trio to the old group of three movements, thereby introducing definite and undisguised dance movements to follow and contrast with the central cantabile slow movement. Between them they had completely transformed the treatment of the orchestra. They not only enlarged it and gave it greater capacity of tone and variety, but they also laid the solid foundations of those methods of art which have become the most characteristic and powerful features in the system of modern music. Even in detail the character of music is altered; all

CLASSIC ORCHESTRAL COMPOSERS 169

phraseology is made articulate and definite; and the minutiæ which lend themselves to refined and artistic performance are carefully considered, without in any way diminishing the breadth and freedom of the general effect. There is hardly any branch or department of art which does not seem to have been brought to high technical perfection by them; and if *the world could be satisfied with the ideal of perfectly organized simplicity without any great force of expression*, instrumental art might well have stopped at the point to which they brought it."

Dr. Parry has, in the passage which I have italicized, touched the marrow of the matter. Haydn's and Mozart's symphonies, however they may have impressed their contemporaries, appeal to us through their perfect transparency, their balance of form, their fluency of instrumental language, and their simple beauty of style. The working-out parts of their symphonies, for instance, are devoted wholly to the exposition of the musical fruitfulness of their subjects. There is nowhere any evidence of an attempt to employ the apparatus of the symphony for a systematic communication of emotion. These works do, indeed, at times arouse our feelings, but there is no conviction that their composers designed them to speak a message of the inner life to us. They are the perfect embodiments of pure musical beauty, and it was not till Beethoven took up the form which they had perfected that it became the definite embodiment of feeling, the systematic means of expression.

What has already been said about Beethoven's piano sonatas applies with equal propriety to his symphonies. But something may be added, because the symphonies exhibit Beethoven's characteristics in their most imposing garb, and it is through them that he comes into his most influential relations with the great mass of music lovers. But as Beethoven's symphonies mark a transition from the classic to the romantic era, it will be more logical to consider them in a chapter including the romantic writers.

Chapter XIII
The Romantic Orchestral Composers

Beethoven and his nine symphonies — Significance of his work — His technical alterations — His romanticism — Meaning of classicism and romanticism — The symphonic poem and the programme overture — The Liszt piano concertos — Successors of Beethoven — Berlioz and his programme symphonies — Tschaikowsky and Dvorak — The music of Johannes Brahms.

THE classical period in musical history is that in which composers appear to have been engaged in perfecting the form and technic of composition. The impulse which led them to make their improvements was the romantic impulse, for by romanticism in music we mean an impulse which urges the composer toward expression. Such an impulse has always been at work in music, but it was impossible for the classical composers to give it free exercise, because they had not fully established a method of composition. Beethoven found the method pretty well formulated. His material was ready to his hand. In the sonata form his predecessors had prepared for him a vehicle which they had fully proved to be capable of a clear, logical, and luminous presentation and development of beautiful musical ideas. It remained for Beethoven to prove that the symphony, the orchestral sonata, was not only the most complex, diversified, and yet organically unified of all musical forms, but that most thoroughly suited to the embodiment of great mood-pictures, outpourings of love, suffering, despair, joy, triumph. It remained for Beethoven to show how the four movements of a symphony, without any merely technical links, could be made to picture a succession of emotional states which should have a natural variety and an equally natural homogeneity.

Because Beethoven's symphonies stand today as the highest types of absolute music, and because all of them are living music, heard in concert rooms, I quote the list with dates of production, etc., from Sir George Grove's admirable work: "Beethoven and his Nine Symphonies."

No.	Key.	Opus No.	Title.	Date of Completion when ascertainable.	Date of First Performance.
1	C	21	....	....	April 2, 1800
2	D	36	....	....	April 5, 1803
3	E-flat	55	Eroica	August, 1804	April 7, 1805
4	B-flat	60	....	1806	March, 1807
5	C minor	67	....	....	Dec. 22, 1808
6	F	68	Pastoral	....	Dec. 22, 1808
7	A	92	....	May (?) 13, 1812.	Dec. 8, 1813
8	F	93	....	October, 1812	Feb. 27, 1814
9	D minor	125	Choral	August, 1823	May 7, 1824

In the chapter on the sonata I have already mentioned some of the details of Beethoven's developments. As displayed in his symphonies the technical changes which call for especial mention are first strikingly seen in the "Eroica." Here we find that Beethoven made the progress from his first to his second subject (see outline of first movement form, Chap. X.) in a thoroughly logical and organic manner. In the working-out he introduced new melodic episodes, but he never forgot that they were subordinate to the two melodic topics of his movement. In the third part of the first movement he introduced a coda of 140 measures, in which new subject matter is introduced, and part of it made to act as a "descant" above the first principal theme.

174 HOW MUSIC DEVELOPED

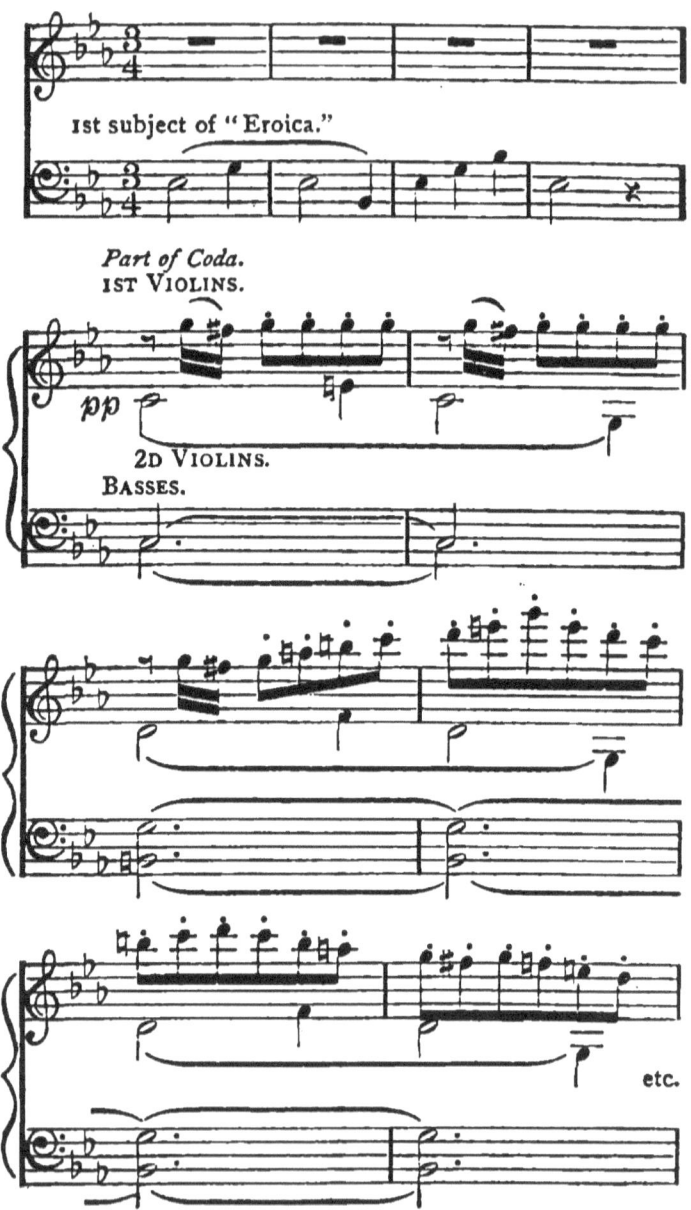

As Sir George Grove has said, "this coda is no mere termination to a movement which might have ended as well without it. No, it is an essential part of the poem, and will be known as such. It is one of Beethoven's great inventions, and he knows it, and starts it in such a style that no one can possibly overlook what he is doing." In the same symphony Beethoven entitles his slow movement "March," and his third movement "Scherzo." Both of these titles were new to the symphony. The finale is made more important and more expressive than it has ever been in any previous work. In his sixth symphony Beethoven gave each of the movements descriptive titles, such as "Scene by the brook." This was a distinct innovation in symphonic writing, and the artistic beauty and eloquence of the work prove that the symphony as a form was capable of the most free expressiveness. In the fifth symphony the composer demonstrated in the convincing manner the complete organization of the form by using a single motive, that which introduces the work, as the germ and the connecting instrument of the whole. The fifth symphony is the most convincing of all Beethoven's works. Its portrayal of man's struggle against fate and his final triumph is superb; yet in form the symphony is absolutely perfect. In his seventh symphony he developed the slow introduction to the first movement, which has previously occupied a dozen measures, to sixty-two. In his ninth symphony he made his only confession of the inadequacy of his instrumental means. He introduced voices. The ninth symphony is a work of transcendent genius, and its effect justifies its method; but the use of voices in instrumental works since has almost inevitably failed. Only Beethoven could bridge the chasm between musical mood-pictures without words and music leaning on the shoulder of text.

Beethoven's symphonies are the connecting link between the classic and romantic schools. They are classic because they adhere to the classic form; they are romantic because they are the instruments of direct, intentional, and highly designed expression. Beethoven was satisfied to accomplish the full achievement of expression within the limits of the classic form. His successors, despairing of succeeding on the same lines, and urged by a desire for personal and representative expression as strong as his, broke away from the classic form of the sonata, but to this day have never been able to escape the sovereignty of its fundamental principles. The kinds of musical devices which Beethoven employed in making his designs expressive, in the widest and deepest sense of that word, may not be discussed here. To attempt to discuss them would lead the reader into the field of pure musical technics. The great fact for him to keep in mind is this: Beethoven seized upon the musical material left him by his predecessors, and instead of employing it to produce simple beauty, used it to express his inner life, treating that life as typical and hence as capable of representation in the broad tints of orchestral music. His successors in the composition of symphonic music have followed his lead, some adhering to the classical form and others departing from it, according to the bent of their genius. All of them, however, have sought to employ the power of music to express emotion, some following plans with broad outlines and others endeavoring to enter into detail. Because these composers have proclaimed the expressive power of music, they are classed as romanticists. It should be noted, however, that many historians include in the classic school all those who adhere strictly to the classic form.

A product of the romantic school is called "programme music." This means music which is intended to illustrate a definite story, and its best examples are those which endeavor to illustrate wholly by voicing in music the sequence of emotions contained in the tale, with the aid of such descriptive music as will convey some idea of the scenic surroundings. The reader will readily understand that some acquaintance with the composer's purpose is necessary to an appreciation of such music. A key to the plan is offered usually by the title. A composition labelled "Macbeth" would, of course, be understood as intended to illustrate Shakespeare's tragedy, and the hearer would naturally call to his aid in listening to it his knowledge of the drama. Two familiar forms of programme music have grown out of the attempts of the romanticists. One of these is the symphonic poem, and the other the programme overture. The symphonic poem is a composition symphonic in style and general treatment, but shorter than a symphony and without pauses between its movements and designed to illustrate a story. An attentive listener will find that a symphonic poem contains definite principal themes, development or working-out, climaxes, and conclusion; for no matter what the sequence of emotions in the story may be, the fundamental laws of musical form must be observed. The programme over-

ROMANTIC COMPOSERS 179

ture is an overture built on lines much the same as those of a symphonic poem, but designed as a musical prelude to a play, or a poem of dramatic contents, as, for example Tschaikowsky's "Hamlet" overture, or Goldmark's "Sakuntala" overture. The latter belongs to a poem.

In addition to these forms the romanticists have made certain alterations in the old sonata form. One of Schumann's symphonies, that in D minor, is in the usual four movements, but without any pauses between them, and the principal subjects of the work are heard in various forms in the various movements. This plan was followed by Liszt in his piano concertos, which are played without pauses and have their several movements largely developed from the themes announced at the beginning of the works.

The principal symphonic writers since Beethoven have been Ludwig Spohr (1784–1859), Franz Schubert (1797–1828), Felix Mendelssohn-Bartoldy (1809–1847), Robert Schumann (1810–1856), Hector Berlioz (1803–1869), Franz Liszt (1811–1886), Johannes Brahms (1833–1897), Peter Ilitisch Tschaikowsky (1840–1893) and Antonin Dvorak (1841,— still living). Spohr's symphonies are generally classic in form, but romantic in subject and treatment, as is indicated by their titles, " Lenore " (on Burger's poem), " Power of Sound," " Consecration of Tones." Schubert's symphonies are also classic in form, and only mildly romantic in content. Schubert was one of the leaders of the romantic school, but his romanticism found its most complete embodiment in his songs. Mendelssohn's symphonies are absolutely classic in form and in the finish of their style and instrumentation, but they are romantic in tendency. His overtures — such as " Hebrides " and " Melusine " — are unquestionably of the romantic spirit. Schumann was an ultra-romanticist and his piano music teems with compositions with suggestive titles, such as " Papillons " and " Carnival." His symphonies are romantic in the fulness of their plan to embody emotion. Hector Berlioz, the famous French symphonist, was one of the extreme romanticists. His symphonies are really symphonic poems in several detached movements and are all original in form. Sometimes he uses voices to help him out, but usually he is content with the orchestra, which he handled with a marvellous insight into its capacity. His symphonies all bear suggestive titles, — as "Romeo and Juliet" or " Harold in Italy," and are designed to illustrate stories. Franz Liszt was the inventor of the symphonic poem, and is included in this catalogue chiefly for that reason. His works are very rich in color, and occasionally rise to a level of real power.

Tschaikowsky was a Russian composer and produced six symphonies, all of which depart from the strict classic form, make free use of Russian style in their melodies, and are intensely romantic in spirit. His fifth symphony introduces a slow waltz instead of a scherzo. His sixth, the "Symphony Pathetique," is one of the noblest of modern symphonies. Its second movement is a waltz in five-fourth measure (five beats to the bar), its third a scherzo which turns into a march, and its last is the slow movement. In the first movement a partial working out of each theme follows immediately upon the first appearance of the theme. Dvorak is a Bohemian, and most of his works are Slavonic in color. He has introduced as a slow movement the "Dumka," or elegy, and in place of the scherzo the "furiant," which is explained by its name. During a stay in the United States he conceived the idea that an American element could be introduced into music by using themes resembling those of negro songs and Indian chants. His chief exemplification of his theory is found in his symphony in E minor, " From the New World." Dvorak's symphonies adhere closely to the principles of the sonata form, and are very popular in style without descending from the level of artistic music.

The music of Johannes Brahms has given rise to a great deal of controversy. Most recent writers have shown a tendency to break away from the strict letter of the sonata form, and too many commentators have come to mistake manner for matter. In calling those writers classic who have adhered to the classic sonata they have too often denied to them the possession of romantic feeling. At the same time some commentators have seemed to think that it was a work of virtue to preserve the sonata form precisely as it was left to us by the hand of Beethoven, while others held that any man who adhered to it was a mere formalist. It was criticism of this kind which obscured the merits of the late Johannes Brahms in his early days. It was not difficult for the commentators to perceive that Brahms employed the sonata form, and that he preserved the outlines laid down by Beethoven. For that they praised him, as if it were a *sine qua non* of absolute music that it should be in the sonata form. It is generally conceded that that form is the most intellectual, the most highly organized, which has yet been devised; but it is not and ought not to be conceded that a man is bound to adhere to that form. If he can produce another which presents an equally convincing process of musical development and conclusion, he deserves laudation as one who is not a mere student of forms, but is a master of the philosophy of form.

A piece of music is not necessarily formless because it is not built on the model of one of the acknowledged forms. A composer is not a heretic because he builds a new pattern. But there are certain fundamentals of form, and these we should demand in every work. In the simplest music we should require that there be recognizable a beginning, a middle, and an end. We should demand discernible rhythms and symmetrical phrases, and we should require that these be exhibited throughout the composition with evident design. In the higher forms there ought to be melodic subjects, and these subjects ought to be discussed and developed. It is almost impossible to escape the cyclic form, with its proposition, discussion, and conclusion; but if the composer does escape it, we must insist upon it that he adhere to the essential principle of repetition and that he distribute his repetitions in such a manner as to preserve the symmetry and balance of his work and to effect an organic unity. His work should contain nothing that does not belong to it. Every phrase should be, as W. A. Hadow suggests, "inevitable."

On the other hand a man is not necessarily a mere formalist because he clings to the old-fashioned sonata form. Brahms's compositions show a completeness of architectonic detail, superimposed upon a symmetrical and inevitable organic development, such as are to be found in those of no other symphonist, except Beethoven. Why deny to the late Viennese master depth of feeling because he fashioned the expression of that feeling with all the force of a gigantic musical intellect? Brahms's music grows slowly in popular favor because it is not easy for the careless hearer to grasp its inner spirit. But it is not true that music, to be real music, demands a Swinburnian diction.

> "The low downs lean to the sea; the stream,
>   One loose, thin, pulseless, tremulous vein,
> Rapid and vivid and dumb as a dream,
>   Works downward, sick of the sun and the rain ;
> No wind is rough with the rank rare flowers ;
> The sweet sea, mother of loves and hours,
> Shudders and shines as the gray winds gleam,
>   Turning her smile to a fugitive pain."

That is great poetry, and the rhythm and the melody and feeling of it are as the music of Chopin and Schumann. But this also is great poetry:—

> "And chiefly thou, O spirit! that dost prefer
> Before all temples the upright heart and pure,
> Instruct me, for thou knowest; thou from the first
> Wast present, and, with mighty wings outspread,
> Dovelike sat'st brooding on the vast abyss,
> And madest it pregnant; what in me is dark
> Illumine! what is low raise and support!
> That to the height of this great argument
> I may assert eternal Providence,
> And justify the ways of God to men."

But the melody and the rhythm and the emotion of it are as the music of Brahms. Some day, I think, if not soon, the world will see how profoundly representative of his nation and his time Brahms was, and he will be hailed, as Milton was, an organ voice of his country. The irresistible seriousness of Germany has never spoken with more convincing accent than in the music of Brahms. There is a feeling in this music which is far removed from the possibility of a purely sensuous embodiment. It may take time for the entire musical world to come under the spell of this austere utterance; but Brahms had the happiness of knowing ere he died that wherever music was cultivated his individuality at least had made itself known.

Chapter XIV

The Development of Chamber Music

Corelli and the "Sonata da Camera" — His distribution of instruments — John Adam Reinken and the "Hortus Musicus" — Music at the Court of Weimar — Bach and Gossec — The quartets of Haydn — Mozart's chamber music — Beethoven and romanticism in quartets — Brahms and Dvorak.

BY chamber music is meant all that class of compositions written for small collections of instruments and therefore suitable for performance in small rooms only. It embraces trios, quartets, quintets, sextets, septets, and octets, named according to the number of instruments employed. The trio is most frequently written for piano, violin, and 'cello, but other combinations, such as piano, violin, and horn, etc., are used. When the word "quartet" is used alone, it signifies a string quartet, consisting of first violin, second violin, viola, and 'cello. A "piano quartet" is one in which the second violin is absent and a piano appears. A quintet for

CHAMBER MUSIC 187

strings may be for two violins, two violas, and 'cello (the usual arrangement), or two violins, one viola, and two 'celli. A piano quintet has a piano instead of the second viola or second 'cello. Compositions for more than five instruments seldom use the piano, but frequently introduced wood or brass instruments. But it is not possible to fix any definite distribution of instruments in chamber music, as there are compositions for almost every conceivable combination, including those of wind instruments only.

It is not difficult to understand that chamber music originated in the early medieval custom of accompanying banquets with music. Small bodies of instrumental players formed for this purpose soon created a demand for a separate kind of music for their performance, as well as a desire to hear such music. Indeed chamber music, as such, existed before orchestral music, for the old sonatas in four-voiced counterpoint, written *da cantare e sonare*, when performed as instrumental compositions, constituted what we should class to-day as chamber music. But genuine modern chamber music began to take form when the violin began to assert its true position and the correct balance of strings began to be perceived. This, as we have seen, was subsequent to the time of the violin maker Maggini (1581-1631) and previous to that the violinist Corelli (1653-1713). In his labors tending toward the development of the sonata form Corelli wrote real chamber music. His compositions were classed either as "Sonate di Chiesa" or "Sonate da Camera," — church sonatas or chamber sonatas. The sonatas employed small combinations of instruments in which the violin and the organ were the chief principals, together with lutes and other stringed instruments. Their relation to the development of the sonata form has already been pointed out. The distribution of instruments, as leading toward modern chamber music is what now concerns us. Corelli's first publication in this line was "XII Sonate a tre, due violini e violoncello, col basso per l'organo," opus 1, Rome, 1683. In 1685 (the year of Bach's birth) he published twelve "sonate da camera" for two violins, 'cello, and cembalo. He published other collections, one of which contained sonatas for four violins, violoncello, and bass, two violins and the 'cello playing the principal parts and the other instruments reenforcing them in the ensemble passages. The successors of Corelli followed his lead and produced many compositions for small collections of instruments, though it must be borne in mind that the idea of formal concerts of chamber music, such as we have now, did not exist then.

When the development of instrumental music began to take a definite direction in Germany, chamber music pure and simple made its appearance, and Germany is the home of this kind of composition. John Adam Reinken (born at Deventer, Holland, 1623, died at Hamburg, 1722, an organist, studied under Swelinck, of the last period of the Netherlands school) wrote a composition called "Hortus Musicus" for two violins, viola, and bass, published at Hamburg, 1704. This composition is what we should now call a suite, and it shows that the art of writing music for a quartet had made considerable progress. We get some light as to the sort of encouragement given to this kind of music from the fact that instrumental performances by small bodies were cultivated earnestly at the ducal court of Weimar between 1708 and 1715, chiefly because the duke's nephew, Johann Ernst, "showed considerable talent for playing the violin and clavier, and even for composition" [Spitta's "Life of Bach"]. Frederick the Great played the flute, and it is thought that this had some influence with Sebastian Bach, who was much admired by the king. At any rate Bach wrote a sonata for clavier, violin, and flute. He also wrote a trio for two violins and bass, and other works which belonged to the chamber-music class. Quartet writing had made its way into France, where François Joseph Gossec (1733–1829) published his first quartet in 1759, the year in which Haydn wrote his first symphony.

Chamber music known to the modern concert room dates from the first quartet of Haydn, written in 1755. In the earlier works the form was uncertain, and it was not until the sonata took definite shape that composers discovered that the sonata form was the best adapted to the development of thematic ideas suitable for chamber music, as well as that of those suitable for symphonies. Scientific musicians were at first prone to scoff at the string quartet as too slight in texture to afford a vehicle for the display of genius. That was because they had not fully mastered the art of writing a four-part harmony with occasional transitions into the pure polyphonic style, — a method of writing which is indispensable to quartet composition, — and also because they did not yet thoroughly understand the scope and value of each individual instrument. It cannot be said that even Haydn penetrated the secrets of the capacities of his

CHAMBER MUSIC 191

four instruments, for his quartet writing shows frequent baldness in this respect; but he did write in four-part harmony, and his quartets beyond all question set the pattern for all that have followed them. Haydn wrote seventy-seven quartets, and naturally his latest show an advance in style and treatment over his earliest. These quartets are characterized by the fluency and simplicity of their melodies, the conciseness and symmetry of their form, the clearness and balance of their part writing, and the sunny sweetness of their prevailing mood. There is nothing in the shape of instrumental music much pleasanter or easier to listen to than one of Haydn's quartets. The best of them hold their places in the concert rooms of to-day, and they seem likely to live as long as there are people to appreciate clear and logical composition which attempts nothing beyond " organized simplicity."

Mozart wrote a great quantity of chamber music, including string quintets, a quintet for clarinet and strings, a quintet for horn and strings, thirty quartets, a quintet for piano, oboe, horn, clarinet, and bassoon, two piano quartets and eight trios. His six early quartets, dedicated to Haydn and published in 1785, do not make any alterations in the form fixed by Haydn. But, to quote the words of Mozart's biographer, Otto Jahn, "following a deeply rooted impulse of his nature, he renounced the light and fanciful style in which Haydn treated them [the features of the form], seized upon their legitimate points, and gave a firmer and more delicate construction to the whole fabric. To say of Mozart's quartets in their general features that, in comparison with Haydn's, they are of deeper and fuller expression, more refined beauty, and broader conception of form, is only to distinguish these as Mozart's individual characteristics, in contrast with Haydn's inexhaustible fund of original and humorous productive power." What is here said of Mozart's early quartets applies fairly to all his chamber music. His part-writing is always delightful in its clearness and in its preservation of the balance of power among the instruments. Every one has something agreeable to say, and the saying of it never becomes a muddle of sound. The composer's peculiar feeling for vocal style, already mentioned, gives his various parts a fluency of melody not to be found in the works of some more pretentious composers.

The complete establishment of the quartet as an art-form worthy to rank beside the symphony is due to Beethoven. The list of Beethoven's chamber music comprises the following: two octets in E-flat for wind, one septet for strings and wind, one sextet in E-flat for strings and wood, one sextet in E-flat for wind, two quintets for strings, sixteen quartets for strings, two "Equali" for four trombones, five trios for strings, one trio for strings and flute, one trio for wind, three duos for wind, one quintet for piano and wind, one quartet for piano and strings, eight trios for piano and strings, ten sonatas for piano and violin, five sonatas for piano and 'cello, and a few other works. The trios are uncommonly fine compositions, but the quartet was Beethoven's especial choice among chamber-music forms, and he used it for the embodiment of some of his noblest thoughts. All that has been said about his treatment of the piano sonata and the symphony applies to his treatment of the quartet. Beethoven could not by any possibility take up such a peculiarly intimate form of music without infusing into it a new life. He made it the vehicle for the expression of a marvellous depth of feeling. In doing so he made variations in the established form, but without overthrowing or ignoring any of its fundamental principles. Sir George Grove says, "The obscurity and individuality of the thoughts themselves, and their apparent want of connection until they have become familiar, is perhaps the cause that these noble works [the later quartets] are so difficult to understand." But it is generally conceded by critics and musicians that Beethoven's quartets, particularly those in F, E minor, and C, dedicated to Count Rassoumoffsky, and called the " Rassoumoffsky Quartets," are the noblest specimens of chamber music extant. In his " Life of Mozart " Otto Jahn says : —

" The string quartet offers the most favorable conditions for the development of instrumental music, both as to expression and technical construction, giving free play to the composer in every direction, provided only that he keep within the limits imposed by the nature of his art. Each of the four combined instruments is capable of the greatest variety of melodic construction; they have the advantage over the piano in their power of sustaining the vibrations of the notes, so as to produce song-like effects; nor are they inferior in their power of rapid movement. Their union enables them to fulfil the demands of complete harmonies, and to compensate increase of freedom and fulness for the advantages which the pianoforte possesses as a solo instrument."

CHAMBER MUSIC 195

OPENING OF SLOW MOVEMENT OF BEETHOVEN'S SEVENTH QUARTET.

196   HOW MUSIC DEVELOPED

The listener to Beethoven's quartets will be impressed with the applicability of these words to them, and he will in a measure be prepared to see where some of Beethoven's successors have failed. Schubert, Schumann, Mendelssohn, Spohr, and other German composers wrote admirable chamber music. So have some of the French and Italian composers. But it cannot be said that this branch of instrumental art, its purest and most thoroughly symmetrical form, has made any advance since Beethoven's day. On the contrary, it has retrograded. This is from two causes: first, the frequency with which piano parts are written in a style so massive and brilliant as to overwhelm the strings in trios or piano quartets and quintets; and second, the unwise attempts of some composers to imitate heavy orchestral effects with only four or five stringed instruments.

Among those who have produced the best chamber music in recent years must be mentioned Brahms and Dvorak, who have been named in the chapter preceding this. The chamber music of Brahms includes a sextet for strings, three piano quartets, a piano quintet, several trios, three string quartets, a string quintet, and a quintet for clarinet and strings. These works are conspicuous for the completeness of their musical organism, the originality, profundity, and artistic reticence of their style, the deep learning with which they treat modern thoughts in a revised polyphony, and the breadth of their intellectual earnestness. It is difficult to understand how any one can deny the genius of Brahms after hearing a good performance of such music as the slow movement and scherzo of his piano quintet.

Dvorak has written a considerable quantity of chamber music, but no final criticism can yet be passed upon it. The composer himself realizes that his earlier quartets and trios, though melodious and clear, contained a great deal of discursive matter. His later writings show an immense improvement in conciseness, strength, and closeness of development. His American quartet and quintet are admirable as examples of form and of treatment of instrumental voices.

Chapter XV

The Birth of Oratorio

Religious character of the Greek drama — The early Christian plays — The liturgical drama — Miracle plays and their introduction of abuses — Reformatory efforts of St. Philip Neri — Ascent of the music to a place of importance — Recitative and Cavaliere's work — Improvements of Carissimi, Stradella, and Cesti — Alessandro Scarlatti and the aria — Advent of Handel and Bach.

HAVING traced the development of piano music, chamber music, and the symphony, from the time at which these began to be separate branches of art up to the present, it now becomes necessary to return to the point of departure and follow a new line of progress. It is the task of the reader now to accompany me in an examination into the origin of oratorio. Difficult as it may be to realize it now, the oratorio was in its infancy a dramatic performance, and it took its origin from the ancient religious drama, which, indeed, is the source of all modern drama. Greek plays, as imitated very badly by the Romans, most directly affected oratorio. The Greek drama began at the altar of Bacchus, where the priestesses sang about the sacrificial goat the goat song, the "tragos ode," the tragedy. At Delphi grew up representations of the slaying of a serpent by Apollo, and at Eleusis the "Eleusinian mysteries" portrayed in dramatic action the rape of Persephone and the wanderings of Demeter. So originated the Greek drama, which until the death of Æschylus was chiefly an embodiment of the religious beliefs and hopes of the Greeks.

When Christianity was introduced in Greece and Rome the people clung to the play form and continued to use the old mythological personages. The fathers of the Church speedily perceived that such plays were distinctly hostile to the progress of the true faith, so they set about writing religious dramas which should present to the people the facts of Christianity quite as attractively as the older plays presented those of Paganism. This work began in the second century (if not earlier), but the old ideas clung firmly. A curious drama called "Christ's Passion," long supposed to have been written by St. Gregory Nazianzen, Patriarch of Constantinople near the end of the fourth century, contains a curious mix-

THE BIRTH OF ORATORIO 201

ture of Biblical personages, church hymns and extracts from Greek plays. About one-third of the verse, for instance, is taken from Euripides. Dr. Brambs, of Leipsic, has proved that this "Christ's Passion" dates from the tenth, not the fourth century. It is not difficult to see how the early Christian dramas could have developed from the elaborate liturgical presentations of such events as the nativity, the annunciation, and the crucifixion. Indeed there are extant some twenty-seven or twenty-eight liturgical arrangements which are purely dramatic in form and style. Their musical part was provided by the old Latin hymns. In one of these dramas, "The Shepherds," occur passages used in Handel's oratorios, such as "Glory to God in the highest," and "Behold, a virgin shall conceive and shall bear a son."

It was a natural outcome of the social condition of the era that in the course of time these dramas, enacted frequently in the open air, forced to appeal to a heterogeneous mass of densely ignorant persons, and bound to employ their very superstitions in order to gain their comprehension, should have permitted the introduction of all kinds of triviality and vulgarity. In "The Fall of Lucifer" the devil was introduced with horns, tail, cloven hoof, and a glaring red beard. Noah's wife, in another play, refused to go into the ark, and Noah took a stout cudgel to her. Adam and Eve appeared naked, and donned their fig leaves in the presence of the audience. One very popular play in the fifteenth century was performed on a three-story stage, of which the top story represented heaven, the middle one earth, and the lowest one hell. The devil had now become the buffoon of the drama, and was driven about by the populace with blows from inflated bladders tied to the ends of sticks. In one play there were four devils to keep the fun going, and jugglers, acrobats, and buffoons were introduced, until the medieval religious drama resembled the modern "farce comedy."

A reform, which led to the establishment of the oratorio, was caused by the work of St. Philip Neri (born in Florence, 1515), founder of the Congregation of the Fathers of the Oratory at Rome. An old Italian writer, Crescembini, says: "The Oratorio, a poetical composition, formerly a commixture of the dramatic and narrative styles, but now entirely a musical drama, had its origin from San Filippo Neri, who in his chapel, after sermons and other devotions, in order to allure young people to pious offices, and

THE BIRTH OF ORATORIO 203

to detain them from earthly pleasure, had hymns, psalms, and such like prayers sung by one or more voices. . . . Among these spiritual songs were dialogues." The truth is that St. Philip Neri induced capable Italian poets to make his librettos, which consisted of dialogues interspersed with choruses. The music he had written by the best composers, even Palestrina contributing to the good cause. The beauty and purity of these works caused them to become popular among the more intelligent young Romans, and St. Philip's oratory (whence the name oratorio) was always crowded.

The invention of dramatic recitative near the close of the sixteenth century produced a marked effect on oratorio. It very quickly took the place of the dialogue, and thenceforward for many years there was little difference between opera and oratorio except in the nature of their subjects. The first oratorio with dramatic recitative, of which any account has come down to us, was " L'Anima e Corpo," written by Laura Guidiccioni and composed by Emilio del Cavaliere, one of the little band of musical explorers who gave us opera. This oratorio was performed in Rome in 1600. The orchestra, consisting of a double lyre, a harpsichord, a large guitar, and two flutes, was placed behind the scenes, and the oratorio was presented as a musical drama. The chorus sat on the stage, but when singing arose and made appropriate gestures. Complete stage directions were given in the work for the action of the various characters. The oratorio ended with a chorus "to be sung, accompanied sedately and reverentially by the dance," and there was provision for a ballet, "enlivened with capers or *entrechats*."

The new form of religious drama soon won its way to general appreciation, and composers were not slow to avail themselves of the opportunities it gave them. Giovanni Carissimi (1582–1672) wrote a number of oratorios, excellent for their time, among them "Jephthah," "Solomon's Judgment," "Belshazzar," and "David and Jonathan." Carissimi made great improvements in the recitative, giving it more character and real musical expressiveness than his predecessors had. He also showed much skill in his choral writing, which was not so completely polyphonic as that of the earlier church writers. He often used bold successions of broad and simple chords and often his writing for the voices is much like that of Handel, a century later. On the whole his work shows a tendency to abandon a close adherence to the methods of the early opera composers and to move toward the style subsequently formulated by Handel. Alessandro Stradella (1645(?)–1681(?)) and Antonio Cesti (1620–?), the latter, a pupil of Carissimi, did much toward developing the choral part of the oratorio. Dr. Parry says : " Stradella had a very remarkable instinct for choral effect, and even piling up progressions into a climax; and his solo music, though apparently not so happy in varieties of spontaneous melody as Cesti's, aims equally at definiteness of structure. His work in the line of oratorio is especially significant, as he stands comparatively alone in cultivating all the natural resources of that form of art — on the lines which Handel adopted later — at a time when his fellow composers were falling in with the inclination of their public for solo singing, and were giving up the grand opportunities of choral effect as superfluous."

The tendency of dramatic music, the state of public taste, and the skill of solo singers all had their influence upon oratorio during the sixteenth century, and the most popular oratorio composers were those who also wrote the most successful operas. Alessandro Scarlatti, who has been mentioned earlier in this book, was the musical dictator of his day, and his oratorios show a great gain in the elasticity and direct expressiveness of the recitative, which is quite as dramatic as that of the contemporaneous opera. But perhaps his treatment of the aria was more influential. It was he who made the aria the central sun of the operatic system, and he naturally gave to the solo parts of his oratorios more definiteness of melody. His treatment of the aria, with its passages of pure vocal display combined with clearly formed tune, led the way directly to the Handelian style.

George Frederick Handel was born at Halle, Germany, Feb. 23, 1685. He studied first under Zachau of Halle, and began his musical career as an opera composer at Hamburg. He went to Italy and studied faithfully the works of the Italian masters, some of whom (the Scarlattis, Corelli, and others) he met personally. His three years in Italy saturated him with the spirit of Italian music, and he was always influenced by it. On his return to Germany he became chapel master to the Elector of Hanover. In 1710 he made his first visit to England and wrote his opera " Rinaldo." In 1712 he went to live in England, where he remained till his death, April 13, 1759. Handel, having failed pecuniarily as an opera composer, took up the work of ora-

THE BIRTH OF ORATORIO 207

torio writing. His principal oratorios are: "The Messiah" (Dublin, April 18, 1742, and London, 1749), "Israel in Egypt" (1740) "Judas Maccabæus" (1747), and "Saul" (1740). The oratorio as we know it to-day dates from Handel, and it was in his day that Dr. Gibson, Bishop of London, gave a decision which put an end to acting in this branch of art and removed it entirely from the realm of dramatic representation.

Contemporaneous with Handel was Sebastian Bach (1685–1750) who is believed to have made five different settings of the story of Christ's passion. Of these only two have been preserved: that according to St. John (1724), and that according to St. Matthew (1729). The latter is regarded as the greater, and is esteemed by most critics as the noblest of all compositions in the oratorio form. The reader has seen how the oratorio in Italy developed up to the time of Handel, who took up that line of progress and advanced it. His oratorios are strictly in the line of Italian development, with such modifications as the character and nationality of the man would naturally produce. We shall best understand the subsequent development of oratorio if we now review the history of passion music and examine the peculiar character of this product as compared with the oratorio of Handel.

Chapter XVI

Work of Handel and Bach

History of "Passion" music — Heinrich Schütz and his "Seven Last Words" — His "Passions" — The text of Brockes — Distinguishing features of the forms of Handel and Bach — The former as a development of Italian oratorio — The latter as essentially German — Protestantism and the chorale — Bach's intimacy and Handel's popularity.

THE history of passion music previous to that of Bach is voluminous. Early in the middle ages the history of the passion according to the four evangelists was sung on the four days of Holy Week. This was done in the Roman Catholic churches. A priest intoned the words of the narrative, a second priest the words of Christ, and a third those of the other personages in the story. The words of the populace, the crowd, were sung by the choir in the polyphony of the time. The Protestant authorities saw the value of this form of service as a means of impressing the story upon the popular mind and continued its use, but with German instead of Latin text. As early as 1530 there were passions according to St. Matthew and St. John, with German text and music by Johann Walther. The first published edition is a passion according to St. Matthew, with music by Clemens Stephani, printed at Nuremberg in 1570. Various versions written by Melchior Vulpius, in 1613, Thomas Mancinus, 1620, and Christopher Schulz, 1653, are known.

An important contribution to the development of passion music was that of Heinrich Schütz (born at Köstritz, Saxony, Oct. 8, 1585, died at Dresden, Nov. 6, 1672). Schütz was a pupil of Giovanni Gabrieli, of the Venetian school of organists, and was made chapel master at Dresden by the Elector George I. In his " Seven Last Words of Christ" (produced in 1645) we find a fusing of all the elements which appear in the earlier passion music, and also a definite foundation for the form employed by Bach. The work begins with a four-part chorus set to the words of the old hymn : —

> "Since Christ our Lord was crucified
> And bore the spear-wound in his side."

An instrumental "symphony" follows and leads up to a recitative by the Evangelist (alto voice) who tells the story: "And it was close upon the third hour when they crucified the Lord, and Jesus spake." The words of Christ are then sung by a baritone: "Father, forgive them, for they know not what they do." The narrative is not confined to one voice, tenor and soprano also taking part in it. The words "And at about the ninth hour he cried aloud and said" are set for a quartet. So also are the words "And after he had thus spoken," etc. An instrumental symphony follows the close of the story, "And he gave up his spirit," and the work ends with a chorus expressing the thoughts of the Christian Church. Significant features of this work are its use of recitative instead of plain chant, which was used in the narrative and recitative parts of the earlier Passions, its preservation of choruses of the old polyphonic motet style, its employment of a carefully made instrumental accompaniment, and its introduction of the two picturesque orchestral interludes. Schütz's recitative, it should be noted, was not so much like the modern oratorio recitative as like the arioso style,— that in which the recitation has a melodious character.

In the years 1665 and 1666 Schütz produced four settings of the Passion. In

WORK OF HANDEL AND BACH 211

these the composer, in an effort to combat the growing influence of Italian opera music in Germany, abandoned the instrumental accompaniment and wrote his choruses in the pure *a capella* church style. But his individual characters, the evangelist, Christ, and others, used dramatic recitative. The Passion music of Giovanni Sebastiani, written in 1672, approaches the form of Bach's very closely. The Evangelist, who tells the story in a recitative of melodious character, is a tenor, and his recitation is accompanied by 2 violins, viola, and bass. The sacred aria makes its appearance in this setting, and so also does the four-part Protestant chorale. This introduction of the chorale grew out of the custom, which had formerly prevailed, of asking the congregation at convenient points in the Passion to sing a hymn.

There were other versions of the Passion, but that which most concerns us at present was an arrangement of the text in 1712 by Barthold Heinrich Brockes, a member of the Town Council of Hamburg. This was set to music by several composers, among them Handel, and it was known to Sebastian Bach. This text appears to the taste of the present to be overloaded with ornate figures of speech.

The reader may now be able to perceive the differences between the form and style of the oratorio proper as cultivated by Handel and of the Passion oratorio, as a special variety, cultivated by Bach. In the St. Matthew Passion, the master-work of Bach, the narrative part of the text, according to the writings of Matthew, is sung by a tenor in a form of recitative. The speeches of Jesus, St. Peter, the High Priest, and Pontius Pilate are always delivered by a bass. The Jews are represented by a chorus. A second group, representing the ideal Christian congregation, introduces moral observations, while a third group sings chorales, representing the spirit of Protestantism.

In Handel's "Messiah" the text, taken from various parts of the Bible, gives an outline of the story of the coming of the Saviour, of his suffering and death. There are solos by tenor, soprano, alto, and bass voices, which are used entirely for musical effect. There is no attempt to identify any voice with any personage. "He was despised and rejected" is sung by the alto; "I know that my Redeemer liveth," by the soprano; "But who may abide the day of His coming?" by the bass. The entire treatment of the text is regulated by musical considerations. It is not possible to discover that the chorus represents the populace or the church. For instance, the bass sings the air "The people that walked in darkness have seen a great light" with text from Isaiah; and this is followed by the chorus "For unto us a son is born" from the same book. Then comes the pastoral symphony, a bit of purely descriptive instrumental music, which serves as a prelude to the scene of the shepherds, which is narrated by a soprano voice. This wholly undramatic style is not unlike the purely musical manner of setting the mass and the other parts of the church liturgy, and has been closely followed in its form by modern composers in many works in which the element of personality is not a factor. It was followed by Handel himself in some of his other works, by Haydn in "The Seasons," and by Mendelssohn in his "St. Paul" to a considerable extent.

But Handel himself thoroughly understood the value of the old-fashioned form of Carissimi, in which the personages were treated dramatically and uttered direct speeches. The familiar number, "Total Blindness," from his "Samson," is an example of this. But the difference between the oratorios of Handel and Bach is not merely one of form. It is still more noticeable in the style and the spirit. The Handelian oratorio, although it may not at first sight appear to be so, is a direct descendant of the Italian. Handel was completely saturated with the spirit of Italian music, and he developed his musical style from it. It was plainly his purpose in building the great choruses of his oratorios to follow the ecclesiastical polyphonic style of Italy. But this in itself had undergone certain technical changes. In the first place, the disappearance of the old church scales and the introduction of the modern major and minor keys had placed polyphony on a new basis and compelled a more free and unrestricted treatment of the voice-parts in order that the new laws of harmony might not be broken. Again the old church choruses were designed for performance without accompaniment, while the oratorio choruses had to follow the later custom and make use of the orchestra. Hence Handel's polyphony had to be cast in broader and more powerful masses, while his orchestral accompaniment had a certain amount of independence, and at times even considerable descriptive power. His entire musical scheme, however, was devised to reproduce in broad tints the emotional spirit of the text.

WORK OF HANDEL AND BACH 215

Handel's choruses are full of musical characterization, and it is this spirit, even more than the style, which distinguishes them from those of his Italian forerunners, and which has made them stand the test of time and manifold changes of musical taste. "The Messiah" is the most popular oratorio in the United States, because its broad mass effects are instantly influential, even among those who neither perceive their musical character nor comprehend their artistic purpose. Strongly marked rhythms, fluent melody, and powerful climaxes are among the easily discernible elements of the greatness of Handel's choruses, but the deeper secret of their power is their admirable adaptation of old means to the promptings of a new spirit. Handel never forgot his public, however, and it is largely because he kept always before him the necessity of achieving his artistic purposes with attractive means that his "Messiah" continues to be popular. The fundamental elements of popularity in music do not change radically, after all, and hence Handel's music holds its own in the absence from the domain of oratorio of anything of a more influential nature.

Two great characteristics mark the difference between Bach's work in the development of oratorio and Handel's. In the first place Bach was essentially German in thought and practice, and in the second place he cared comparatively little about producing beautiful melody and attractive musical effects, but devoted his energies to the most accurate, detailed, and subtle expression. The Teutonism of Bach's music is to be seen not only in the intense earnestness and high intellectuality of it, but in its wide and significant employment of the German chorale and of a musical style developed therefrom. As Dr. Parry has noted, Bach's early life was given up to the study of organ playing, and hence the voice-parts in his choruses follow the method of organ counterpoint. His choruses are, therefore, not so broad and massive as Handel's, but present a more scholarly and varied polyphony. "Where Handel aimed at beauty of melodic form, Bach strove for characteristic expression." Handel's counterpoint is the smooth, mellifluous, facile counterpoint of the Italians; Bach's, seeking always to fit the musical phrase to the immediate context, is severe, intricate, and evasive. Its demands on the hearer present themselves as a series of numberless details, demanding of him unusual closeness of attention and delicacy of perception. Han-

WORK OF HANDEL AND BACH 217

del's melodic form and mass effects are easily appreciable by the masses; Bach requires more attention than the masses ever give, but he repays study with a revelation of great riches. To sum up this part of the matter, Handel was Italian in his knowledge of how to please, while Bach was German in his conscientiousness and thoroughness.

The employment of the German chorale in Bach's Passion music was not only the result of his adherence to established custom, but the outcome of his life-long devotion to this characteristic embodiment of the spirit of Protestant Germany. Bach treated the chorale melodies in many of his works, such as his organ chorales and his motets, as the medieval composers treated the *cantus firmus*, the liturgical chant. He used it as the subject of a contrapuntal work, weaving around it a rich, yet austere polyphony, which voiced the plain methods of the Protestant Church as fully as the medieval counterpoint reflected in music the artistic method pictorially embodied in Gothic architecture. It was altogether natural and fitting that when he came to set the Passion he should have used the chorale as the most complete and satisfying exponent of the Protestant faith, for that was what it had come to be in Germany. To this day the Lutheran hymn " Ein feste Burg ist unser Gott " is the battle-hymn of the German Protestant.

Bach lacked the impulse of the Italian to write tune for tune's sake. Striving as he did " for characteristic expression," it was impossible for him to reach a simple song-style in the solo parts of his Passion. His recitative is too intricate, too detailed, and too thoughtful to produce the broad declamatory effects of Handel's. The same assertion may be made as to his airs. Bach's music always has a reflective quality which robs it of the conventional dramatic appearance and stands as an obstacle in the way of its immediate appreciation by a miscellaneous and unprepared audience. There is nothing popular about Bach's music. He never comes down from his elevation to meet the crowd. If you wish to understand Bach you must climb up to his height, and that is never easy to do.

Both the forms, that of Handel and that of Bach, have individuality and distinct limitations. Bach's style, capable as it is of intense feeling, is essentially intimate, personal, and undramatic. It is always the voice of Bach in direct address to you that you hear. Handel's method is productive of broad and imposing effects, and while it is frequently only theatrical, it is quite as often sincerely and convincingly dramatic. One of Handel's biographers says of his great choruses: "They are choral recitatives, uttered by the voice of a multitude instead of a man. And strangely enough, the path that led to this embodiment of the composer's aspirations was the dusty path of Italian opera, where great combinations were impossible, science all but wasted, and where a giant intellect found little to grasp." Yet it is precisely the development of Handel's oratorio style from his work as an Italian opera composer that establishes its direct connection with the progress of the original Italian school of oratorio founded in Rome. It was the outcome, the climax, and the end of this school. Bach's Passion oratorios were the product of a purely German and Protestant ancestry, and they, too, were the highest achievement of their school. The subsequent history of oratorio will show us how attempts were made to fuse the elements of the two schools.

Chapter XVII

Haydn and Mendelssohn

Decadence of oratorio after Handel and Bach — Haydn and "The Creation" — Development of descriptive orchestration in oratorio — Haydn's oratorios descriptive and contemplative — Mendelssohn and the fusion of styles — His dramatic German Protestant oratorios — Mingling of elements from Handel and Bach.

FOR a considerable period after the deaths of Handel and Bach nothing of note in oratorio form was produced. One must seek for the cause of this in the vitiated state of public taste. Europe was addicted to the Italian opera habit, and in those days Italian opera was quite as empty, meaningless, and insincere as it has been at most periods in its history. There were no Italian composers who had sufficient genius to combine dramatic truth with musical beauty, so those who were writing contented themselves with the easily attainable, and turned out watery arias to please the superficial multitude. It was much easier for people to listen to that sort of music than to the imposing works of Handel or the subtle productions of Bach. Indeed the work of the latter was not known far outside of his own country. The large and comprehensive " History of Music," by Sir John Hawkins, published in 1776, when England was not yet through mourning the loss of Handel, contains a very brief mention of Bach, and says nothing at all about his Passions. They indeed were quite forgotten till Mendelssohn found that according to St. Matthew and resurrected it a hundred years after it was written. In the meantime Sacchini, Paisiello, Jomelli, and other Italian opera composers, whose works are now as dead as the Pharaohs, were writing worthless oratorios in operatic style.

Josef Haydn (1732–1813) began his career as an oratorio composer by writing an Italian work, in 1774, called " Il ritorno di Tobia." It was in the accepted form of its time, and though it contained some melodious solo parts and some well made fugal choruses, it shared the fate of other oratorios in the same style and sank into oblivion. Before Haydn reached the closing years of his life, however, two influences combined to change the public attitude toward operatic and oratorio music. Gluck had made a determined stand against the meaningless jingle of Italian opera music and had shown how to write operas which should be simple, melodious, and dramatically honest. Mozart had taken the entire extant apparatus of Italian opera and shown how it could be made the vehicle of the fullest dramatic expression and the most faithful characterization. The people in general were led to revolt against the employment of the unsuitable style of the old-fashioned opera in church music, of which they felt oratorio was a close connection. They saw that if Italian opera music was unfit for the stage, it was certainly less suited to a form closely allied to worship.

Meanwhile Haydn had been in London and had heard some of Handel's oratorios. The knowledge gained therefrom he was now to put to good use in constructing the choruses of his new works. His own developments in orchestration had been supplemented by Mozart's revelation of the wide possibilities of tone-coloring, and Haydn, equipped with all this knowledge, was to make a most important contribution to the growth of oratorio in its orchestral department. In the latter days of his great career, in 1798, Haydn produced "The Creation," a work which has survived its worthless predecessors of the post-Handelian period, and which is welcomed to-day wherever music-lovers have not lost their ability to appreciate simplicity and unpretentious beauty. In form "The Creation" is much more closely allied to the epic form of "The Messiah" than the dramatic shape of "Samson" and other works. The solo parts of "The Creation" are assigned to persons in the drama, as Adam and Eve, but these persons have no dramatic character or function. Their voices are employed only as those of narrators or commentators. They narrate the events of creation and comment on its wonders. The reader will at once see that this method deprived the work of the powerful element of personal characterization. The emotions of Adam and Eve never come to the surface. There is no passion, no grief in "The Creation." Thus it makes a step backward toward the music of pure religious contemplation, such as we found at the close of the era of church counterpoint. But Haydn's means were more modern. His arias for the solo voices have all the beauty of melody and style to be found in the best Italian writing for the stage, while they add to these elements a sincerity never wanting in the music of Haydn.

The choruses are naturally designed on a less imposing scale than those of Handel, which, as we have seen, had a certain dramatic quality. The general style and purpose of Haydn's oratorio writing made it inevitable that his choruses should be more contemplative or descriptive and less dramatic, and his development of the instrumental accompaniment emphasized this condition. It was Haydn who introduced into the oratorio purely descriptive orchestral music, and in doing this he paved the way for later composers to make stronger dramatic effects. Descriptive music in the orchestra, and instrumental accompaniments with special significance, are now a familiar part of the apparatus of the lyric drama as well as of the oratorio. Haydn employed these means as a part of his general scheme of descriptive writing. In order to give his instrumental description full scope, he was obliged to cast his choruses in a simpler mould than those of Handel, but his contributions to the art of descriptive writing were quite as valuable within their field as Handel's to the art of building huge choral climaxes. The prelude to "The Creation" is an instrumental representation of chaos; in the recitative beginning "And God made the firmament" are instrumental illustrations of storms, winds, thunders, and floods; the air "Rolling in foaming billows" has an accompaniment designed to suggest to the hearer the movement of waves. These were Haydn's original devices, and as such, although they sound simple and even naive to us to-day, they claim an important place in the advancement of musical art.

Haydn's second oratorio, " The Seasons," was produced in 1801, and although the composer's powers failed rapidly thereafter, there is no evidence of weakness in this work. In all essentials the form and style of this oratorio, which is secular, being founded in Thomson's poem of the same name, are the same as those of " The Creation." It is a descriptive, contemplative work, and must please by its thoughtful beauty and illustrative power. It is without the dramatic element. Ludwig Spohr (1784-1859) wrote oratorios, one of which, called " The Last Judgment " — though its name literally means " The Last Things " has some claims to consideration, inasmuch as by reason of its purely contemplative method and its instrumental descriptions it stands in the direct line of oratorio progress. It is, however, not frequently performed. It was produced at Cassel in 1826.

We come now to the master who established a new form of oratorio, — a form which is unsurpassed in its possibilities, and in which he left us the greatest masterpiece of dramatic oratorio. Felix Mendelssohn

(1809–1847) wrote two oratorios : "St. Paul," produced in 1836, and " Elijah," first performed in 1846. Though Mendelssohn was never a writer for the stage, for which his style was not at all suitable, he was not undramatic in his musical instincts. He was inordinately fond of programme music, and was somewhat more inclined to attribute to music a definite directness of utterance than most thoughtful commentators are willing to concede to it. He certainly went far toward justifying his theories by his " Midsummer Night's Dream " overture, but one must be careful to note that this composition is almost wholly made up of what has happily been called scenic music, — music descriptive of the externals of a drama, not of its subtler emotions. That Mendelssohn, however, had on the whole the right conception of the expressive power of music is shown by his reproof of the man who tried to give titles to the "Songs Without Words," and by his quotation of the opening measures of his own Hebrides overture as his attempt to express his own feelings aroused by the winds and waves. On the whole, it must be conceded that Mendelssohn had a correct idea of the dramatic expressiveness of music and a deep sympathy with it.

At the same time Mendelssohn, though of Jewish blood, was intensely German. Furthermore, he was baptized and brought up as a Protestant Christian. It is not at all surprising, then, that he was prepared to be powerfully attracted toward the Protestant oratorio, when he approached that form of composition, and to show little sympathy for the Italian form, as perfected by Handel. As early as 1823 the score of Bach's "St. Matthew Passion" was copied from the manuscript and placed in his hands for study. It is not difficult to imagine the effect of the work on the mind of an eager, ambitious boy of fourteen, already a composer, and just passed through the severe process of German preparation for confirmation. Mendelssohn became an enthusiastic propagandist of the teachings of Bach, and revived the "St. Matthew Passion" in Germany, where the general public had quite forgotten it.

In preparing himself for the task of composing his first oratorio, "St. Paul," Mendelssohn undoubtedly gave close study to the works of his great predecessors. That he should have rejected almost instinctively the Italian style of Handel followed as a matter of course. That he should have put aside with equal readiness the austere style of Bach was inevitable. Mendelssohn was from the outset an exponent of graceful, fluent melody. His genius was deeply tinged with the sentiment of song, and he could no more have sacrificed beauty of theme and perfect simplicity of form to subtlety of detail than Handel could. But at the same time his dramatic instincts told him that the sure way to the hearts of the people was the old Italian way, which made the oratorio in all essentials, except scenery and action, a religious drama. He knew at once that Bach's method of presenting the speeches of the principal personages in direct recitative was good, but that it had fallen short of complete effectiveness from two reasons: first, because the speeches were led up to and quoted by the evangelist narrator; and second, because the musical character of the recitative was too detailed to appeal to a general audience. But Mendelssohn saw one tremendous factor in the Bach oratorio,— the chorale as an embodiment of the Protestant faith of Germany.

In his "St. Paul" he did not arrive at the true method of dealing with the elements which appeared to him to be essential to an influential and permanent form of oratorio. The book is episodic and lacks dramatic continuity. The plan is religious rather than dramatic. The martyrdom of St. Stephen is the first episode, and it is without direct connection dramatically with the other two, the conversion of St. Paul, and his later career as a preacher. Both Stephen and Paul are deficient in definiteness of characterization. They appear to us rather as representations of an idea, which may be expressed in the words, " Go ye unto all the world and preach the gospel." But in " Elijah " we have the genuine modern dramatic oratorio, and in it we find that Mendelssohn made use of those parts of the apparatus of his predecessors suitable to his designs. " Elijah " is eclectic. It is a fusion of forms and styles, made with great skill and with the finest possible discrimination. It is a logical evolution, and Mendelssohn showed in its composition an instinctive grasp of the evolutionary principle of the survival of the fittest, — that is, the fittest for his design.

He dispensed with the narrator and directed his attention to placing the speeches of his personages before the auditor in the most direct, dramatic, and characteristic manner. He used the choruses as Handel did, to impersonate the mass of people. He employed the chorales exactly as Bach did, to signify the thought of the Church as it had come to be understood in Germany. His scenes are all arranged in dramatic form, and without doubt could be placed upon the stage effectively if the whole feeling of contemporaneous audiences were not opposed to that method of giving oratorio. His characters are drawn clearly and sharply. Indeed, there is no oratorio in which the musical characterization is so finely worked out. The contrasts between the choruses of the priests of Baal and the Jews are sufficient evidence of this. But everywhere throughout the score there is evidence of a consistent and successful effort to adapt to the production of a powerfully dramatic, yet specifically Protestant and German, oratorio, the most influential elements of the forms of Handel and Bach, together with Haydn's instrumental coloring.

The very beginning of the oratorio strikes a new note, and one of tremendous dramatic power. Three broad chords are followed by the portentous prophecy of Elijah, "As God the Lord of Israel liveth, before whom I stand, there shall not be dew nor rain these years, but according to my word." After that single passage, set to a style of recitative wholly different from that of either Bach or Handel, yet containing some of the qualities of both, follows the overture, a

HAYDN AND MENDELSSOHN

piece of music descriptive of the misery of the land of drought. Thenceforward everything moves dramatically. The people cry, "Help, Lord; wilt Thou quite destroy us?" Then they beseech, "Lord, bow Thine ear to our prayer." Obadiah calls them to repentance with warning and with the lovely air, "If with all your hearts ye truly seek me." Later an angel comes and commands Elijah to go to Cherith's brook, and then follows the double quartet, "For He shall give His angels," a new employment of Bach's commentary chorus. The episode of Elijah and the widow is treated with dramatic directness, and is followed by the commentary chorus, "Blessed are the men who fear Him."

The whole scene between Elijah and the priests of Baal is magnificent in the eloquence of its dramatic form and style. Yet the superb air of Elijah, "Lord God of Abraham, Isaac, and Jacob, this day let it be known that Thou art God," is followed by the pure old Bach species of chorale, "Cast thy burden upon the Lord." The climax of the oratorio is reached in the great scene of the coming of the rain. This scene is constructed and composed with a fine sense of dramatic values, and its effect is so sure and strong that it puts before the imagination a vivid picture. It is no wonder that in England, where dry and dusty works are produced year after year by native composers, such a masterpiece as " Elijah " is always heard with unabated enthusiasm. Here it is overshadowed in the popular mind by " The Messiah," and perhaps this is due in some measure to the public absorption in opera.

Since Mendelssohn achieved his fusion of the most influential elements of the Italian and German oratorios, no significant advance has been made in the oratorio form. This, of course, is due to the fact that no musician of genius has found in that form a vehicle suitable to the character of his thought. Good, workmanlike compositions have been produced in England, where oratorio is more popular than it is in any other part of the world, but so far as can be judged from the disadvantageous position of close proximity to the novelties, nothing of large worth has been written there. It seems safe to say, however, that the greatest choral composition written since Mendelssohn's day is the German Requiem of Brahms. But it lies outside the field of oratorio. Edgar Tinel, born at Sinay, Belgium, on March 27, 1854, has made an attempt to return directly to the Italian dramatic form of Carissimi, but employing modern musical material. His oratorio, " St. Franciscus," produced in Brussels in 1888, employs the entire musical apparatus of modern German opera, including the full resources of Wagnerian orchestration. The result is that the music smells of the theatre, and the whole style of the work is foreign to the religious atmosphere of the oratorio. Charles François Gounod (1818–1893), the famous French opera composer, made an attempt in his " Redemption " to produce a modernized treatment of Bach's passion form. Gounod was always a student of Bach, and was thoroughly acquainted with the various forms employed by that master. In " The Redemption " he followed the Bach plan of giving the narrative to one or two separate male voices and having the direct speeches of Jesus quoted by a baritone. He employs the chorale to represent the voice of the Church, while modern chorus forms are used to represent the crowd. Gounod also uses a single typical theme to embody the love of Jesus, and this, of course, is a device of later date than Bach. But the ground plan of "The Redemption" is plainly modelled on that of the "St. Matthew Passion." There the resemblance ends, for Gounod's recitative and choral writings are modern and sweetly melodious without subtlety.

Chapter XVIII

The Birth of Opera

Festival plays and intermezzi — Dreary character of music in plays — Influence of Greek learning — Attempt to resuscitate the dramatic declamation of the Greeks — Galilei and his " Ugolino " — Caccini's Nuove Musiche — Peri's setting of " Daphne " — Production of Rinuccini and Peri's " Eurydice " — The character of the new music.

THE modern opera was the result of a deliberate attempt to revive the Greek drama, and that attempt was caused chiefly by dissatisfaction with the music of medieval festival plays. The direction of the attempt was guided by the revival of Greek learning in Italy, a revival of which the reader has already been informed in Chapter VI. In order, however, that the reader may have a clear understanding of the conditions which led to the birth of opera, it is necessary that the author should briefly review the state of vocal music employed in plays in the sixteenth century. The reader will best understand this by recollecting that

THE BIRTH OF OPERA 235

the entire art-music of the time was colored by the use of the ecclesiastical scales and the complete devotion of composers to church counterpoint. The result was that in the beginning there was no difference, except in the subjects of the libretti, between the religious dramas, from which the oratorio was developed, and the secular plays with music, which may be regarded as the forerunners of the opera. These plays contained no recitative, because recitative had not yet been invented. They consisted of dialogue interspersed with choruses, and these choruses were always written, like the madrigals and other secular songs of the time, in one or the other of the ecclesiastical scales and in three, four, or five part polyphony.

Accounts have come down to us from a time as early as 1350 of the employment of plays with musical accompaniment performed to bring to a close the carnival festivities in Florence. This accompaniment at first consisted of a single chorus sung at the end of a scene, to a text bearing some relation to that of the play. The absurdity into which it fell at times may be understood from the fact that the text sung in a polyphonic chorus was frequently supposed to be the utterance of one of the personages of the drama. Toward the end of the fourteenth century the custom of introducing these pieces of music grew until they were known as intermezzi. The intermezzo grew in importance till it became a separate play of lighter character than the principal drama. As our fathers used to go to the theatre to see "Richard III.," followed by a one-act farce, so these medieval Italians went to see a serious drama relieved by a humorous or fanciful intermezzo; the difference being that the intermezzo was performed between the acts of the play. The intermezzo subsequently rose to such an importance that it developed into opera buffa, the comic Italian opera. But for the present we are concerned with it only as a forerunner of opera.

In 1589 Giovanni Bardi, Count of Vernio, wrote, as the festival play for the marriage of the Grand Duke Ferdinand with Christine de Lorraine, "L'Amico fido" with "grand, spectacular intermezzi." There were five intermezzi: "The Harmony of the Spheres," by Rinuccini, Cavaliere, and Malvezzi; "The Judgment of the Hamadryads," by Rinuccini and Marenzio; "The Triumph of Apollo," by Rinuccini, Marenzio, and Vernio; "The Infernal Regions," by Strozzi and Caccini; and "The Fable of Arion," by Rinuccini, Cavaliere, and Marenzio. This production naturally stimulated the movement in the direction of true opera, while it served to emphasize the utter unfitness of the extant style of music for dramatic purposes. The more frequently the composers undertook to set to music dramatic libretti, even of the simplest nature, the more firmly they became convinced that their music was not the right kind. The musical artists of the time had followed the methods of the religious drama, described in the chapter on the birth of oratorio, and were now gradually awakening to the fact that its style of music was incapable of illustrating the human passions and emotions of the secular drama. The dissatisfaction first found general voice in 1579, when a festival play, with music by Claudio Merulo and Andrea Gabrieli, was performed in honor of the marriage of Francesco I., Duke of Tuscany, with Bianca Capella, of Venice. The text of the choruses was full of joyous praise of the beauty of the bride; the music was in strict canon and in four parts, and made the wedding songs sound like funeral hymns. The artistic nobility of Florence was deeply displeased, and it was then that the Count of Vernio and a circle of his friends set out to see how they could improve the state of dramatic music.

The reader will recollect that in Chapter VI I spoke of the great influence of the revival of Greek learning in Italy on the simplification of musical style. The friends and associates of Count Vernio were all enthusiastic students of Greek literature; and to them the masterpieces of Æschylus and Euripides had come as revelations. It became their fondest ambition to restore the Greek drama, but they soon learned that in order to do this they must find their way back to something like the Greek music used in that drama. It was in searching for this that they hit upon the much desired substitute for the unsuitable polyphonic choruses. The Greek drama resembled the opera rather than the play of the present day. Music was an essential part of it. The dramatic and lyric elements were inseparable, and the one modified the other. The spirit of the text was as faithfully represented in the music as it was possible to represent it with the music of that age. We have abundant evidence that the Greek tragic writers were also composers. H. E. Krehbiel, in his " Studies in the Wagnerian Drama," has excellently summarized this evidence. A fragment of a theoretical work on rhythm by Aristoxenus is filled with lamentations over the decadence of dramatic music since the days of Æschylus. The author accuses contemporary composers of pandering to a depraved public taste. Sophocles was not only a poet and a composer, but an actor and a singer. In his own drama "Thamyris" he appeared as a singer stricken blind by the muses. Special note is made by the Greek writers that Euripides had to call in the aid of a composer to supply the music for one of his plays. In the Greek play the actors did not declaim their lines ; they chanted them. The odes which filled the pauses between the various stages of the dramatic action were sung by the chorus which gravely danced around an altar between the stage and the audience. These choruses were sung in unison, and were accompanied by instruments.

It was this dramatic recitation in music as practised by the Greeks that the little circle of enthusiasts, habitually assembled at the Palazzo Bardi, set out to resuscitate. But they had no specimens of it and hence were forced to do the best they could from descriptions. The most significant fact that struck home into their minds was that a single personage sang or intoned his part alone, and with an accompaniment of lyres or instruments of that class. Of course solo singing was not unknown to the medieval

Italians. The troubadours and minstrels were practising it, and furthermore it is inconceivable that they themselves did not often hum the catch of a madrigal. Musical historians too often speak of solo singing as if it were a sudden invention of the Bardi circle. What they did was to begin the artistic cultivation of it on certain lines and to produce something which became dramatic recitative. Vincenzo Galilei, father of Galileo, the famous astronomer, was a most enthusiastic advocate of the ancient music. He entered into a published controversy with the composer and theorist Zarlino, who warmly defended the music of his time. Galilei's "Dialogo della Musica Antica e Moderna," published in 1581, presents Count Vernio and Pietro Strozzi, one of the poets of the Vernio circle, as discussing ancient and modern music. It seems strange to us to find Galilei condemning modern music — that of the church in 1581 — as suitable only for uncultivated persons and not for the scholar. Galilei, however, was not content with precept; he added example. He selected a passage from Dante's "Inferno" and under the title of "Il Conte Ugolino" he set it to music for a single voice with lute accompaniment. He was an admirable lutenist and his perform-

THE BIRTH OF OPERA

ance of this, the first artistic monody of which we have any record, must have been very effective. The work itself is lost.

Giovanni Battista Doni, in his "Compendio del Trattato de' Generi e de' Modi della Musica" (Rome, 1635), tells us that Galilei was the "first who composed songs for a single voice," but he declares that Giulio Caccini, another member of the circle, "in imitation of Galilei, but in a more beautiful and pleasing style, set many canzonets and sonnets written by excellent poets." Caccini collected a number of these songs, which are in pure recitative style, and published them in 1601, under the title of "Nuove Musiche." He wrote a long preface, in which he claimed the honor of the highest achievement in this new kind of music and stoutly upheld its superiority to that of the contrapuntists. Here is a specimen of this "new music," which will give an excellent idea of the kind of musical recitation those enthusiasts of Florence evolved from their attempts to revive the Greek drama.

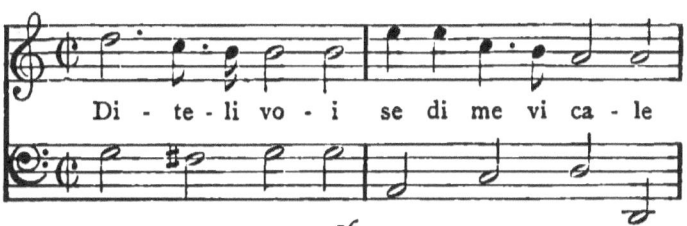

(From Grove's "Dictionary of Music.")

THE BIRTH OF OPERA 243

The bass part is intended to be figured by the thorough-bass system to indicate the harmonies. The only point necessary for the reader to note is that this recitative showed a tendency to abandon the church scales and use the modern major and minor keys. This tendency soon became a fixed practice, for composers learned from their dramatic experiments that the church modes were not suitable to the embodiment of human passions, and that they also lost much of their musical effectiveness when not employed in polyphony. The reader will recollect what has already been said about the change from polyphonic to monophonic writing. This excerpt from Caccini's book is one of the earliest specimens of monophonic composition, for it was in the search after the Greek recitative that composers found the new thing in music. This particular quotation presents an unusually well-formed piece for that time, for most of the music of the Vernio coterie lacked that definite movement which we call figure. Its rhythm was exceedingly vague, for the purpose of the composers was to follow as closely as possible the inflections of the voice in speech. It was their belief that this method was the true path to dramatic expressiveness. Their theory has been proved by the experience of their successors to be fundamentally correct, though their practice was naturally uncertain, tentative, and often unsuccessful. Nevertheless to Galilei, Caccini, and the other members of the assembly at the Palazzo Bardi must be attributed the invention of modern dramatic recitative, upon which the whole structure of opera rests. It is not possible to tell which of these men was the actual inventor. Probably the product was the result of consultation and joint effort extending over some twenty years.

Although the labors of Galilei and Caccini produced recitative, it is plain that they had not up to 1595 (or thereabout) written anything more than scenes for a single voice. In 1592 the Pope appointed the Count of Vernio his Maestro di Camera, and he accordingly removed from Florence to Rome. The meetings of the Florentine coterie were held thereafter at the palace of Giacomo Corsi, who was also an enthusiast in regard to Greek literature and art in general. It was at the house of Corsi that the first work of the coterie in the form of a play was made known. This was a pastoral called "Daphne," performed privately in 1597. The book was written by Ottavio Rinuccini, the poet, who wrote some of the intermezzi previously mentioned, and the music was by

THE BIRTH OF OPERA

Jacopo Peri, a member of the coterie, not a very learned musician, but a firm believer in the new style. The work is lost, but Peri tells us in the preface to his later work, "Eurydice," that he wrote "Daphne" at the solicitation of Corsi and Rinuccini to try the power of the new vocal music. Rinuccini, in his dedication of the libretto of "Eurydice" to Mary de Medicis, wrote:

"It has been the opinion of many persons, most excellent queen, that the ancient Greeks and Romans sang their tragedies throughout on the stage, but so noble a manner of recitation has not, that I know of, been even attempted by any one till now; and this I thought was owing to the defect of the modern music, which is far inferior to the ancient. But Messer Jacopo Peri made me entirely alter my opinion, when, upon hearing the intention of Messer Giacomo Corsi and myself, he so elegantly set to music the pastoral of 'Daphne,' which I had composed merely to make a trial of the power of vocal music in our age; it pleased to an incredible degree those few who heard it. From this I took courage. The same piece, being put into better form and presented anew in the house of Messer Peri, was not only favored by all the nobility of the country, but heard and commended by the most serene grand duchess, and the most illustrious Cardinals dal Monte and Montalto. But the 'Eurydice' has met with more favor and success, being set to music by the same Peri with wonderful art, and having been thought worthy to be represented on the stage by the bounty and magnificence of the most serene grand duke, in the presence of your Majesty, the cardinal legate, and so many princes and gentlemen of Italy and France. From whence, beginning to find how well musical representations of this kind were likely to be received, I resolved to publish these two, to the end that others of greater abilities than myself may be induced to carry on and improve this kind of poetry to such a degree that we may have no occasion to envy those ancient pieces which are so much celebrated by noble writers."

It is evident that Rinuccini had a high opinion of the value of his libretti. Posterity has awarded the palm, however, to Peri's music. Peri, in his preface to " Eurydice," says he wrote " Daphne " at the suggestion of Corsi and Rinuccini " to test the effect of the kind of melody which they imagined to be the same as that used by the ancient Greeks and Romans throughout their dramas." The success of the private performances of " Daphne " led to the writ-

THE BIRTH OF OPERA 247

ing of "Eurydice," which was prepared as the festival play for the marriage of King Henry IV., of France, with Mary de Medicis. This work, the first Italian opera, was produced in 1600 in Florence, after careful preparation. Its success was immediate and almost sensational. It was pronounced by all the dilettanti of Florence to be a genuinely new thing in art, and the recitative music, by its fidelity to the text, made a profound impression. Fortunately this work has been preserved and there is a modern reprint of it. In the preface Peri set forth his theory of recitative. It is evident that he had a deep insight into the true nature of the new form. He tried to imitate ordinary conversational speech with music half sung and half spoken — what came to be called "parlando." More complex emotions seemed to him to call for a "melody with greater intervals and a lively tempo, the accompanying instrumental harmonies changing more frequently." It appears also from Peri's preface that he had some assistance from Caccini in writing his score. But, as Rinuccini credits Peri alone with the work, as only Peri's name appeared in the published score, and as Caccini afterward set the entire libretto to music of his own, I suspect that he, being a singer, simply helped Peri with some of the more troublesome parts for the solo voices.

The author was present at a performance of "Eurydice," given by The American Academy of the Dramatic Arts in New York on March 15, 1894. The work of course sounded antiquated and tentative, and it is impossible for us to-day to realize the impression which it must have made on the Florentines three hundred years ago. To approach such a realization would require the power to free one's mind from familiarity with some of the most ordinary harmonic and melodic sequences of modern music, which came into existence after the days of Peri. One would, furthermore, have to bring his mind into the state of those whose only vocal music of an artistic kind had been contrapuntal and ecclesiastical, and to whom the vocal solo was a startling novelty. Viewed from a standpoint as near this as a modern person can reach, Peri's recitative — and his music is never anything more than recitative — becomes pregnant with meaning and fruitful in possibilities. It certainly sounds somewhat timid to us, lacking, as it does, the bold melodic sequences of later music. But it reveals itself as a sincere and — within its limits — successful artistic effort. It is in some measure hampered by the antiquated conventionalities of Rinuccini's book, but we must remember that he, too, was laboring in the field of experiment. Here is a specimen of Peri's recitative, quoted in my "Story of Music," with harmony arranged by Dr. F. L. Ritter.

250 HOW MUSIC DEVELOPED

With the exception of a few measures of their choral writing, the whole opera was in recitative of this kind. The orchestra in "Eurydice" consisted of a violin, a large guitar, a lyre, a large lute, and a harpsichord. These instruments played a very bald sort of accompaniment. There was no attempt at instrumental effects, except in one place where three flutes were employed to imitate a pandæan pipe, played by one of the characters. The whole value of the opera lies in its vocal part.

In closing this account of the first opera, I must endeavor to convey to the reader a clear idea of the peculiarities of its music. I have already pointed out the fact that the composer sought to impart dramatic significance to his music by imitating the inflections of the voice in speech. Naturally this method precluded the possibility of arriving at any definite musical form, such as we should now call a tune. The composers of the time had not yet acquired such

THE BIRTH OF OPERA 251

familiarity with the monophonic style as to understand that, as I have shown earlier in this book, all single-voiced tunes were dependent upon a harmonic basis.

Not having a definite succession of chords, they mixed their harmonies up in unrelated masses, and the voice-parts, built upon those harmonies, were consequently shapeless. There being no definitely shaped tunes, there could not be any strong musical contrasts. To-day a composer expresses grief through a slow movement, such as a largo or an adagio, and usually in a minor key, while a change to joy is indicated by a transition to a major key, a lively movement, and an incisive rhythm. But in Peri's "Eurydice," where everything is in recitative, such strong contrast is impossible. When Orpheus bewails the loss of Eurydice he does it in recitative which is somewhat broken and spasmodic in its phrasing; when he pours out his joy at her recovery, he does it in recitative which flows more smoothly and approaches more nearly what we call melody. But that is as far as Peri advanced, and it is as far as he could advance in the then state of monophonic composition. A good singer can make Peri's recitative sound fairly expressive. Caccini's setting of Rinuccini's poem is similar in general style to that of Peri. But as skill in writing homophonic music developed among instrumental composers, the opera writers began to see how they could adapt to their needs some of the new material, and the development of operatic writing in the direction of definite forms was remarkably rapid, — so rapid, indeed, that it led dramatic music out of its province, as we shall see.

It should be noted, before proceeding further, that Peri called his "Eurydice" a *Tragedia per Musica*. The other titles of the lyric drama in its inception were *Drama per Musica*, *Melodrama*, and *Tragicomedia*. It was about 1650 that the title *Opera per Musica* was first used, and this was soon afterward abbreviated to Opera. The new style of music, the recitative, was called *Stile rappresentativo* or *Stile parlante*.

Chapter XIX

Italian Opera to Handel's Time

Work of Monteverde — His development of recitative and orchestration — Cavalli and his attempts at melodic form — Alessandro Scarlatti — Recitative stromentato and aria da capo — Tune for tune's sake — Reign of the singer — Operatic law in the eighteenth century — The Opera Buffa.

THE rapidity with which the new style advanced may be judged from the fact that seven years after the production of "Euridice" we meet with an opera containing a duet, and a few years later with one containing instrumental descriptions. The composer, who appears to have been the first gifted with a real genius for operatic composition, was Claudio Monteverde (1568–1651). Already many other composers had sought to follow Peri, and Mantua, Bologna, and Venice became homes of opera. Monteverde was a student of the old contrapuntal style, but his entire genius was out of sympathy with it. He became chapel master to the Duke of Mantua, and at his invitation prepared, as one of the festival plays for the marriage of Francesco Gonzaga with Margherita, Infanta of Savoy, in 1647, his "Arianna," which, according to the testimony of a contemporary, "visibly moved the whole theatre to tears." The lament of Arianna over the departure of her faithless lover must have amazed the public of that day by its simple, melodious pathos. It approaches the modern arioso in style, and is really expressive. So successful was "Arianna" that Monteverde was asked to compose another opera for 1608. This was his "Orfeo," the libretto being on the same story as that of Peri's "Euridice."

The work begins with a prelude, eight measures in five-part harmony for trumpets and other instruments, followed by a short passage of contrasting nature. This is to be played three times before the rising of the curtain. After this overture there is a prologue of five speeches in recitative delivered by a character called La Musica Prologo, who represents the genius of music. In his prologue he invites attention to the story which he relates. The opera begins with a recitative by a shepherd, and this is followed by a five-part chorus, with accompaniment of the full orchestra, consisting of

ITALIAN OPERA TO HANDEL 255

the instruments enumerated in Chapter XI. The work then proceeds in recitative, varied by choruses, duets, and trios. There are no solo arias. The aria form had not yet been developed. Here is part of a duet from Monteverde's "Orfeo."

APOLLO AND ORPHEUS ASCEND TO HEAVEN, SINGING:—

ITALIAN OPERA TO HANDEL 259

The opera ends with a dance. In his "Tancredi e Clorinda," an intermezzo produced in Venice in 1624, Monteverde introduced special instrumental effects which were to become of so great importance in opera. These effects I have already described in Chapter XI., and it is necessary to add here only the statement that they were used, not simply as descriptive of action, but also to aid in conveying to the minds of the auditors the impetuosity and passion of the combatants in the remarkable scene of the fight. It gives one something of a shock to find Monteverde indicating the galloping of horses and the fierceness of their riders, rudely indeed, but with the same musical methods as Wagner employed, with their modern development, in his "Ride of the Valkyrs." Monteverde was, indeed, the Wagner of his time. He broke so completely away from old conventions that Artusi, a writer of Bologna, accused him of having lost sight of the true office of music, "to please the ear."

One of the remarkable things (remarkable at that time) done by Monteverde was to introduce the chord of the dominant seventh unprepared. I shall not undertake to explain the nature of this novelty in harmony, lest I merely confuse the lay reader, but shall ask him to content himself with the statement that such an introduction produced one of those sharp dissonances so common in the music of to-day, and used to express passion. Monteverde began to use these dissonances in his madrigals, of which the Fifth Book, published in 1599, aroused Artusi's ire. But the tremendous effect of the dissonant progressions in "Arianna" quite demolished all the arguments of the opponents

ITALIAN OPERA TO HANDEL 261

of the novelty. Their employment was one of the practices which led directly away from the tonality of the old ecclesiastical scales and toward the modern major and minor keys. Dr. Parry's comments on the work of Monteverde are so pertinent and so lucid that I cannot do better than to quote a part of them : —

"The methods of choral art did not provide for dramatic force or the utterance of passionate feeling; and under such circumstances it was natural that Monteverde should misapply [in his madrigals] his special gifts, which were all in the direction of dramatic expression. The new departure, when it came, was his opportunity. He was not ostensibly a sharer in the first steps of the movement; but directly he joined it he entirely eclipsed all other composers in the field, and in a few years gave it quite a new complexion. For whereas the first composers had not laid any great stress on expression, Monteverde's instinct and aim were chiefly in that direction; and he often sought to emphasize his situations at all costs. His harmonic progressions are for the most part as incoherent as those of his predecessors, and, as might be expected with his peculiar aptitudes, he did very little for design. But he clearly had a very considerable sense of stage effect, and realized that mere monotonous recitative was not the final solution nor even the nucleus of dramatic music. It is true he introduces a great quantity of recitative, but he varies it with instrumental interludes which now and then have some real point and relevancy about them; and with passages of solo music which have definite figure and expression, and with choruses which are more skilfully contrived, and to a certain degree more effective, than those of his predecessors. By this means he broke up the homogeneous texture of the scenes into passages of well-defined diversity, and interested his auditors with contrast, variety, and conspicuously characteristic passages, which heighten the impression of the situation as all stage music should."

Soon after the production of Monteverde's "Tancredi e Clorinda" the opera ceased to be a strictly aristocratic form of entertainment and became public and popular. In 1637 the Teatro San Cassiano was opened to the public as a regular opera house. Opera houses became numerous. Up to 1727 no less than fifteen operatic enterprises were started, and up to 1734 four hundred operas by forty composers had been produced. This, however, carries us far ahead of the period which we are now discussing. The statement

ITALIAN OPERA TO HANDEL 263

is made merely to show that only those Italian composers can now be mentioned who made actual contributions to the development of the lyric drama.

The next who did so contribute after Monteverde was his pupil, Francesco Cavalli (1599–1676), a native of Crema, a town near Venice. He was at one time chapel-master of St. Mark's. His first opera, " Le Nozze di Tito e di Peleo," was produced in Venice in 1639. Its recitatives are varied in style and it has instrumental interludes, notably one for hunting horns, of striking character. But it was in his " Giasone," produced in 1649, that Cavalli's most influential music appeared. He was opposed to the banishment of rhythmical music and song-forms from opera simply because the Greeks did not have them. Instrumental forms were beginning to show the influence of folk-music and the popularity of the early collections of dance tunes suggested to Cavalli the possible effectiveness of something similar in vocal style. In his " Giasone," therefore, he foreshadowed the *aria da capo* (aria with a repeat at its close of the passage with which it began) by making a return to the first part. Cavalli's melodies show a strong movement toward clearness of rhythm and definiteness of shape, though the style continued to be tentative and uncertain.

But it is easy to perceive that even in his day Italian opera had begun the movement toward elementary rhythms and harmonies and tunefulness for tune's sake, which were to be its special characteristics for more than two centuries. The improvements in the dramatic recitative and the choral part of oratorio made by Carissimi, Cesti, and Stradella (see Chap. XV.) also influenced composers of opera. The general tendency was in the direction of definitely shaped melodies as a substitute for the formless recitative of Peri and Monteverde. The recitative itself became more characteristic and was diversified with short arioso passages. Furthermore the accompaniment of the recitative was much improved. Peri and Caccini fashioned the slight chords of their accompaniments to recitative so that they might be played on one instrument, for they were jealous of the slightest instrumental interference with their newly invented *stilo parlante*. Monteverde improved the instrumental part of opera, as we have seen, and frequently accompanied his solo parts with small groups of instruments. Meanwhile Giovanni Gabrieli wrote his church music with orchestral accompaniment, and the opera composers began to see how grand dramatic effects might be produced by using similar means. The result is that in the latter half

ITALIAN OPERA TO HANDEL 265

of the sixteenth century we find different kinds of recitative clearly defined and the *aria da capo* thoroughly established. The composer who exhibited the most complete mastery of these forms, and who was so influential that he became the founder of the great Neapolitan school of opera writers, was Alessandro Scarlatti.

He was born at Trapani in Sicily in 1659. The record of his early life is lost, but his career as a famous composer seems to have been fairly begun when he produced his opera "Pompeo" at Naples in 1684. He wrote 115 operas, of which 41 are extant in score. They have all ceased to be performed, but their historical interest is great. Scarlatti died Oct. 24, 1725. It is hardly necessary for the purposes of this volume to specify in which operas the special features which he contributed to the development of the form are to be found. It will perhaps be more instructive to the reader to enumerate these features and explain them. Scarlatti made a systematic distinction of the characteristics of three kinds of vocal music in opera. Two of these were recitative, which had hitherto been treated in one way, the accompaniment being confined to a small group of instruments, or one instrument alone, playing chords. In one of Scarlatti's operas appeared recitative accompanied by the whole orchestra, and he made a clear distinction in the character and purpose of two kinds of recitative. The first of these was the *recitativo secco*, which means "dry recitative." This is the pure dialogue form of recitative, used to carry on the ordinary passing conversation of the scene. It was accompanied in the early works by the harpsichord generally, and it is the custom to this day in artistic opera houses to play the chords to the *recitativo secco* in "Don Giovanni" on the piano. In England it became the custom to play these chords in broken form on the double bass and violoncello, but this custom has not prevailed elsewhere. *Recitativo secco* is not used so much now as it was in the earlier days of opera, but short passages of it are found in many modern works, even those of Wagner, while in oratorio it is not at all infrequent. Here is an example of it from Mozart's "Don Giovanni":—

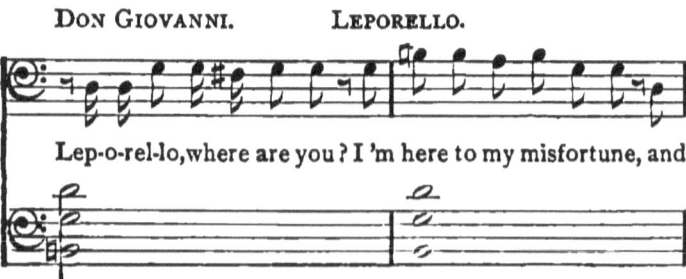

Lep-o-rel-lo, where are you? I'm here to my misfortune, and

ITALIAN OPERA TO HANDEL 267

you, sir? I'm here. Who's dead, th' old man or you, sir?

Alessandro Scarlatti was the first to make systematic use of that richer form of recitation known as *recitativo stromentato*. Indeed, some historians declare, and with fairly good ground, that he invented this species. *Recitativo stromentato* is recitative with an especially designed orchestral accompaniment instead of the simple chords of the *secco* style. Usually the most significant orchestral passages are placed in the pauses between the phrases uttered by the voice. The whole recitative thus becomes more passionate, more varied, and more filled with meaning. The extreme development of *recitativo stromentato* is to be found in Wagner's later dramas, in which entire scenes are made of it. Excellent examples of it in its customary modern form, however, are to be found in his earlier works. Here is one from the first act of "Lohengrin":—

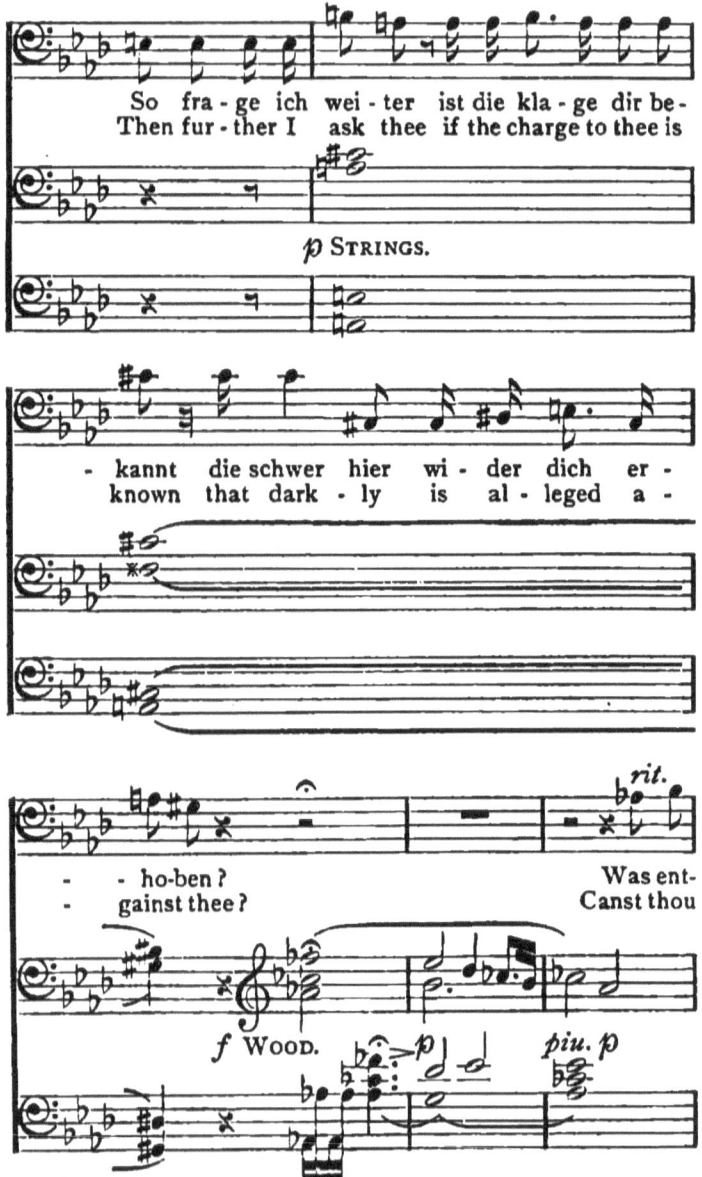

ITALIAN OPERA TO HANDEL

It will readily be perceived that these improvements in diversification of the recitative gave the Italian opera a livelier musical character, and made it appeal more directly to the popular taste. But significant as Scarlatti's labor in this department was, its influence did not equal that of his development of the *aria da capo*. We have already seen that Cavalli made a step in the direction of this form by repeating the first part of a tune to make its close. It was Alessandro Scarlatti, however, who completely established the position of the aria in opera and defined its form. He himself was a noted singer and a teacher of singing, and he saw in the aria abundant opportunity for the display of pure vocal ability. His success in making music that enabled singers to reveal the beauties of their voices decided the direction in which Italian opera was to move until almost the present day, and led to the birth of a numerous body of composers upon whom I am fond of placing the title " Neapolitan school." The theory of the *aria da capo* is a purely musical one, and its inventors did not perceive that it was distinctly opposed to dramatic fidelity. The conception of a melody in three sections, of which the first and third are the same and the middle one strongly contrasting, belongs to the realm of absolute music. When the composer asks a soprano to be mildly pathetic in the beginning of an air, work herself into a passion in the middle, and suddenly become mildly pathetic again at the close, simply in order that she may repeat the opening measures, he violates emotional truthfulness and is guilty of false art. The Italian opera writers seem to have arrived at a realization of this fact very soon, and finding that their symmetrical tunes pleased the public, they threw overboard all pretence of dramatic sincerity and wrote the tunes for their own sake, no matter whether they fitted the spirit of the text or not. Francesco Rossi, Antonio Caldara, Antonio Lotti, and Giovanni Maria Buononcini were among Alessandro Scarlatti's immediate successors, and all of them devoted themselves to producing operas which consisted of strings of arias, duets, etc., united by brief passages of recitative.

One important result of this practice was that the voices and abilities of the principal singers had to be considered in order that the arias might be effective. The singers were thus enabled to make such great personal impressions upon the public that they soon became the reigning power in opera, and actually made laws for the composers. This was the period of the famous male soprano singers Farinelli, Cafarelli, Senesino, Gizziello, and others, whose marvellous singing was due to long processes of training, and who were the adored and inexorable monarchs of the musical world. The state of Italian opera in the time of Handel

(1685–1759) is more easily described than imagined. I have already told how the famous composer of "The Messiah" began his career as an opera composer. He wrote some forty operas, all of which have now only an historical interest. Arias and duets from them are frequently heard in concert, and are excellent examples of the manner in which composers treated text in those days. To two lines of text one frequently finds half a dozen pages of music, the words apparently being employed simply to give the singer syllables to pronounce. It must be said for Handel that he was too great a composer to turn out mere rubbish. While he displayed remarkable dexterity in writing passages of pure vocal exhibition work for the singers, he contrived to put a considerable quantity of very good music into his operas. Nevertheless he was under the control of the singer and the formulæ of the time.

The laws of Italian opera in that day prescribed six persons — three men and three women — as the proper number of singers. The men were always sopranos or tenors. The use of the baritone voice was quite unknown; sometimes a bass part was written for one of the men, but as there are only a few fine bass parts in any of the old

ITALIAN OPERA TO HANDEL 273

operas, and no records of the fame of any great basses except Boschi, we must conclude that only the male soprano and tenor had any wide vogue. In Handel's "Teseo" there was neither bass nor tenor; all the parts were sopranos and contraltos. Of course there were male characters, so it is easy to conceive how far away from anything like dramatic truth the whole thing must have been. The common use of the baritone voice, the voice of the average man, did not begin till the latter part of the last century. The French composers, who, as we shall see, clung more faithfully to dramatic fidelity than the Italians, were the first to use it extensively. Gluck made frequent use of it, but it remained for Mozart to discover the full scope of its usefulness.

The rules made by the singers and in force in Handel's time did not stop at the distribution of the voices. They prescribed also the kinds and number of arias, duets, etc. There were five kinds of aria: *aria cantabile, aria di portamento, aria di mezzo caraterre, aria parlante, and aria di bravura. Aria cantabile* was slow and flowing and usually pathetic in style. *Aria di portamento* was also slow, but with stronger rhythm and wider intervals. *Aria parlante* was declamatory. *Aria di mezzo carattere* was an air of medium character, containing a fusion of styles. *Aria di bravura* was one in which every possible opportunity was given the singer for a display of agility in the way of runs, trills, jumps, *et cætera*. The rules also commanded that every scene in an opera should end with an aria, and that in each act every principal singer should have one aria. No singer could have two arias in succession, nor in any circumstances might two arias of the same kind stand together. The hero and heroine had each to have one *aria di bravura* and one duet. The opera ended with a dance and chorus. At one time no trios, quartets, or concerted pieces were allowed.

A natural result of such rules was that opera librettos were very poor stuff generally, and had little dramatic sense or force. Composers often took a lot of good airs and duets from operas which had failed, and strung them together with new text to make a new opera. It was an experiment of this kind which led Gluck, as we shall see, to doubt the possibility of producing anything artistic according to the extant methods of Italian opera. As Gluck's movement of reform was undertaken in Paris, and as his works lie rather in the line of development of French opera than of Italian, I shall recount the story of his battle in the narrative

ITALIAN OPERA TO HANDEL 275

of the growth of the French school. It is sufficient for the present to say that his labors had no very serious influence on Italian composers. They continued to write tune for tune's sake, and their modifications in style and form would have come about without the intervention of Gluck.

Immediately after Handel the Neapolitan school of composers was conspicuous through its development of opera buffa, comic grand opera. The principal writers were Logroscino, Leo, Hasse, and Pergolesi. The last was popular both as a serious and a comic writer somewhat later than 1770. Later still came forward Sacchini, Galuppi, Paisiello and Piccini. The last named, a contemporary of Gluck and Mozart, and Gluck's opponent in Paris, was a most melodious writer. He deserves special mention for his development of the operatic finale. His finales were long concerted pieces in which the various voices were united in rich harmonies so as to produce a strong effect.

Chapter XX

Italian Opera to Verdi

Cimarosa, Rossini, Donizetti, and Bellini — The last writers of the Neapolitan school — Tune for tune's sake — Rossini's improvements in methods of opera writing — Verdi and his three styles — "Aïda," and "Otello," "Falstaff," and the new school of Italian opera.

DOMENICO CIMAROSA (Naples, Dec. 17, 1749 — Venice, Jan. 11, 1801) wrote seventy-six operas, none of which are heard to-day outside of Italy, where recently there has been a movement to revive some of the operas of the end of the last century. Cimarosa's masterpiece is "Il Matrimonia Segreto," a genuinely fine work in the department of Italian opera buffa. The music is distinguished for its flow of genuine and spirited humor and its constant melody. The ensembles are excellently made and have served as models to later masters.

The most celebrated, original, and influential of Italian masters of the present century before Verdi was Gioachino Antonio Rossini, born at Pesaro, Feb. 29, 1792. His principal works are: "Tancred" (1813), "Otello" (1816), "Il Barbiere di Siviglia" (1816), "Semiramide" (1823), and "Guillaume Tell" (1829). The last-named opera was written for Paris and it was not warmly received. Rossini appears to have taken its failure greatly to heart, and finding himself independent he wrote no more for the stage. He died in Paris, Nov. 13, 1868. "William Tell" is usually classed by historians among French operas, because it was written for the French stage and was a deliberate attempt to follow the French style. But it was its pure Italianism that prevented it from winning immediate success in Paris. Nevertheless it is Rossini's masterpiece.

Rossini was not a man of musical genius, nor was he one of profound musical learning. As soon as he had enough musical science to write a score, he dropped study once and for all and embarked upon his career as a composer. He had a keen perception of the nature of those musical means which could be employed to produce a stage effect, and wrote always with these in his mind. There is no depth, no sincerity, in the music of Rossini. It is always theatrical and full of imposition. Perhaps the most heartless music ever written for an opera by a man of real talent is that of "Semiramide." Hardly an air in it will stand the test of comparison with its own text, and the manner in which a plotting priest, supposed to be a dark and mysterious villain, goes about expressing his desperate soul through trills and scales is almost ridiculous. Yet "Semiramide" is full of melody, and it contains musical effects which were new and striking at the time of its production. The employment of four horns together with clarinets in the finale, for instance, was an innovation.

Rossini must be credited with several improvements, although he wrote for the singer, and his "Semiramide" is a survival of the style of opera produced in Handel's day. In his "Otello" he abandoned the old *recitativo secco* and produced an opera with *recitativo stromentato* throughout. He enriched the instrumentation greatly, largely through his employment of the horns. He was a fine horn-player himself. He introduced the use of long crescendi and also introduced the *cabaletta*, a quick movement to follow a slow cantabile aria, as the "Dolce pensiero" after "Bel raggio" in "Semiramide," or the "Semper libera" after "Ah, fors e lui" in Verdi's "La Traviata."

Rossini also tried to abolish the custom of permitting singers to make their own ornamental cadenzas, insisting that he could write good ones and that singers must use them. The most important of all these improvements was the abandonment of *recitativo secco*. While all other composers did not at once follow his lead, the superiority of operas containing only *recitativo stromentato* gradually became clear, and *recitativo secco* almost disappeared. It is written by composers of to-day only in very brief passages.

Rossini's "Barber of Seville" is a genuinely good example of opera buffa. It is full of melody and it sparkles with vivacity. When well performed it must always give pleasure to intelligent hearers. "William Tell" is a melodious, fluent, and in places really eloquent piece of dramatic composition. It is fine enough to make one regret that Rossini, who finished his life under the influence of French dramatic theories, did not again write for the stage. The popularity of Rossini's operas in the first three quarters of the present century was enormous. At one time it seemed as if all the bands and half the pianos in Europe were playing "Di tanti regi." His works preserved all the essential elements of the

Neapolitan school founded by Alessandro Scarlatti, of whom Rossini and his immediate Italian successors were artistic descendants.

Gaetano Donizetti was born at Bergamo, Nov. 29, 1797. His first successes were achieved after Rossini had retired. His most important works are: " Elisir d'Amore" (1832), " Lucrezia Borgia " (1834), " Lucia di Lammermoor" (1835), " La Favorita" (1840), " Linda di Chamounix " (1842), and " Don Pasquale " (1842). Donizetti cannot be said to have contributed anything to the development of Italian opera except a simpler and less pretentious style than that of Rossini. Weak and watery as his grand operas appear to us now, they had a good influence at the time of their production. His opera buffa " Elisir d'Amore " is, when well performed, a very pleasing trifle. Donizetti had an excellent flow of melody, but he sacrificed dramatic truth to musical effectiveness at all times in his operas.

Vincenzo Bellini (1802–1835) wrote also in a sweet, melodious, and generally sentimental style, except in " Norma" (1832), in which one of the most dramatic librettos in the whole field of opera inspired the composer to the production of some really admirable music. Bellini's " Norma " went far toward showing how a pure Italian style

ITALIAN OPERA TO VERDI 281

and a powerful dramatic utterance might be reconciled. His " La Sonnambula " (1831) is occasionally performed, for the glory of some light soprano. Bellini might have achieved much if he had not died so young.

Saverio Mercadante (1795–1870) wrote sixty operas. His most important works are : " Elisa e Claudio " (1822), and " Il Guiramento " (1837). The latter work not only contains powerful ensembles and solos, but differs from the style of Rossini more than any other of Mercadante's works. It contains passages which are original, yet remind us of the style of Meyerbeer and of Wagner in his " Rienzi."

We come now to the greatest opera composer that Italy has produced, — a composer who ranks with the representative masters of other schools and whose career is an epitome of the history of Italian opera in his time. Giuseppe Verdi was born at Roncole, near Busseto, Oct. 9, 1813. He took his first lessons from a local organist, but in 1833 was sent to Milan to study. His first opera, " Oberto, Conte di San Bonifazio," was produced at Milan in 1839. His principal works since have been: " Ernani " (1844), " Rigoletto " (1851), " Il Trovatore " (1853), " La Traviata " (1853),

"Aïda" (1871), "Otello" (1887), and "Falstaff" (1893).

Verdi's music has been divided into three styles. It will, perhaps, be somewhat difficult for the average listener to distinguish more than two, yet there are musical grounds for the statement. His earliest operas are in the old Neapolitan style as it had come to exist in Verdi's time. They consist of series of tunes, strung on threads of recitative, without any consideration of dramatic fidelity except a vague, general fitness of color. Their music is designed strictly to tickle the ear. In "Ernani" we meet with Verdi's second style, which is characterized by immense vigor, boisterous instrumentation, and contrasts of tremendous dramatic power with cheap dance music. "Rigoletto" is the best and most familiar specimen of this period. "Il Trovatore," though of later date than "Rigoletto," is rather in the style of the first period. The third period began with "Aïda," in which Verdi parted company forever with elementary rhythms and harmonies, common dance tunes, coarse instrumentation, and operatic clap-trap in general. "Aïda" is a grand and inspiring masterpiece in which the Verdian stream of melody is quite as rich as in the earlier works, but is guided in artistic channels. The music is intense in its dramatic passion, and by the use of rich harmony and changeful melody Verdi creates an atmosphere full of local color. In "Aïda," however, Verdi preserved all the familiar forms of the older Italian operas. He uses even the *aria da capo* in its modern shape. But into everything is infused a true dramatic spirit. It is in characterization that the greatest shortcoming of the "Aïda" music is to be found. Nevertheless, "Aïda" is the best opera written by an Italian up to its date of production.

In his next opera, "Otello," written at a time when most composers would have retired to rest on their laurels, Verdi made another tremendous stride upward, and stamped himself as one of the world's genuine masters. In "Otello" he abandoned all the old forms. There are no set instrumental introductions to arias, not set arias, no cabaletti. The only lyrics are Desdemona's "Ave Maria" and "Willow" song, which are introduced as songs might be in a spoken drama. Verdi named "Otello" a lyric drama, and that is precisely what it is. The single speeches are treated as speeches, not as songs, and the dialogue is pure dialogue, not as duets or trios. Much of the score is in the modern style of arioso, a species of recitative in which the phrases are highly melodic in style without forming a complete tune, and yet preserve their dramatic truthfulness. The orchestration is immensely rich and expressive, and is quite independent of the voices. One or two leading motives of the Wagnerian kind are employed with much judgment and moderation. The libretto, a remarkably fine adaptation of the Shakespearian play, is by Arrigo Boito (born 1842), himself the composer of a very fine opera, "Mefistofele," intensely modern in style.

Verdi was accused of imitating Wagner in both "Aïda" and "Otello," chiefly because he modified and afterward abandoned the recognized forms of the Italian school. The charge cannot be sustained. Verdi has never for an instant sacrificed his individuality, and his music is as purely and intensely Italian as Wagner's is German. The same charge was made against Gounod when he wrote "Romeo et Juliette," a thoroughly French work. Verdi in these operas was simply following the dictates of his mature genius, which was leading him toward one of the most significant developments of our time. He was struggling to adapt to the fundamental theories of opera, as expounded by its founders, Rinuccini and Peri, the vast and complicated materials of modern musical expression. In "Aïda" he endeavored to reconcile the formulæ of the Neapolitan school with the esthetic principles of the Greek drama and approached as closely to complete success as the opposing nature of the two chief elements would permit. In "Otello" he confessed the unsuitability of the Neapolitan forms to the full and detailed union of text and music. He preserved the Italian beauty of the vocal part of opera, constructed it with a consistent, determined, and generally successful attempt at organic union with the text, and so produced an opera which will, I believe, live. That he was wholly uninfluenced by Wagner's style, though he was attentive to Wagner's proclamations of the true theory of dramatic composition, is demonstrated by "Otello," and still more conclusively by his last work, "Falstaff," which is as far away from Wagner's style as is Mozart's "Nozze di Figaro," and yet which is built on precisely the same dramatic principles as Wagner's "Die Meistersinger."

In "Falstaff" we hear the voice of Mozart. If Mozart had lived in the latter part of this century he might have written this noble work. In "Falstaff" Verdi has, as in "Otello," declined to use any of the Neapolitan paraphernalia. There is not a single number that approaches the old aria form except two small lyrics in the last scene. There are quartets, but they are in disguise. They are dialogues for four persons, written with profound musical learning, and with the unaffected freedom of the most playful fancy. But the great bulk of the dialogue is in the true Verdian arioso style, that glowing recitation which is the chief means of expression in this master's last works. There are no Wagnerian leading motives in the orchestration, but the orchestra independently accompanies and explicates the drama in a series of picturesque phrases whose beauties and significance will not be exhausted in many hearings. But what will most delight and amaze every hearer of this music is its youthful vigor. It is as fresh and spontaneous as the work of a young man in the blush of his first love, yet it is full of the wisdom and experience of him who is the epitome of more than half a century of Italian opera. It bustles, it glows, it inspires, yet it never transcends the modesty of art. Rich, complex, brilliant, and eloquent as the orchestration is, it never strains for effects and it is never blatant. Subtle, varied, polished as the recitation is,

ITALIAN OPERA TO VERDI 287

it has not a measure that cannot be sung, and neither the voice of the singer nor the ear of the hearer is ever outraged. In short, "Falstaff" is the work of a man whose genius is inexhaustible, whose natural fire burned in his eightieth year with all the glow of that dawn when "Ernani" was the morning star.

The latest development of Italian opera is the short work as seen in the "Cavalleria Rusticana" and "Pagliacci,—" probably a passing fashion. It shows no evidences of permanency, for its composers have produced no new style. They have employed the whole material of Verdi's later operas, and the only new feature is the condensation, which does not always give good musical results, because the emotions shift too constantly to permit a complete and influential musical embodiment of any one state. These young composers have tried to advance beyond Verdi in complexity of rhythm and boldness of modulation. Some of their modulations are made obviously for the sake of oddity. The *aria da capo* has disappeared entirely from the modern Italian opera. But the greatest achievement of the latest writers, chiefly Verdi, is the development, to what seems to be the highest possible point, of the beautiful arioso style of Italy, — the style which combines most of the power of German declamation with all the elegance and singable quality of the Neapolitan manner.

Arrigo Boito, born at Padua, Feb. 24, 1842, and still living, produced one remarkable opera, " Mefistofele," first performed on March 5, 1868, at La Scala Theatre, Milan. The work, in its original form, was so subtle, so philosophical, so undramatic, so thoroughly in sympathy with the spirit of Goethe's " Faust," and withal such a radical departure from everything recognized as opera by the Italians, that it caused the most heated controversy. In 1875 a revised version, that now known to the public, was put forward, and this has pleased the majority of opera-goers. The work is episodic and disjointed, but its characterization is most graphic, and the dramatic force of some of its scenes, notably that in the prison, is enormous. " Mefistofele " shares with " Aïda " the honor of having restored dramatic truth to the Italian lyric stage, but it lacks the skill in theatrical construction shown in Verdi's work. Boito has contented himself in later years with writing Verdi's libretti, but Verdi himself is authority for the statement that Boito has written an opera called " Nerone," which is a masterpiece.

ITALIAN OPERA TO VERDI 289

The opera music of the Italian school, in its entirety, is marked by greater floridity than that of other schools. The superficial, sensuous charms of the human voice have always appealed powerfully to the Italian race, and its composers have catered to this taste. An honorable ambition for a fame wider than the limits of their own country has led Italian composers to select from other schools their most immediately popular elements. The present Italian opera is eclectic. Its excellence lies largely in the fact that it does not run to extremes in any direction.

Chapter XXI

Beginnings of French Opera

Beaujoyeux and his " Ballet Comique de la Royne "— Production of Cambert's " Pomone " and founding of the Grand Opera — Advent of Lulli — His acquisition of the opera patent — Character and influence of his operas — Rameau and his improvements on Lulli's style.

THE history of French opera begins with the performance of a curious little pastoral in which the germs of some parts of the lyric drama may be found. The age of the work leads French writers to claim precedence over Italy in the invention of opera, but such claims are easily overthrown by the accumulation of evidence that the advent of Peri's " Daphne " was the result of a systematic series of experiments looking toward the revival of the Greek drama. In 1577 an Italian violinist named Baltazarini was imported from Piedmont into France by Marshal de Brissac. Catherine de Médicis made him her intendant of music and *valet de chambre* to the king. He changed his name to Balthasar de Beaujoyeux, and is so known in musical history, which, however, is generally silent about him. He introduced the Italian ballet to Paris, and also produced the first pastoral opera there. This pastoral is entitled "Circe," but is better known as the " Ballet Comique de la Royne." It was produced as the festival play for the marriage of the Duke de Joyeuse and Mlle. de Vaudemont. It is purely pastoral in character and has little or nothing of the true dramatic character of opera, though it has some of the operatic forms. There are choruses in four parts, dances, and accompanied solos. The last are written in a slow and melodious form of recitative, which is pleasing, but not especially expressive. Doubtless Beaujoyeux, who left Italy about the time when the experiments in monodic writing were beginning, must have known something of the nature of the movement. This he communicated to Beaulieu and Salmon, who wrote most, if not all, of the music of the ballet which he arranged.

These French ballets, of which "Circe" was apparently the first performed at court, owe probably quite as much of their origin to the old pastoral plays of the country as

292 HOW MUSIC DEVELOPED

they do to the Italian monody. As far back as the thirteenth century the troubadours had constructed little pastorals, with solo vocal music, and at least one of these, Adam de la Halle's " Gieus de Robin et de Marion," contained well-formed songs. These little works, performed in Picardy and Provence, declined with the troubadours, but some record of them may have helped the court composers of the latter end of the 16th century in the formation of their recitative. The French ballet differed from the earliest Italian opera in that most of its music was designed as an accompaniment to action, largely pantomimic and wholly terpsichorean in its nature. The solo parts were short and built on lines wholly dissociated from those of the Florentine recitative.

FROM THE " BALLET COMIQUE DE LA ROYNE,"
BY BEAUJOYEUX.

BEGINNINGS OF FRENCH OPERA

It was not until Italian opera made its way into France that a genuine French opera was developed. The first attempt was made by Rinuccini, who took " Eurydice " to Paris in 1600. Its total failure to touch the popular taste is an excellent demonstration of the difference between it and the musical shows to which the French were accustomed; and during the entire reign of Louis XIII. (1610–1643) the ballet remained the favorite

BEGINNINGS OF FRENCH OPERA 295

form in France. An attempt was made in the minority of Louis XIV. by Cardinal Mazarin to revive the Italian opera, but again it did not meet with favor. The earliest attempt at a genuine opera in French, so far as is known, was "Akebar, Roi de Mogol," by the Abbé Mailly, produced in 1646.

Pierre Perrin, a French poet (1616–1676) was a conspicuous figure in the establishment of opera in France. He was a sort of major domo in the employ of Gaston, Duke of Orléans, and his post enabled him to make the acquaintance of some powerful personages. Of these the Cardinal Mazarin took a liking to him and became his patron. He also met the composer Robert Cambert (1628–1677), who, after hearing a performance of "Eurydice," acceded to Perrin's proposition to set to music his "Pastorale," described as the "première comedie Française en musique." This was performed at Issy in 1659, and afterward at Vincennes before the king. It was successful and led to the production by the two men of "Ariane," "Adonis," and other works. On Nov. 10, 1668, Perrin obtained from Louis XIV. a patent for the performance of opera, and founded the Académie de Musique, now known to all the world as the Paris Grand Opéra. Perrin and Cambert carried on this enterprise for thirty-two years. Their principal work was "Pomone," produced on March 19, 1671. The success of this embryonic opera was something remarkable. It ran eight months and paid to the poet alone 30,000 francs. The score of " Pomone," as well as that of the " Ballet Comique de la Royne " and other early French works, is published by Theodore Michaelis, in a collection of the "Chefs-d'œuvre de l'opéra Français," with piano arrangement and an historical introduction by J. B. Wekerlin. The following example of Cambert's recitative, leading to a duet, is taken from this score: —

BEGINNINGS OF FRENCH OPERA

FAUNE.

C'est bien à toi, dieu mi-sé-ra-ble, De pré-tendre à tes maux quel-que sou-la-ge-ment!

LE DIEU DES JARDINS.

C'est bien à toi, monstre effroy-a-ble, De-se-vir un ob-

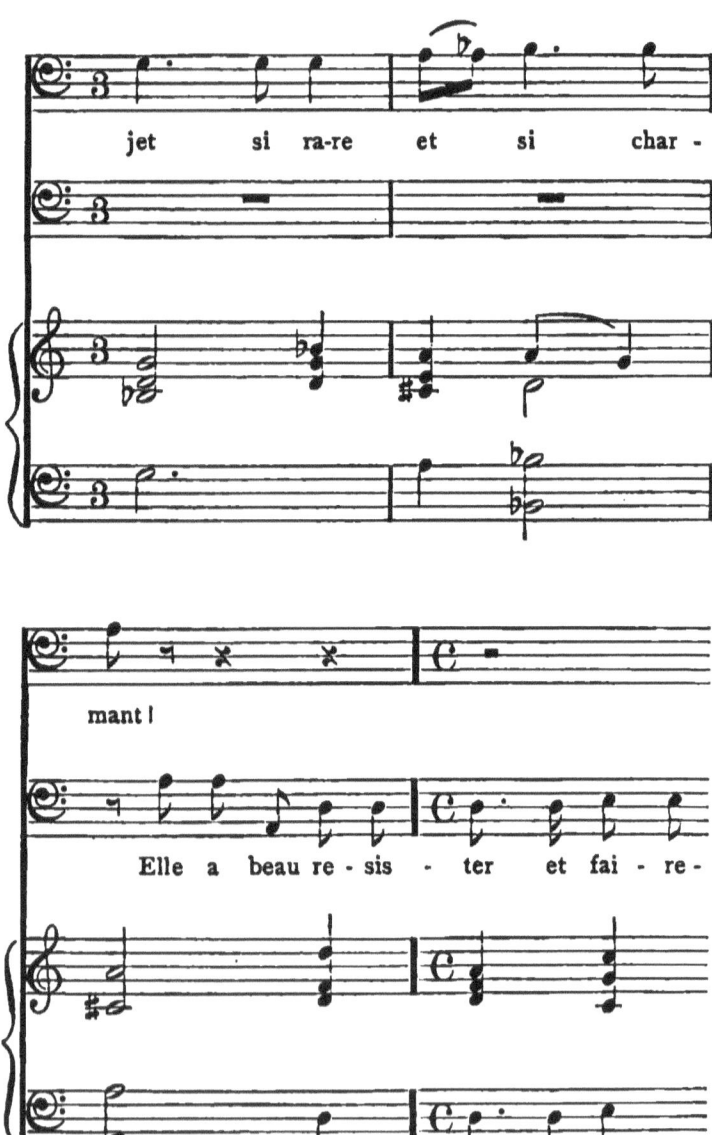

BEGINNINGS OF FRENCH OPERA

It is not difficult to see that this recitative shows an advance in flexibility and directness over that of Beaujoyeux. Undoubtedly Cambert had profited by his study of the Italian works produced under the auspices of the Cardinal Mazarin, but he did not penetrate the secret of the Italian method. The influence of the ballet style is discernible throughout the work. Probably Cambert would have hesitated at a complete adoption of the Italian method, even if he had been capable of it, for it would hardly have been approved by the public taste of France at that time.

Perrin and Cambert had associated with themselves in the Académie the Marquis de Sourdeac, with whom Perrin, for some reason not on record, had a quarrel in the course of the run of " Pomone." Perrin resigned from the partnership, which continued without him. But he was not content to be idle, and in company with Henri Sinchard, a poet, and the Sieur de Sablières, a musician, started a rival enterprise.

It was at this point that the famous composer, Giovanni Battista Lulli, usually known by his French name, Jean Baptiste Lully, entered upon the scene and became the virtual founder of French opera in the grand style. Lulli was born in 1633 near Florence, and as a boy received some musical instruction. He was taken to Paris by the Chevalier de Guise and placed in the service of Mlle. de Montpensier. He became a fine violinist and was made a member of her band. But he was stupid enough to write an indecent poem referring to his mistress, and she dismissed him. In spite of this temporary downfall he succeeded in working his way into the orchestra of Louis XIV., known as " Les Violons du Roi," and in 1652 became its director. He appears to have been an expert courtier, for he won the favor of the king and set to music some ballet-comedies by Molière.

When Perrin parted company with Cambert and Sourdeac, the opera suffered from his rivalry. Lulli, who had now acquired great influence with the king, saw in the battle of the two houses his opportunity. He proposed to purchase the interest of Sourdeac and Cambert in the opera patent and they accepted his terms. He then induced the king to remodel the patent so as to make its provisions exclusive. The new patent conferred upon Lulli the sole right to the performance of opera. It prohibited the managers of other theatres from employing more than two singers or six players of stringed instruments. This, of course, made grand operas out of the question for Lulli's rivals, and he set about producing such large works as he alone could present.

Discreditable as Lulli's conduct was in this whole matter, it must be admitted that he did all that he could for the elevation of French operatic art. In this direction he had a powerful ambition, and although it was selfish it was not altogether narrow. His most important operas were : " Alceste " (1674), " Thesée " (1675), " Persée " (1682), " Roland " (1685), " Armide " (1686), and — his last — " Acis et Galathée " (1686). The influence of his operas may be judged from the fact that they held the stage till 1774. Lulli's works were inferior to those of his Italian contemporaries in purely musical beauty. The aria as written by Lulli possesses far less distinctness and symmetry of form, and he showed no such ability as the Neapolitans did in dealing with voices in mass. Neither in duets nor in ensembles was he especially happy. His choral writing is generally thin and poorly developed, and his duets are rather dialogues. But on the other hand Lulli far excelled the contemporary Neapolitan composers in sincerity of purpose and in the dramatic fidelity of his method.

BEGINNINGS OF FRENCH OPERA 303

He endeavored to the limit of his ability to fit the music to the text. In this he followed the fundamental principles of Peri, and established that tradition of dramatic sincerity which has never left the French school of opera. He increased the value of the chorus by making it an integral part of the drama. The Neapolitans used the chorus merely for musical effect. Lulli gave it a dramatic reason for existence. Its music is always appropriate to the situation and fits well into the general tone-picture. His recitative is built largely after the Italian model of his time, and it is a vast advance over that of Beaujoyeux and Cambert. Here is an example from " Armide " : —

BEGINNINGS OF FRENCH OPERA

It must be understood that Lulli's recitative was not always dramatically correct. Sometimes it is merely grandiose in style, but it is much more animated, flexible, and capable of expression than that of his predecessors. Lulli was undoubtedly influenced in his solo writing by the works of Monteverde, which were performed in Paris under the direction of Cavalli. Lulli is said to have written some of the ballet music which had to be inserted in these works to please the Parisians. The love of ballet has never died out in France. It was a fight over it which killed Wagner's "Tannhäuser" in Paris in 1861. Lulli's early training naturally made him an eclectic, and when he set

BEGINNINGS OF FRENCH OPERA 307

out to provide the Parisian public with grand operas to its taste, he chose from French ballet and Italian opera such features as he believed would be popular, and upon these as a foundation reared a new version of the Greek drama, thoroughly Gallic in its conception.

Courtier, man of the world, and selfseeker, Lulli knew how to plan an opera, with such musical materials as there were in his day, so that it should present some effect of contrast and shape. For one thing, he fairly rid himself of everything pertaining to the ecclesiastical style of composition. As I have said, he wrote arias, but their indistinctness is owing largely to the fact that the conventional form had not yet become fully established. It is, perhaps, in the general plan of his operas that Lulli shows the most important advance over his predecessors. He was certainly far ahead of Peri, Monteverde, Cavalli, Beaujoyeux, and Cambert in the manner in which he distributed his scenes so as to give variety of emotion, and in the effective way in which he arranged the succession of recitatives, arias, choruses, and ballets. The plan was, indeed, designed wholly with a view to stage effectiveness, and thereby led away from the dramatic directness of Peri; but on the other hand Lulli's music followed the development of his story with much sincerity. The breadth and force of the recitative in many places suggest that the public taste to which he catered was by no means to be despised.

Lulli was the founder of a school, but among his followers there was no man of genius, and only one of noticeable talent. This was Marin Marais (1656–1728), who showed a broader style than Lulli in arias, and who made some attempts at instrumental description in his accompaniments. But the other members of the school were mere imitators, and French opera became little more than an adherence to the traditions and conventions of Lulli. Its vitality seemed in a fair way to desert it completely, when a new master arose and put fresh life into it. This master was Jean Philippe Rameau, born at Dijon, Sept. 25, 1683, died at Paris, Sept. 12, 1764. He showed musical gifts when a child, and his parents gave him a musical education. He went to Milan in 1701 to study, but was dissatisfied with Italian music. After considerable travel he arrived in Paris in 1717, whence he was driven away by the rivalry of the organist, Marchand. He went into retirement in the provinces, and wrote his "Traité de l'Harmonie." His theoretical works gave him

BEGINNINGS OF FRENCH OPERA 309

reputation, and at the age of fifty he succeeded in having his "Hippolyte et Aricie" produced. The conservative followers of Lulli and the new admirers of Rameau now entered into a controversy which lasted till the success of an Italian opera buffa company in 1752 united the forces, under the title of Anti-buffonists, in defence of French opera. Rameau's principal works were: "Castor et Pollux" (1737), "Zoroastre" (1749), and "Les Surprises d'Amour" (1759).

Rameau's operas show certain decided improvements upon those of Lulli. He was a more sincere artist, with a self-sacrificing devotion to high ideals of which Lulli was quite incapable. The story of Rameau's early struggles and of his late recognition by force of sheer merit is far different from that of Lulli's courtier-like machinations. But Rameau recognized the value of Lulli's art-forms and did not set out to overthrow them. He took them up and improved upon them by reason of his strong grasp of dramatic truth and his larger conception of musical organism. To put the matter in the plainest possible terms, Rameau was a much more truthfully dramatic composer than Lulli, and at the same time he was a better musician. His mastery of the science of harmony enabled him to build an instrumental background for his vocal parts far richer and more expressive than anything within the reach of Lulli. His instrumentation was much broader and more highly colored than his predecessor's, and his declamation is more musical, and hence more fruitful in melodic beauty. Rameau's works are full of evidence that he sought earnestly after dramatic expression in the grand style; and that he was not wholly able to escape affectation is due largely to the taste of the period in which he lived, — the period of Racine, Voltaire, and Rousseau.

His music, however, abounds in strong and varied rhythms and in a generally richer style. Previous to his time, for instance, the French composers accompanied the voices with strings in five parts, and flutes and oboes in two parts. Rameau insisted upon giving each instrument a special part, and he introduced the now familiar custom of writing solo passages for the different wood wind instruments. He also greatly improved the character of the choral writing in French opera. But Rameau was not highly skilled in writing for the voice. He recognized that fact himself when it was too late for him to remodel his style. And he had a foolish idea that a good composer

BEGINNINGS OF FRENCH OPERA 311

could set any kind of a libretto to music. Many of his works failed to please the Parisians simply because their books were so weak. But on the whole, Rameau left his mark on the French opera. There can be no doubt that so great a composer as Gluck learned much from him, and he must at any rate be credited with a faithful preservation of those principles of the real grand-opera style which entered the French school at its inception and which have never wholly departed from it. It was the influence of such works as his that prepared Paris to receive the sincere dramatic operas of Gluck, the next composer of importance in the line of development of French opera.

Chapter XXII

The Reforms of Gluck

His early Italian operas — His conversion and the cold reception of his new ideas in Vienna — Recognized in Paris as Rameau's successor — The conquest of Piccini. — Gluck's theory of the lyric drama — How he developed it in practice — His immediate successors and imitators.

IN spite of the labors of Rameau the prevailing style of Italian opera gained a footing in Paris, where its cheap melody and direct appeal to the unthinking gave it a dangerous popularity. Its unreality, its dramatic infidelity, and above all its exaltation of the singer above the composer, went far toward leading the Parisians astray from the true opera given them by Lulli and Rameau. It required the work of a man of true genius, guided by the sincere dramatic purposes of the earlier composers, to restore opera in France to its position of artistic nobility and to fix it there. The man who achieved this was Christopher Willibald

THE REFORMS OF GLUCK 313

Gluck, who turned to Paris only when he found that his work failed of appreciation elsewhere.

Gluck was born July 2, 1714, at Weidenwang, near the frontier of Bavaria and Bohemia. He received his early musical instruction in a Jesuit seminary. In 1737 or 1738 he went to Italy in the service of Prince Melzi. In Italy he wrote and produced, in 1741, his first opera, " Artaserse." In five years he wrote eight operas, all of which are utterly forgotten. They were built on the conventional plan of the Italian opera seria of the time. In 1745 Gluck went to England, where two important things occurred: he produced a wretched work called " Piramo e Tisbe," which failed; and he heard Handel's oratorios. His " Piramo e Tisbe " was a *pasticcio*, — an opera made up of tunes selected from his earlier works. Gluck's innate genius led him to perceive that the failure of the opera was due to its lack of dramatic sincerity, its complete want of organic unity. He began to understand that the opera must be a drama expressed in musical terms. He went to Paris, heard Rameau's operas, and learned something about French recitative.

But he was not yet ready to put his half-formed theories to the test. He wrote several operas in his early style, but at length he felt that he must break with the artificial conventions. Raniero di Calzabigi became his librettist, and the result of their joint labors was "Orfeo," produced at Vienna, Oct. 5, 1762. He followed this with several minor works in his old style, but on Dec. 16, 1767, produced "Alceste," a complete and unyielding embodiment of his reformatory theories. In 1769 he produced "Paris and Helen." After this he decided that his operatic purposes would be better understood in Paris than in Germany, and he set out for the French capital. There he made an operatic version of Racine's "Iphigénie en Aulide," which was produced April 19, 1774. The work aroused the greatest enthusiasm among those who had been lamenting the decline of French opera since Rameau. "Orfeo" and "Alceste" were produced, and Gluck became the favorite of the nobility and the artistic circle.

The admirers of Italian opera were aroused by the success of Gluck, and selected as the champion who should overthrow him the gifted Italian composer Piccini. The musical warfare was quite as warm as the subsequent Wagner and anti-Wagnerite controversy. Men of letters bombarded each other with impolite phrases in the public prints, and ladies

THE REFORMS OF GLUCK 315

of fashion pelted each other with expressions unfit for publication at private dinners. The supporters of Gluck awaited eagerly a new work. On Sept. 23, 1777, he produced "Armide." It was only a success of esteem. On May 18, 1779, he brought out "Iphigénie en Aulide," and all Paris bowed its head before him. Even Piccini acknowledged his superiority. Gluck's last work was "Echo et Narcisse," Sept. 21, 1779. He became ill, and, after suffering for several years, died Nov. 15, 1787.

The simple fact that Gluck in beginning his labor of reform in opera selected for the subject of his libretto the story used by Rinuccini and Peri in "Euridice" shows that he embarked upon his undertaking with a sincere desire to get at the fundamental principles of the true *drama per musica*. From the miserable incongruity of his own "Piramo e Tisbe" he proceeded to the conviction that the ultimate purpose of opera music must be a correct and moving embodiment of the emotions expressed by the text. The methods which he regarded as efficient are best enumerated by himself in the preface to his "Alceste." He says:—

"I endeavored to reduce music to its proper function, that of seconding poetry by enforcing the expression of the sentiment and the interest of the situations without interrupting the action, or weakening it by superfluous ornament. My idea was that the relation of music to poetry was much the same as that of harmonious coloring and well disposed light and shade to an accurate drawing, which animates the figures without altering the outlines. I have therefore been very careful never to interrupt a singer in the heat of a dialogue in order to introduce a tedious ritornelle, nor to stop him in the middle of a piece either for the purpose of displaying the flexibility of his voice on some favorable vowel, or that the orchestra might give him time to take breath before a long-sustained note.

" Furthermore I have not thought it right to hurry through the second part of a song, if the words happened to be the most important of the whole, in order to repeat the first part regularly four times over; or to finish the air where the sense does not end in order to allow the singer to exhibit his power of varying the passage at pleasure. In fact my object was to put an end to abuses against which good taste and good sense have long protested in vain.

" My idea was that the overture ought to indicate the subject and prepare the spectators for the character of the piece they are about to see; that the instruments ought to be introduced in proportion to the degree of interest and passion in the words; and that it was necessary above all to avoid making too great a disparity between the recitative and the air of a dialogue, so as not to break the sense of a period or awkwardly interrupt the movement and animation of a scene. I also thought that my chief endeavor should be to attain a grand simplicity, and consequently I have avoided making a parade of difficulties at the cost of clearness. I have set no value on novelty as such, unless it was naturally suggested by the situation and suited to the expression. In short, there was no rule which I did not consider myself bound to sacrifice for the sake of effect."

Gluck, of course, meant for the sake of dramatic effect. His artistic creed, as set forth in this preface, is singularly clear and concentrated. Any one who examines a Gluck opera, or goes to hear his "Orfeo," which is still performed, in the expectation of finding a vast difference in the outward shape from that employed by the Italian opera composers of the time will be disappointed. The ground plan of opera had not been long enough before the world to satisfy serious thinkers that it might beneficially be subjected to a radical reform, a reform tending toward a restoration of the continued recitative of Peri. Opera had to pass through the middle stages of development, in which its forms were perfected and exhausted, before men could discover that as mere forms they were valueless for the purposes of dramatic expression, but that the materials out of which they were made could be utilized. This time has but recently arrived. Gluck was ahead of it. He was not prepared to discern the artificial restraints put upon free expression by the old formulas. And even if he had done so, he could not by any possibility have induced his public to follow him in an overthrow of all that they regarded as a necessary part of opera.

Gluck was compelled to use the aria form in his operas, because there was no other definite form in his day, and operatic art was not sufficiently comprehended by the public to admit of the introduction of a new form. The French ballet was a necessary part of his scheme. Even a century later the Parisians refused to accept opera without it. But Gluck restored to the aria its dramatic purpose. In his hands it was no longer a mere show piece for the singer, but a definite, carefully designed, and generally successful embodiment of an emotional state. The famous " Che faro senza Euridice" in his " Orfeo" is an admirable example of the Gluck aria at its best. To be sure, it sounds somewhat placid to us, accustomed as we are to the impassioned and highly colored musical diction of recent composers. But to the French of Gluck's day with their by no means incorrect conception of the purity and dignity of Greek art, which Gluck was trying to imitate, the "grand simplicity" of this style must have been highly influential. Indeed if there is one quality above all others in the music of Gluck's "Orfeo" which strikes the thoughtful listener of to-day, it is its classicism. It is a full and satisfying embodiment of what we believe to have been the Greek art spirit. One can think of Gluck's "Orfeo" as being performed in a Greek theatre of the age of Pericles, and the fancy does not shock the mind.

As in the case of the arias, so Gluck also endeavored to make his recitative purely expressive rather than merely conventional. In this his task was easier, because he was advancing along the path already trodden by Lulli and Rameau. He strove furthermore to make the ballet and the chorus integral parts of the action of the play. No finer example of this is to be found anywhere in his works than in the scene in Hades in "Orfeo." The dance of the demons, tentative in style as it seems to us to-day, is at least an honest attempt to give the dancing a pantomimic value, and the whole action of the chorus in this scene, with its expressive gestures and its vigorous shouts of "No" to the pleadings of Orpheus, is an example of dramatic organization of the highest kind. In this scene poetry, painting, music, and action are as firmly and indissolubly joined as they are in any scene in those dramas which a century later were called "the artwork of the future." Even the instrumentation is as carefully designed for dramatic purposes as that of Wagner. The differences are in the state of development of the art, not in design. In Gluck's day orchestral effects had not been developed as they are now, but I am quite prepared to adopt the words of Dr. Parry: "Mozart was the first to show real natural gift and genuine feeling for beautiful disposition of tone, but Gluck anticipated modern procedure in adapting his colors exactly to the mood of the situation. A good deal had been attempted already in a sort of half-hearted and formal manner, but he was the first to seize firmly on the right principles and to carry out his objects with any mastery of resources."

Gluck's immediate influence was confined to French opera, and it is because of this

THE REFORMS OF GLUCK 321

that I have placed him in the history of opera in France. He seems to have had absolutely no effect on Italian opera. Less than thirty years after his death all Europe was whistling or strumming " Di tanti palpiti." On French opera, however, the influence of Gluck was permanent. He fastened upon it the sound traditions of Rameau, and he pointed out the true path of progress. That his immediate successors so frequently mistook the means for the end, and became merely prosy and prolix where he was simple and chaste, or in their endeavors to avoid this fate fell into pretentious bombast, was due to the fact that Gluck was unquestionably ahead of his time. In his attempts to put his theories into practice he himself was hampered by the incomplete development of musical material in his day. We find him constantly struggling for full dramatic expression and missing it because he had not the later composer's palette of color at his command. His imitators, less gifted than he and moved less by unyielding artistic convictions than by the desire to gain general approval, could hardly be expected to equal him. It was not till French opera had reached the period in which its composers by the study of the works of German and Italian masters had formulated an eclectic system of expression that it was able to take its place in the high seat of dramatic art. Yet one seeks in vain through the contents of French musical drama for any works which are so pure in their attempt at dramatic sincerity as those of Gluck.

His immediate successor, and the one who best succeeded in maintaining his traditions, was Étienne Henri Méhul (1763–1817). His principal works were : " Stratonice " (1792), " Ariodant " (1799), and " Joseph " (1807). His music is simple and dignified in style and full of expressive force. But his operas had to give way to the more easily popular Italian works in all countries outside of France. Luigi Cherubini (1760–1842) was an Italian, but passed most of his life in Paris when he was director of the Conservatory of Music. His principal operas were: " Les deux Journées " (1800) and " Faniska " (1806). Cherubini began his career by writing old-fashioned Italian opera, but became a convert to the theories of Gluck. He was a writer of no small force and originality. Beethoven was his enthusiastic admirer, and it is certain that, although the antiquated style of his recitative and arioso makes his music unpalatable now, he was sincere in his attempt at dramatic fidelity. Another Italian who wrote for the French stage and tried to imitate the French manner was Gasparo Spontini (1774–1851). His principal operas were: "La Vestale" (1807), "Ferdinand Cortez" (1809), "Olympie" (1819), and "Agnes von Hohenstaufen" (1829). The last-named opera was written for Berlin. Spontini's style seems very dry and stilted to us now, and it is quite certain that he had neither the melodic gift of Méhul nor the dramatic inspiration of Cherubini. In his attempts at scenic display, glittering stage pictures, and the employment of imposing effects, he foreshadowed Meyerbeer. Daniel François Auber (1784–1871) wrote "La Muette de Portici," generally known by its Italian title "Massaniello," and "Fra Diavolo" (1830). The former work is directly in the line of transition from Spontini to Meyerbeer. The latter belongs rather to the school of opéra comique. Jacques François Halévy (1799–1862) wrote several operas, of which only "La Juive" (1835) holds the stage. The works of Auber and Halévy show a decided tendency away from the simple directness of the earlier French composers towards a cheap and easy theatrical effectiveness. "La Juive," however, contains some passages of singular beauty and genuine power.

Chapter XXIII

Meyerbeer and his Influence

The grandiose style and its ground plan — External display and internal emptiness — Gounod and his dramatic power — Bizet and "Carmen" — Works and tendency of living writers of French opera.

THE gradual drift of French opera away from the pure style of Gluck led to the success of one of the most remarkable figures in the history of music, a composer whose works persist in pleasing the public, while they enrage both critics and musicians. This composer was Jacob Meyerbeer, born of wealthy Jewish parents at Berlin, Sept. 5, 1791. He studied music under Lauska, Clementi, and Vogler, and began his public career as a juvenile pianist. His first opera was "Jephthah's Vow,"— a failure, as were several other early works. His successful operas were: "Robert le Diable" (Paris, 1831), "Les Huguenots" (Paris, 1835), "The Camp in Silesia"

(Vienna, 1843, and afterwards remodelled as " L'Étoile du Nord," Paris, 1854), "Le Prophète" (1849), "Le Pardon de Ploermel, generally called "Dinorah" (Paris, 1859), and "L'Africaine" (Paris, 1865). He did not live to see the production of the last work, but died May 2, 1864. Of these works "Robert" is now performed infrequently, and "Dinorah" only to please some light, colorature soprano. "L'Étoile du Nord" is practically dead. "Les Huguenots," "Le Prophète," and "L'Africaine" are still popular. The most consistent and sustained of these three is "L'Africaine," though the greatest heights to which Meyerbeer ever ascended are to be found in "Les Huguenots." It is generally conceded that the duet between Valentine and Raoul in the fourth act is a genuinely great piece of dramatic writing. Even Schumann and Wagner, the severest critics of Meyerbeer, admitted that.

The operas of Meyerbeer are remarkable examples of a skill entirely devoted to the production of *ad captandum* effects. Everything imposing, grandiose, delusive in splendor, or dazzling in cheap finery is to be found in these works, which are arranged on a grand plan. Meyerbeer's distribution of arias, duets, ensembles, and finales is the result of a deliberate eclecticism. He took for his purpose all that seemed most effective in the Italian and French schools. His finales, for instance, are often ridiculously weak in melodic ideas, as in that of the second act of " Les Huguenots," but they are always worked up with a clever combination of action, stage pictures, and pretentious orchestration. His arias are deliberately designed to catch the applause of an audience. He uses ballets, processions, pageants, and glittering masses of people on the stage to hide his poverty of ideas, and, as Dr. Parry well notes, when he has absolutely no idea at all, he distracts your attention from that fact by a cadenza for the clarinet. His most successful combination of music and pageantry is in the return of Selika to her kingdom in "L'Africaine." His poorest is the wedding festivities of Valentine in " Les Huguenots." There is no heart in Meyerbeer's works. He was capable of taking infinite pains, but all for the sake of instantaneous effect. To quote Dr. Parry again: "The scenes are collections of the most elaborate artifices, carefully contrived and eminently effective from the baldest theatrical point of view. But for continuity, development, real feeling, nobility of expression, greatness of thought, anything that may be truly honored in the observance, there is but the rarest trace."

A good deal has been said about Meyerbeer's powers of characterization, and his works have been compared to historical novels. But a very little analysis will show that the characterization in " Les Huguenots," for instance, is almost purely pictorial. What impression would be left of St. Bris without his black velvet clothes and courtly bearing? And how prominent would Marcel be without his costume, and his war cry " Ein feste Burg"? Marguerite de Valois is characterized by white satin, diamonds, and *arias di bravura*. The truth is that Meyerbeer's characterization is altogether superficial. The best that can be said of Meyerbeer is that he was amazingly clever, and that in a few places in his works, finding theatrical effectiveness and dramatic sincerity not incapable of achieving in combination his desired result, he wrote like a master.

The most recent French composers have shown a tendency to utilize the general plan of the Meyerbeer opera, but to try to infuse into it a genuine dramatic sincerity. They have written fewer cadenzas and more sincerely expressive melody. They have in general adhered to the traditions which have belonged to French opera from its earliest days, the traditions of Lulli, Rameau, and Gluck, but they have superimposed upon the classic outlines of the works of those masters a more attractive sensuous beauty. They have made concessions to the demands of a not profound public, yet they have persistently declined to do everything for mere empty effect, as Meyerbeer did. They have striven to give adequate expression to the dramatic ideas of their librettos, and they have aimed at organic unity in their music; but they have demonstrated their belief that they would achieve their purpose with music of the kind loved by the mass of opera-goers. In this line of practice the most successful of all the French masters was Charles François Gounod, born in Paris, June 17, 1818, and died in the same city, Oct. 18, 1893.

He was a student at the conservatoire, where he won the second "prix de Rome" in 1837 and the "grand prix" in 1839. He studied theology for two years, and the effect of his religious pursuits, and his study of the works of Palestrina during a stay of several years in Rome is manifested in some of his compositions. He himself declared that the most powerful musical influence of his career was his first hearing of Mozart's "Don Giovanni." His first opera, "Sapho" was produced April 16, 1851. It had no lasting success. "La Nonne Sanglante" (Oct. 18, 1854) had eleven performances only. These works were produced at the Grand Opéra, but Gounod was now obliged to try his fortunes at the Théâtre Lyrique with "Le medécin malgré lui" (Jan. 15, 1858). Meanwhile he had begun in 1855 the work which was to make his fame. "Faust" was completed in 1857, and produced at the Théâtre Lyrique on March 19, 1859. The work was not remarkably successful at first, but it grew in public favor, till to-day its only rival on the operatic stage is Wagner's "Lohengrin." On Feb. 18, 1860, Gounod produced "Philémon et Baucis," a delicate little opéra comique. This was followed by "La Columbe," comic opera, (Baden, 1860), "La Reine de Saba," grand opera (Paris, Feb. 28, 1862), and "Mireille," grand opera (1864). None of these had any large measure of success. "Romeo et Juliette" (April 27, 1867) has held the stage, largely because of M. Jean de Reszke's popularity as Romeo. "Polyeucte" (Oct. 7, 1878), "Cinq-Mars" (April 5, 1877), and "Le Tribut de Zamora" (1881) are all dead and buried.

Gounod's fame and his influence as a composer of opera will rest on "Faust" and "Romeo et Juliette." The ground plan of both these operas is distinctly Meyerbeerian. The differentiating factor is Gounod's dramatic sincerity. In every scene of "Faust" one finds evidence of the composer's earnest search after the correct and convincing musical embodiment of the emotions of his personages. There is no attempt at establishing musical connecting-links between the different scenes, except in the simple expedient of causing Marguerite, in her insanity in the last act, to recall the music of her early acquaintance with Faust. For the rest, Gounod has treated each scene as a separate entity and has aimed at giving it an adequate and finished musical setting. His forms are very free, and the recitative is almost wholly in the arioso style with full orchestral accompaniment. There is some successful characterization in "Faust." The music of Mefistofeles is thoroughly suitable to the personage as set forth by the librettists. The influence of Rameau and Gluck may be found in this work, in its definite and consistent attempt at dramatic fidelity. That of Meyerbeer may be seen in the distribution of the vocal numbers and the stage pictures, such as the

Kermess scene and the return of the troops. Compare the sextet of men in "Les Huguenots" with the trio of men in the duel scene of "Faust," if you desire to hear the very echo of Meyerbeer's song. But Gounod's honesty forbade him to write claptrap, and he does not make many concessions to the singers. The artistic value of "Faust" is very high. It is one of the purest and most beautiful lyric dramas now on the stage. The scene in the cathedral and the death of Valentine are not equalled in beauty and dramatic truth by anything in the works of any other French composer, and have been excelled perhaps only by Mozart, Wagner, and Verdi. "Romeo et Juliette" shows less originality and inspiration than "Faust," but contains scenes of genuine beauty and dramatic power. The evidences of Meyerbeer's influence are quite as notable as they are in the earlier work, but in general Gounod's style of music prevents him from falling into mere empty display.

Georges Bizet, born at Paris Oct. 25, 1838, and died in the same city, June 3, 1875, wrote several operas, of which "Carmen," produced March 3, 1875, remains one of the most popular works of the time. The ground plan of this drama is formed on essentially French lines, and in the dramatic fidelity of its music and its general freedom from meretricious display it stands directly in the line of the development of the lyric drama in France. There is some employment of leading motives in the Wagnerian style, but it is discreet and moderate. The work displays great originality in its use of Spanish rhythms and in its scheme of harmonic color. It is a noble work, a true music drama, and its fame is well deserved.

Other French composers are still living, and their works have not yet had that test of time which is necessary to a correct estimate of their value. France has no one great representative master like Verdi whose works epitomize the tendencies of the time. Her living composers show in their operas the results of various influences acting upon the fundamental principles of Lulli and Rameau, and for that reason a brief mention may be accorded to the leading writers. Camille Saint-Säens, born Oct. 9, 1835, is perhaps the most gifted of living French composers, but he has not earned his highest distinction as a writer of opera. His dramatic works are : "Le Timbre d'Argent" (1877), "Samson et Dalila" (1877), "Étienne Marcel" (1877), " Henri VIII." (1883), " Proserpine " (1887), " Ascanio " (1890), and "Phryne" (1893). None of these works has made a serious impression except "Samson et Dalila," which is more effective as an oratorio than as an opera, owing to its lack of action. Saint-Säens's opera music is always scholarly, dignified, and pure in style. It belongs strictly to the French school. His more spectacular works, such as "Henri VIII.," show the influence of Meyerbeer in their plan, but they make a more earnest attempt at dramatic truth.

Jules Émile Frédéric Massenet, born at Montaud, near St. Étienne, May 12, 1842, has written several operas, of which the principal are: "Don Cæsar de Bazan" (1872), "Le Roi de Lahore" (1877), "Herodiade" (1881), "Manon" (1884), "Le Cid" (1885), "Esclarmonde" (1889), "Le Mage" (1891), and "Werther" (1892). In his more idyllic works, such as "Werther" and "Manon," he follows the lead of Gounod, while his more pretentious operas, such as "Le Roi de Lahore," "Esclarmonde," and "Le Cid," are decidedly Meyerbeerian in general plan, though usually more refined than those of Meyerbeer in general treatment. At the same time, in "Esclarmonde" at least, Massenet has sought to follow Wagner in the use of leading motives and in the gorgeous coloring of his orchestration. His best works, however, are genuine lyric dramas, distinctly French in plan and style.

The French composer who has tried most earnestly to select the best features of Gounod, Meyerbeer, and Wagner, and weld them into a genuinely French opera, is Ernest Reyer, born at Marseilles, Dec. 1, 1823. His principal works are: "Sigurd" (1884) and "Salammbô" (1890). Neither has attained wide success, but they deserve mention here as illustrating the devotion of the present French composers to the high dramatic traditions of their nation. Alfred Bruneau, born March 1, 1857, in his "Le Rêve" (1891) and "L'Attaque du Moulin" (1893), has shown himself to be greatly influenced by the works of Richard Wagner. Indeed, the spirit of Wagner broods over much of recent French dramatic music. It will readily be understood that it is easier for Frenchmen to follow Wagner than it is for composers of almost any other nation, because Wagner's dramatic theories are not different in their fundamental principles from those of Lulli, Rameau, and Gluck. The chief difficulty encountered by the modern French writers is the survival of a public fondness for the popular features of the Meyerbeer opera, and the composers in taking account of this fondness have preserved much of a ground plan which cannot be wholly reconciled with the Wagner theories. But the French writers deserve respect for their sincerity and for the infrequency with which they compose mere show pieces for singers. They write very favorably for the voice, but they try to make beautiful arias with real expressive power.

Chapter XXIV

German Opera to Mozart

Schütz and his version of "Dafne" — Hamburg and its opera — Works of Reinhard Keiser — The "Singspiel" — Mozart and his dramatic works — "Don Giovanni," Italian in form and German in tendency.

THE story of the introduction of opera into German is sufficiently amusing to form part of an operetta plot. There was no opera of native origin, but the fame of the Italian product having reached the ears of the Elector John George I., of Saxony, he determined to have one of these new lyric dramas performed as the festival play at the marriage of his daughter. Heinrich Schütz, whom we have already met as the composer of the "Seven Last Words of Christ," was the elector's court-director of music, and he was accordingly commissioned to procure from Florence a copy of "Daphne," the pastoral of Peri and Rinuccini. The copy having been obtained, Martin Opitz, a poet,

GERMAN OPERA TO MOZART

was ordered to translate it into German. He did his work with poetic feeling, but without musical knowledge, and when his text was completed it could not be sung to the music of Peri. Consequently Schütz was directed to write new music, and thus the first German opera came into existence. It was performed on April 13, 1627. The work has been lost and there is no account of its reception. It is quite probable that its music imitated the Italian monodic style, with which Schütz had previously become acquainted while visiting Italy. After his second journey to Italy Schütz wrote an opera called "Orpheus," which was produced in Dresden, Nov. 20, 1638. This work is also lost, but it was probably an imitation of Monteverde's "Orfeo."

Meanwhile all attempts at establishing a national German opera were overthrown by the outbreak of the Thirty Years' War. When that had ended, Schütz, who had seemed likely to do something for the lyric drama in his country, devoted himself, except in the case of the work already mentioned, to sacred composition. Italian opera had made its way into Germany, where it became the fashionable amusement of the aristocracy of Berlin, Vienna, Dresden, and Munich. It had no connection with the art life of the

German people, but maintained its purely exotic condition. Only in Hamburg was there anything that seemed to proceed from native impulse. It was a free city; it had grown enormously wealthy by its commerce; and it was far away from the centre of activity in the war.

Hamburg was a musical centre, and was especially famous for its organists and composers of sacred music. The latter were strong advocates of that kind of individuality of expression in sacred music which paved the way for the Passions of Bach. They did not feel that the intense intimacy of Protestant faith could be embodied in music of the Palestrina school. They introduced a semi-dramatic recitative into their works, and their church cantatas had a decidedly dramatic color. A public taste formed on such church music was ripe for the enjoyment of opera, and the first attempt by a native German composer, though it was hardly anything more than an oratorio given with scenery and action, aroused great interest. This work was "Adam and Eve," composed by Johann Theile (1646–1724). It was produced on Jan. 2, 1678.

It was not until 1693, however, — when Johann Sigismund Kusser (1657–1727) went to Hamburg and introduced his own works

GERMAN OPERA TO MOZART

modelled after those of Steffani, and also the Italian method of singing, — that decided progress was made. In 1694 Reinhard Keiser (1673–1739) went from Leipsic to Hamburg, where he produced one hundred and sixteen operas, and was all his life the pet of the public. His works were full of facile melody and they had a sincere charm in that they strove to express character in their music. From 1703 to 1706 Handel wrote for the Hamburg opera, but as his works were strictly Italian in style he did not exert such an influence as might have been expected from a man of his genius. Gradually attempts at sustaining German opera became weaker and weaker, and in 1738 it was discontinued in Hamburg, which now, like other German cities gave itself up to the Italians.

Leipsic and Vienna made earnest attempts to support the German " singspiel " (songplay). It is hard to define singspiel, because it is exclusively German. It is a musical drama in which there is spoken dialogue and light music in the song style. Yet at times the Germans themselves have seemed to lose the distinction between singspiel and opera. In the latter we meet with music designed to develop the dramatic design of the work, while in the former no such attempt is made. Works of the singspiel class were produced in Leipsic and Vienna, and they had considerable influence upon the development of German opera. Their construction gave composers experience in writing for voices. Furthermore, the composers gradually adopted the forms and methods of opera and so gained facility in the use of operatic material. This process continued till the advent of the first German genius in the field of opera and his earliest works, though called song-plays, have been accepted outside of Germany as operas.

Wolfgang Amadeus Mozart (1756–1791) wrote many works for the stage, of which these were the principal: " Bastien et Bastienne," operetta, one act (1768), " La Finta semplice," opera buffa (1766), " Mitridate, Re di Ponto," opera (1770), " Lucio Silla," opera (1772), " Idomeneo," opera seria (1781), " Die Entführung aus dem Serail," comic opera (1782), " Le Nozze di Figaro," opera buffa (1786), " Don Giovanni," opera buffa (1787), and " Die Zauberflöte," opera seria (1791). Mozart's earliest works and, indeed, some of his later works, which I have not mentioned, were in the strictest Italian style. " Don Giovanni," too, is essentially Italian, and is seldom well performed by Germans. But in all Mozart's

GERMAN OPERA TO MOZART 341

dramatic works there is a German spirit, manifested not so much in the style of the music, perhaps, as in the entire sincerity of its character. Mozart made no revolution in operatic forms, and because of that it is by no means easy to define the improvements which he made in the art of the German lyric stage. Yet it is indisputable that before Mozart there was no distinctive school of German opera, and that since his day there has always been one.

"Die Entführung aus dem Serail," often called by its Italian title "Il Seraglio," was Mozart's first attempt at a German work, but the general plan and style follow the Italian opera of the time. What Mozart achieved was the introduction of a more definite and sincere expressiveness in the arias. In "Le Nozze di Figaro" Mozart's music is marvellous in its adaptation to the comic action of the play, and in its suitability to the characters of the various persons. There is absolutely nothing new in the forms or the general plan. The outline is all Italian; the coloring is all Mozart's. And it has that peculiar German solidity which comes from the tendency of the people to get to the bottom of things. Superficiality is opposed to the German nature. It was the fatal weakness of Italian opera. Mozart went below the surface in his "Figaro." A musical feature of this work and of "Don Giovanni," noted by Dr. Parry, is the way in which the composer "often knits together a number of movements into a continuous series, especially at the end of the act. This was the way in which complete assimilation of the musical factors into a composite whole was gradually approached." In "Die Zauberflöte" Mozart again followed Italian forms, but there is a profundity of thought in some parts of the work wholly foreign to all Italian conceptions of beauty. I am unable, however, to find ground for preferring this work to "Don Giovanni," as many writers do. To my mind "Don Giovanni," is not only the greatest of Mozart's works, but of all works in the old form. It was written in the prime of the classical period, before Weber had revolutionized with "Der Freischütz" the German conception of opera, and before Beethoven had become at once the culmination of the classic and the prophet of the romantic school. It has lived through all the changes of a century, and to-day stands forth in its clear, calm beauty, a thing of joy forever, beside the pulsating creations of the romantic school, even in the presence of Wagner's mighty creations.

"Don Juan" possesses the universality of a work of true genius. Its characters are recognizable as types, and its human nature belongs to no period, but to all time. It is uncommon in ideas and unconventional in treatment. Even Lorenzo da Ponte (born at Ceneda, Italy, March 10, 1749, died at New York, August 17, 1838) did something original when he wrote the book, for he gave us an opera without a hero. Don Juan is anything but a hero, and one hardly feels inclined to accept the imposing ghost of the Commendator as one. Don Octavio is a very estimable person, and is ever ready with his good advice, but it is not of such stuff as he that heroes are made; and as for Leporello, he is the prince of cowards. Indeed, so strong is the comedy element in "Don Juan," so fine and faithful the character painting, so significant the exposition of human weakness and folly, that despite the fatal ending of the work, it would require no great ingenuity of argument to establish it as one of the purest and loftiest specimens of true comic opera.

The nobility of its music does not make this classification absurd, for let us remember that in the greatest of all comic music-dramas, "Die Meistersinger," the music is second to none in loftiness of character, beauty of melody, dignity of color, and splendor of instrumental treatment. Mozart's biographer, Jahn, recognizes the presence of the true comedy spirit in Da Ponte's book when he says: "He has endowed his characters with the easy, pleasure-loving spirit of the time; and the sensual frivolity of life at Venice or Vienna is mirrored in every page of his 'Don Giovanni.'" He says further that the librettist furnished the composer with "a number of musically effective situations, in which the elements of tragedy and comedy, of horror and merriment, meet and mingle together. This curious intermixture of ground tones, which seldom allows expression to any one pure and unalloyed mood, is the special characteristic of the opera. Mozart grasped the unity of these contrasts lying deep in human nature and expressed them so harmoniously as to open a new province to his art, for the development of which its mightiest forces were henceforward to be concentrated."

Tempting, however, as the comic aspect of Mozart's opera is, we must not lose sight of the fact that the work has a serious purpose. Don Juan, bold and unscrupulous as he is, fails in every attempt, and finally meets with utter discomfiture and destruction. There is something here of the spirit of the old Greek tragedy, which always voiced a deep moral truth. After all, there is a term which fits "Don Juan" and roundly describes it. One of the names given to the lyric drama of Italy, when it was brought forth by Jacopo Peri and his associates, was Tragicomedia. Where is there to-day a nobler specimen of Tragicomedia than the "Don Juan" of Mozart?

As for the music of the opera, nothing better has ever been said about it than what Schink wrote in the *Dramaturgische Monate* in 1790. He says: "How can this music, so full of force, majesty, and grandeur, be expected to please the lovers of ordinary opera, who bring their ears to the theatre with them, but leave their hearts at home? ... His music has been profoundly felt and thought out in its relation to the characters, situations, and sentiments of his personages. It is a study in language, treated musically.

"He never decks out his songs with unnecessary and meaningless passages. That is the way in which expression is banished from music; expression consisting not in particular words, but in the skilful and natural combination of sounds as a medium of real emotion. Of this method of expression Mozart is a consummate master. Each sound which he produces has its origin in emotion and overflows with it."

This last sentence of Schink's is charged with import. One who studies the music of " Don Juan " carefully must be convinced of the truth of the critic's view. If it is true, however, it proclaims the presence of the essential elements of musical romanticism in this truly classic opera. To some extent what we call romanticism has always been present in art music, while it was and is the vital principle of folk tunes. It was when Weber united to the science and culture of musical art the folk lore and folk melody in which were voiced the poetic imaginations of a people that romanticism threw aside the shackles of tradition and became the ruling element in the tone art.

Mozart was not an iconoclast. He made no new forms; he destroyed no old ones. But proceeding on the principle subsequently enunciated by Schumann, that "mastery of form leads talent to ever increasing freedom," he absorbed all extant forms. There is a saying that if you wish to become an astronomer you must make mathematics your slave. Mozart seemed to feel that if he wished to become a composer he must make form his slave. As a mere child he made himself a consummate contrapuntal

GERMAN OPERA TO MOZART

scholar. In a word, he became literally a master of form.

When, therefore, he came to the composition of his wonderful operas, he saw no necessity for the creation of new forms, because he did not feel the shackles of the old ones. To him they were chains of roses, and the impulse had not come which set all composers thundering against the restrictive barriers of mere formalism. With Mozart there was no such thing as mere formalism; and if there is any lesson which every repetition of " Don Juan " forces home upon us with vital force, it is that fashion is no restraint on genius. Mozart accepted the material of Italian opera as he found it. But he filled the old forms with a new spirit. In the process of the years the spirit waxed too mighty for the old body and took its flight into the infinite regions of free, untrammelled expression. Mozart stood upon the boundary of the promised land; Beethoven and Weber strode boldly across the border; Wagner feasted upon the milk and the honey.

Chapter XXV

Weber and Beethoven

Weber the artistic forerunner of Wagner — Characteristics of "Der Freischütz" — Weber's theory of the lyric drama — Beethoven and his "Fidelio" — Advancement of the overture — Marschner, Conelius, and Goldmark.

MOZART, in "Die Zauberflöte," had touched upon an element which always appeals to the peculiar naïveté of the German character. That element is the supernatural. The Germans love a good fairy tale, and the " Nibelungen Lied," their national epic, is a version of the most imposing fairy tale the world knows. It was Mozart's misfortune, however, that he clung to old traditions and served up his German food in Italian dressing. So it was reserved for Weber to join hands with Beethoven and Schubert in starting the romantic movement. What Beethoven did for absolute music and Schubert for the song, Weber did for German opera. The influence which acted as an incentive to the romantic movement in music was the romantic movement in German literature. The writings of Goethe, Schiller, Heine, Ruckert, and others were intensely romantic in feeling and distinctively German in character; and they seem to have suggested to Weber the importance of national stories as material for opera librettos. At any rate he took up such material with a full knowledge of the awakened German taste for native legend and story. Unfortunately he was easily turned aside from this path, and induced afterward to waste his powers upon librettos of no value whatever.

Carl Maria von Weber (Dec. 18, 1786–June 5, 1826) wrote in his early days several operas of no great importance. The first, written when he was twelve years old, was called "The Power of Love and Wine." He must have known a great deal about it at that age. He wrote also "The Forest Maiden" and "Peter Schmoll." In 1811 was produced his "Abou Hassan," a comic opera of considerable merit. His masterpiece "Der Freischütz" was produced in Berlin, June 18, 1821. His other important stage works are: "Euryanthe," Vienna, Oct. 25, 1823, and "Oberon," London, April 12, 1826.

The story of " Der Freischütz " has existed in German literature as far back as the 17th century, and its incidents are of the kind that appeal most forcibly to the mass of the German people. It presents the conflict of the powers of good and evil in a concrete form, the evil being represented by Samiel, a German Mephistopheles, and the good by the pious Agatha. The superstitious yet religious minds of the average Germans were deeply affected by the manner in which Weber set this struggle to music. His melodies are notable in that they are quite within the grasp of popular comprehension, yet embody both religious sentiment and individual character. One of the salient peculiarities of " Der Freischütz " is its employment of the simple song-form, so dear to the Germans in their folk-tunes. Weber's use of this form went far toward assisting the general public to an appreciation of his work. The old German singspiel form is preserved in the original score of " Der Freischütz," which contains spoken dialogue. The recitatives usually employed now were written by Hector Berlioz for the Parisian production of the work.

The significance of Weber's position in German opera must be found in the fact that in his theory of the musical drama he

WEBER AND BEETHOVEN 351

anticipated Wagner and paved the way for him. He defined opera as "an art work complete in itself, in which all the parts and contributions of the related and utilized arts meet and disappear in each other, and, in a manner, form a new world by their own destruction." He believed that a libretto should not be constructed with a view to its offering pegs upon which to hang strings of pretty music, but that there should be an organic union of the various arts employed in dramatic representation. His theory as to the purpose of lyric music was fully set forth in these words: "It is the first and most sacred duty of song to be truthful with the utmost fidelity possible in declamation." He furthermore had no sympathy with the rigid and restrictive formalism of the old-fashioned Italian opera, but was a thorough believer in the fundamental principle of romantic music, that the content must govern and prescribe the form: "All striving for the beautiful and the new good is praiseworthy, but the creation of a new form must be generated by the poem which is sitting." Mr. H. E. Krehbiel says in "Famous Composers and their Works," "Here we find stated in the plainest and most succinct terms the foundation principles of the modern lyric drama."

These principles rest on the essential laws laid down originally by Peri, followed by Lulli and Rameau, and regenerated by Gluck. It was in following these principles and at the same time recognizing the characteristics of the German people and embodying them in his music that Weber formulated a style which has been a model and an inspiration to all the sincere composers of opera since his day. Wagner's debt to him was freely acknowledged, while Berlioz never wearied in expressing his admiration for the genius of Weber. To quote Mr. Krehbiel's masterly article once more : "To the band he gave a share in the representation such as only Beethoven, Mozart, and Gluck before him had dreamed of. The most striking feature of his treatment of the orchestra is his emancipation of the wood-wind choir. His numerous discoveries in the domain of effects consequent on his profound study of instrumental *timbre* placed colors upon the palettes of every one of his successors. The supernatural voices of his Wolf's Glen are echoed in Verdi as well as in Meyerbeer and Marschner. The fairy footsteps of Oberon's dainty folk are heard not only in Mendelssohn but in all the compositions since his time in which the amiable creatures of supernaturalism are sought to be delineated."

Beethoven's one opera, "Fidelio" (produced Nov. 20, 1805), belongs to the German romantic school, but it cannot be said to have exerted any marked influence upon the general advancement of that school except in the treatment of the overture and in the employment of the characteristic expression of the various orchestral instruments in the development of the story. In both of these movements Beethoven joined hands with Weber, whose overtures were the first written by any German, except Beethoven, with a deliberate purpose to embody in an instrumental prelude the principal emotions and incidents of the drama. Beethoven wrote four overtures to "Fidelio," but their numbers do not correspond to their order. That known as "Leonora No. 1" was written for Prague in 1807 (a performance which did not take place). That called "Leonora No. 2" was played at the original production of the opera. The famous "Leonora No. 3" is a reconstruction of No. 2, and was prepared for the revival of "Fidelio" in 1806. The fourth, known as the "Fidelio" overture, was written in 1814. The "Leonora No. 3" is the finest possible preface to an opera. In writing a dramatic work Beethoven felt hampered by the conventionalities of the stage. As Richard Wagner admirably said: "While in the oratorio and especially in the symphony a noble, perfect form lay before the German master, the opera offered him an incoherent medley of small undeveloped forms, to which was attached a conventionalism incomprehensible to him and restrictive of all freedom of development. If we compare the broadly and richly developed forms of a Beethoven symphony with the different pieces in his 'Fidelio,' we at once perceive how the master here felt himself restrained and hindered, and could hardly ever attain to the proper unfolding of his power. For this reason, as if to launch forth at least for once in his entire fulness, he threw himself as it were with all the weight of desperation into the overture, projecting in it a composition of previously unknown breadth and significance." It must be added that, while Beethoven retained spoken dialogue in his opera after the "singspiel" fashion, he infused into his principal numbers a deeper and more powerful dramatic expression than any previous composer. In all opera there is nothing more eloquent than the scene in the prison, in which the attempted murder of Florestan by Pizzaro is first checked by Leonora, and afterward by the arrival of the minister.

Heinrich Marschner (1796-1861) in his "Hans Heiling" showed that he was strongly influenced by Weber. The music is notable for its flow of melody and its highly wrought orchestration. The work is founded on a story containing elements of the supernatural similar to those in "Der Freischütz." Marschner wrote also "Templar and Jewess," founded on "Ivanhoe," and "The Vampire," a work of the gloomiest character.

More recent German opera has been in a state of confusion, owing to the enormous influence of Richard Wagner. The immense success of this master's embodiment of his own theories of the lyric drama has led to a general abolition of the set forms of the Italian school and equally to an abandonment of such attempts as those of Weber to employ the song-form. That German opera has gained in richness and dramatic power by the disuse of formality and the employment of all the resources of the modern declamatory arioso and orchestration cannot be denied. But only one or two composers have shown sufficient individuality to prevent them from being buried under their own imitations of the Wagnerian style. Peter Cornelius (1824-1874), an earnest advocate of the Wagner ideas, wrote "The

Barber of Bagdad," "The Cid," and "Gunlod." Of these the first is one of the most successful works of the school known as the new romanticists. The score is full of the most characteristic and fluent melody, admirably written and distributed among the various voices and instruments. The themes are rich in meaning and charged with individuality. The musical characterization is faithful and the musical humor simply delicious. Carl Goldmark (1830–   ), in his "Queen of Sheba" and "Merlin," made an attempt to superimpose the modern German style upon a ground plan somewhat Meyerbeerian. The music is full of sensuous richness and at times rises to heights of genuine passion, while every opportunity to introduce spectacular features, such as processions and ballets, is seized.

But it cannot fairly be said that any German has done anything toward the development of opera since Weber except Wagner, and he has influenced operatic composers the world over. It is to him and his theories that I now invite the attention of the reader.

Chapter XXVI

Wagner and the Music Drama

Points of resemblance between Wagner's theories and Peri's — His use of the myth as a subject — How he abandoned the old forms and made a new one — The *leit motiv* system — What it is and its merits — How *leit motive* are made and developed — Not necessary to identify them — Wagner's recitative and independent accompaniment — How combined.

RICHARD WAGNER (born at Leipsic, May 22, 1813, died at Venice, Feb. 13, 1883) was one of the great geniuses of music and the mightiest master of musical drama that ever lived. For many years his works were the subject of bitter differences of opinion. Persons educated to love the old Italian operas of the Neapolitan school, which were simply entertaining, rebelled against Wagner's demand that the lyric drama be taken as the most serious of art works. Yet, as I shall show, he was simply embodying in modern music the principles of Peri, Lulli, Rameau, and

Gluck. He was accused of being an iconoclast, a destroyer of all the laws laid down by Bach, Mozart, and Beethoven, yet he was their most enthusiastic admirer and understood them as few other musicians have done. France, England, and Italy long refused to receive his works, though they were successful in America from the outset. But his principles carried the day, and now Paris vies with London in its admiration of his works, and they have even been applauded in Italy. His first grand opera, "Rienzi," produced in 1842, was an attempt to combine the styles of Meyerbeer and some others in a work built on the old Meyerbeerian plan. It was fairly well received and remains to-day a good work of its school. But it is not in the characteristic style of Wagner. The works which have made him famous are: "The Flying Dutchman" (1843), "Tannhäuser" (1845), "Lohengrin" (1850), "Tristan und Isolde" (1865), "Die Meistersinger von Nurnberg" (1868), "Der Ring des Nibelungen"—a "tetralogy" consisting of four operas, "Das Rheingold," "Die Walküre," "Siegfried," and "Die Götterdämmerung"—(1876), and "Parsifal" (1882).

A great deal that is confusing has been written about the Wagner system. Indeed

Wagner's works have been explained so much that some persons have become convinced that they are quite beyond comprehension. Those who have attentively read the present volume should have no difficulty in understanding the brief account of the Wagner system now to be given, because that system is simply a new application of the original principles of Peri. Three salient resemblances to the Peri scheme of opera are to be found in the Wagner plan: first, the attempt to produce an art-form which should resemble the Greek drama; second, the employment of mythical or legendary stories as subjects for librettos; and third the construction of a form of recitative for the dramatic declamation of the text.

Wagner was utterly dissatisfied with the condition of the lyric drama in his day. The opera bore no relation whatever to the national life or thought of the people. It was a mere show designed to catch the applause of the unthinking, to dazzle the ignorant by empty display. In its popular Italian form the music had no genuine connection with the text, for the words were mere pegs on which to hang pretty tunes. These tunes, too, were designed, not to convey to the hearer the emotion of the scene, but to give the singers opportunities to display their powers. The stories of the operas were unpoetic, undramatic, false to truth, incoherent, and not typical. The characters were small and unrepresentative. The opera could not touch the heart of the people because it did not spring from the thought of the people. In Greece the drama, founded as it was on the great mythological legends of the nation, was almost a form of religion ; and its influence on the life and thought of the people was tremendous. Wagner's high aim was to produce a species of German opera that should have the same relation to the Germans as the Greek drama had to the Greeks. It is only by bearing in mind this fact that one can account for such works as " Lohengrin," " Tannhäuser," and " Parsifal," on the one hand, and " Der Ring des Nibelungen " on the other. The first three are Wagner's embodiment of the Christian mythology of Germany, with its whole content of the fundamental religious beliefs of the nation. " Der Ring des Nibelungen " is his presentation of the old pagan mythology of his country, with its noblest thoughts pushed to the front and its final retirement before a new order of faith strongly suggested by the last scene of " Die Götterdämmerung."

The employment of the myth or legend as a subject for dramatic treatment recommended itself to Wagner also on a purely musical ground, which Peri could not discover in the crude condition of musical art in his day. Myths are embodiments of human types, of fundamental traits of character and of elementary emotions. They have the advantage of universality. They are free from conventions of time and place. Thus Wagner saw that the employment of mythical subjects would permit him to concentrate the whole power of his musical expression upon character and emotion, which are just the things within the scope of operatic music. Every one of his music dramas makes action and the pictorial elements of the drama subordinate and accessory to the expression of the emotions of the scene. In working out this plan he came upon the final and fundamental law of his theory, namely, that there must be in a music drama an organic union of all the arts neccessary to the expression of the emotions of the scene to the spectator. Text, music, action, and scenery must all unite in a common purpose, and their union must be so complete that no one element can be taken away without injury to the whole. From this law Wagner derived the corollary that he must write his own text, and so he did. All his librettos are his own, and they are not mere schemes of dialogue, arias, processions, and ballets, but remarkably fine dramatic poems. The text being written, according to Wagner all the other elements in the drama, music, action and scenery, must be devoted to the fullest and most convincing expression of the emotions contained in that text. Now the conveyance of emotion is within the power of music, and the more completely the music can be devoted to this, the more successful it is likely to be. The use of the myth enabled Wagner to make perfect his organic union of the arts tributary to the drama, because it focussed the music upon the emotions, and so carried the other elements to the same point. This principle — concentrating the musical expression upon the emotion — led Wagner to adopt a new musical form. He writes what has been called "continuous melody." That is, there are no set arias, duets, or ensembles in his later works, but all the dialogue is carried on in a free arioso form, and duets are simply the musical conversation of two people. Wagner wrote voluminously in regard to his theories, and on this point he says : —

"The plastic unity and simplicity of the mythical subjects allowed of the concentration of the action on certain important and decisive points, and thus enabled me to rest on fewer scenes, with a perseverance sufficient to expound the motive to its ultimate dramatic consequences. The nature of the subject, therefore, could not induce me, in sketching my scenes, to consider in advance their adaptability to any particular musical form, — the kind of treatment being in each case necessitated by the scenes themselves. It could, therefore, not enter my mind to engraft on this, my musical form, growing as it did out of the nature of the scenes, the traditional forms of operatic music, which could not but have marred and interrupted its organic development. I therefore never thought of contemplating on principle, and as a deliberate reformer, the destruction of the aria, duet, and other operatic forms; but the dropping of those forms followed consistently from the nature of my subject."

Nevertheless he could not proceed without any form, because music without form would be without design, and hence would not be an art. Form in music is based on the systematic repetition of fundamental melodic ideas. This constitutes the identity of the composition. A tune made of disjointed fragments, no two alike, is not a tune at all. A composition does not exist unless there is repetition of the melodic subjects of it. In the old aria form these repetitions existed within each aria, which formed in itself a separate composition. Wagner, having abandoned the aria form, was obliged to invent a new system of repetitions for his continuous melody. This he achieved by introducing the *leit motiv*, " leading motive " or " typical theme," a melodic phrase employed to designate a certain personality or thought in the drama, and heard, either in a voice-part or in the orchestra, whenever that personality or thought is mentioned or has an immediate connection with the scene before the auditor. It was while composing " The Flying Dutchman " that Wagner invented his new system. In Senta's ballad, which tells the legend, he employed two themes. The first of these

he intended to represent the Hollander, and to convey in some measure his unsatisfied longing for peace. The second theme

WAGNER AND THE MUSIC DRAMA 365

is intended to represent the complement to the former, the sacrificial love of Senta, which is to bring the peace. Wagner says : " I had merely to develop, according to their respective tendencies, the various thematic germs comprised in the ballad to have, as a matter of course, the principal mental moods in definite thematic shapes before me. When a mental mood returned, its thematic expression also, as a matter of course, was repeated, since it would have been arbitrary and capricious to have sought another motive, so long as the object was an intelligible representation of the subject, and not a conglomeration of operatic pieces."

The *leit motiv* system was not so extensively used by Wagner in his earlier works as in his later ones, when the system had become fully developed and he had obtained a complete mastery of its difficult musical technic. In his later works the orchestral score is largely made up of repetitions and elaborations of the various leading motives, and this has led to some grave misconceptions as to the nature and purpose of his system. Many writers have published handbooks purporting to explain the Wagner dramas. These handbooks contain musical reprints of the various thematic phrases, with names which Wagner never thought of giving them. The books simply follow the scores through, page by page, enumerating the various motives as they appear. The result of reading these books is naturally a belief that the principal business of the auditor's mind at the performance of a Wagner drama is to identify each leading motive which is heard, and by doing so to get at the composer's meaning. In other words, those handbooks cause many persons to suppose that the hearer of a Wagner score has to translate the music into definite terms, those terms being labels which will tell him what the music itself does not. This is an utter misconception of the Wagner system, and it has been one of the chief obstacles in the way of its ready acceptance by persons educated in music of the older sort.

It is not necessary to know the name of a single leading motive in any Wagner drama in order to understand the work. Wagner himself did not know all the names found in the handbooks. He did not invent the names.

The quotation given above explains what Wagner was trying to accomplish by the use of leading motives. He tried to embody the " principal mental moods " of his dramas in " definite thematic shapes," and to use those thematic shapes whenever he desired to express those moods. Now if the themes do not express the moods, all the names in the handbooks are worthless, because incorrect. If the themes do express the moods, the names are still worthless, because superfluous. Furthermore, if a passage made up of various leading motives does not fairly convey to the auditor the moods and emotions of the text and action to which that passage is set, the whole system is a failure. If it does convey those moods and emotions, then it makes no difference whatever to the auditor whether he knows the names of the leading motives or not. It does not even matter whether he knows that there are any leading motives at all. An acquaintance with the leading motives immensely increases one's intellectual pleasure in listening to Wagner's dramas and enables one better to appreciate their musical form and their subtler details; but I repeat that it is absolutely inessential to an understanding of the dramatic force, eloquence, and truthfulness of the music. The text is the only test to be applied to any opera music. If the music expresses fairly the emotions contained in the text, it is good dramatic music. That was the test which Wagner himself imposed upon opera music, and it is the test by which his work must be judged. Every leading motive in Wagner's dramas is explained by text, usually on its first appearance, but sometimes not till afterward. What is called the sword motive makes its first appearance in the score of "Das Rheingold," when Wotan simply conceives the idea of creating a race of heroes.

The meaning of this motive is thoroughly explained when Siegmund in "Die Walküre" sees the sword in the tree in Hunding's house, and the trumpet in the orchestra intones the phrase in a manner not to be mistaken. None of the motives in these Wagnerian dramas are composed arbitrarily. The poet-musician used every resource of music — melody, harmony, rhythm, and instrumental color — to make them, in the fullest sense of the word, expressive. Occasionally he fell into the error of trying to embody in music purely intellectual processes, which are quite beyond the scope of musical expression. But no one need ever be at a loss as to his meaning, because the organic union between text and music is so perfect that one always explains the other. For example, in the final scene of " Die Walküre " Brünnhilde announces to Sieglinde that she will become the mother of a great hero, Siegfried, in this passage : —

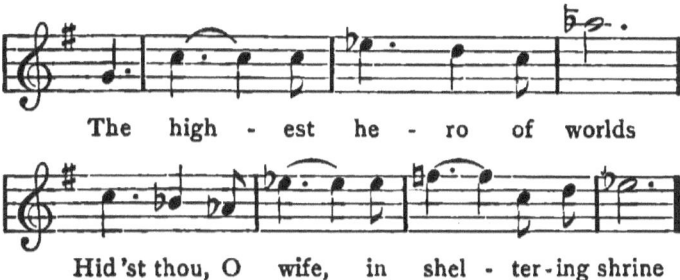

And we forthwith learn to associate that music with Siegfried in his character of hero. Sieglinde answers Brünnhilde thus :

When Brünnhilde, having prophesied the downfall of the gods, throws herself, in the last scene of "Die Götterdämmerung," upon Siegfried's funeral pyre, the orchestra peals out this phrase in majestic tones. There is no mistaking its meaning; it proclaims the divinity of Brünnhilde. Wagner has also employed the sound musical device of thematic development when it can be used with plain meaning, and this is a decidedly unique feature of his scheme. In "Siegfried" the young hero plays on his hunting-horn this theme, which seems to be an utterance of his buoyant youth: —

In "Die Götterdämmerung," when Siegfried has gained his maturity, Wagner presents his theme rhythmically developed from the gayety of six-eighth measure to the solid strength of four-fourth measure and adds to its breadth and dignity by the instrumental treatment.

WAGNER AND THE MUSIC DRAMA 371

As I said before, if it were necessary to go to the handbooks to find out the existence and meaning of these musical devices, they would be valueless. But Wagner's works are self-explanatory. An attentive listener, whose mind is open and who has not entered the opera house with a preconceived idea that an opera must always consist of pretty arias, duets, and ensembles, interspersed with recitatives, will have no trouble in entering fully into the spirit of these masterpieces of dramatic music. One of the features of Wagner's system which will require some attention on the part of the listener is the complete independence of the orchestral part. Wagner seldom writes an accompaniment pure and simple. His orchestral score, made up of the constant weaving and interweaving of thematic fragments, designed to express definite thoughts, is a vast and complex tonal illustration of the text. The orchestra is one of the chief agencies in the development of the plot. Characterization and emotional expression are largely, at times chiefly, confided to it, and it is quite as important a personage in the drama as the tenor or the soprano. While it is voicing the thoughts and emotions of the scene in imposing tone-language the actors are reciting the text in voice-parts wholly independent. These voice-parts are frequently written in a kind of recitative, but it is a recitative which is better described as declamation, because its form is so flexible. At one instant it may be recitative pure and simple, and the next moment it will glide into melodious arioso. The following example is taken from the first act of " Siegfried ": —

374 HOW MUSIC DEVELOPED

The address of Mime to the Wanderer is an admirable specimen of the Wagnerian declamation. The phrase in the accompaniment marked A has previously been made known as illustrative of Mime's labor as a smith, and it is here followed by B, a motive which has been identified in the score with Mime's meditation. The two phrases used here plainly say, " Mime is thinking," and the text and action show us that he is thinking very hard about the question which he is to ask the Wanderer, for he has wagered his head that this Wanderer cannot correctly answer three questions. He has answered two and this is the third. The Wanderer is Wotan, father of the gods, in disguise, and when he is asked who live in the sky, he rises to his feet and, while his face glows with celestial light, he answers in a passage of broad and noble arioso. The orchestra, at the point marked " dolcissimo," begins to accompany him with the Walhalla motive, whose meaning has been clearly brought out in the finale of " Das Rheingold." It makes no difference at all whether you know the names of these motives. Their significance has already been shown on their first appearance in the score. And even if it had not, they form an accompaniment thoroughly suited to the meaning of the text to which they are allied.

I have devoted this chapter to an explanation of the Wagner system, because it is the vital element in this master's work. In it are to be found the novelties in his method of applying the principles of Peri,

Gluck, and Weber. If the reader will refer to the Gluck preface previously quoted and to the excerpts from Weber's letters, he will perceive how in this system Wagner was only carrying out their ideas in a musical form invented by himself. This new method of Wagner's has been imitated with disastrous results by some composers to whose works it was unsuited, and to whose genius it was foreign. Wiser modern writers, like Massenet and Verdi, have adopted the broader features of it — the continuous melody, the arioso declamation, and the independence and illustrative agency of the orchestra — without attempting to make extensive use of leading motives. Massenet has used them moderately, Verdi not at all. But in " Falstaff" Verdi has filled his orchestration with illustrative melodic fragments, which are not repeated. All recent composers have treated the orchestral parts of their operas with much freedom, and have scored them with great instrumental richness. This advance in operatic writing is due chiefly to Wagner. It is quite impossible to estimate at a time so soon after the composer's death how deep and permanent will be his influence upon operatic art, but it is plain that every writer of to-day has yielded some allegiance to him, and every one has striven to attain dramatic fidelity. Better librettos are written for operas; and public taste, in almost every country where opera is given, demands that the lyric stage shall present for consideration a genuine *drama per musica*. This demand for sincerity has spread into other branches of musical art, and it can fairly be said that Wagner has done more for the general advancement of musical taste in his day and immediately after it than any other composer who ever lived.

Chapter XXVII

The Lessons of Musical History

Characteristics of the three great periods : Polyphonic, Classic and Romantic — Purposes of composers and possibilities of music in each — Limitations of the periods and their reasons — The contest between Classicism and Romanticism.

NO critical review of the development of the tone art is complete without notice of the intellectual and emotional impulses which governed that development, and of the characteristics of the three grand periods into which the history of music is divided. Two primary impulses have operated in the formulation of a system of musical art. These impulses are called Classicism and Romanticism. The terms are very glibly used by many music-lovers, but are not definitely understood by all. The ordinary concert-goer, whose terminology is nothing if not vague and unprecise, calls all artistic music, above the level of that heard in operettas or ballrooms, " classic." The term should be strictly applied to those works which have stood the test of time and have by the general consent of enlightened music lovers been accepted as masterpieces. From the fact, however, that the great masterpieces of the classic composers were conspicuous for their development of a clear, symmetrical, and logical form, the term "classical" in music has come to be applied to all works in which pure beauty of form and matter are the most conspicuous features. "Romantic" is applied to music in which the form is made for the immediate purpose of a particular work, and is the direct outgrowth of the thought contained in that work. As Dr. Parry has worded it: —

"'Classical' is used of works which have held their place in general estimation for a considerable time, and of new works which are generally considered to be of the same type and style. Hence the name has come to be especially applied to works in the forms which were adopted by the great masters of the latter part of the last century, as the instrumental works in the sonata form and operas constructed after the received traditions; and in this sense the term was used as the opposite to 'romantic' in the controversy between the musicians who wished to retain absolutely the old forms and those, like Schumann, who wished music to be developed in forms which should be more the free inspiration of the composer and less restricted in their systematic development."

The controversy is now at an end, and it is generally conceded that a modern composer may fully choose whether he will embody his romantic thought in the classic sonata form, as Brahms did, or make new forms to suit his purpose, after the manner of Liszt and Tschaikowsky. The contest between classicism and romanticism began as soon as musical science had formulated sufficient law to enable composers to work according to some system. The very development of the classical era itself was due to the impulses of romanticism. But the process of perfecting form is a purely intellectual operation. Hence the dominance of formal development was due to a belief that form was of paramount importance in music, and to a determination to work according to that belief. The dominance of romanticism, or free emotional impulse, could only come when composers had arrived at the intellectual conviction that this impulse ought to be permitted to make its own forms according to its needs. At this point I must ask the reader to accept a somewhat long quotation from another book of my own (" What is Good Music?"), simply because I cannot present in any different form what I have already said and now desire to say again:

"Music was originally a free dictation of fancy or feeling, and it dates back to the night of time. When I say 'free,' I mean in respect to form. It was probably a kind of intonation employed in the solemn speech of ceremonials, as instanced in the First Book of Samuel, x. 5: 'After that thou shalt come to the hill of God, where is a garrison of the Philistines; and it shall come to pass, when thou art come thither to the city, thou shalt meet a company of the prophets coming down from a high place with a psaltery and a tabret and a pipe and a harp before them; and they shall prophesy.' Further historical support of the probability that song began in mere inflections of the voice is found in the old Neume notation, which preceded the notation now in use. The Neumes were marks, somewhat like the Greek accents, placed over the vowels of a text, to indicate the intervals, up or down, through which the voice should pass in intoning. What we now recognize as melody was developed by gradual growth from intonations of this kind. Rhythm must have made its appearance in music as soon as it did in the verses to which music was set. Eugene Veron, in his ' Æsthetics,' says : —

'A very important characteristic of ancient languages was rhythm. The more or less regular recurrence of intonations and of similar cadences constitutes for children and savages the most agreeable form of music. The more the rhythm is accentuated the better they are pleased; they love not only its sound, but its movement also. . . . The most civilized nations cannot escape this tyranny of rhythm. . . . Rhythm seems, indeed, to contain some general law, possessing power over almost all living things. One might say that rhythm is the dance of sound, as dancing is the rhythm of movement. The farther we go back into the past, the more marked and dominant is it found in language. It is certain that at one period of the development of humanity rhythm constituted the only music known, and it was even intertwined with language itself.'

" The earliest music, then, must have been a kind of intonation, in which the rhythm was simply that of the text, and the melody a derivative of the inflections of the voice, as dictated by the natural utterance of that text. The most artificial attempts in music have been based on the idea that we could return to that primitive form. One attempt

LESSONS OF MUSICAL HISTORY 385

was that of the founders of the church chant; the other was that of the inventors of opera. It is incumbent upon us to consider now only the first of these. At the beginning of modern artistic music (not the music of the people, the folk-songs) we find the Gregorian chant, a musically formless droning of the church liturgy, in which the only rhythm was that of the text, and the melody was the outgrowth of mere intonation. The cultivators of artistic music were the monks, who found as material ready to hand only the folk-songs of the people and the music of the Greeks. The latter appealed to these cloistered mediæval scholars as the only proper material for churchly use, and they set to work to develop a system. It was inevitable that modern scientific music should begin with the invention of the *materia musicæ*. These old monks had first to develop melody, and it was natural that having once started upon that labor they should carry it out to its logical issue. Melodic form is more obvious than harmonic, hence they developed it. Having once got the melodic idea firmly fixed in their minds, they conceived a composition to be a combination of melodies, and when at some period about the end of the eleventh century the device of imitating in a second voice the melody uttered by the first was invented, counterpoint, single and double, grew with great rapidity."

In their exploration of the possibilities of melodic combinations, Okeghem, Des Prés, and their successors laid down the primary laws of music and consequently established the first forms, for in music form is the first manifestation of law. The first of all musical forms was that found in the songs of the people in which the rhythmic dependence of the music upon the text was the controlling principle. But the earliest scientific composers, the monks and church writers, having only the liturgy in mind, ignored the folk-songs and so robbed themselves of the aid of the simple rhythmic forms dependent upon verse. They naturally could not avail themselves of these forms because the liturgy was not written in verse.

Having, therefore, nothing to serve as a model, they were obliged to start from the foundation and build a wholly new musical system. Thus they produced, in a series of developments occupying nearly 700 years, the most closely knit and purely intellectual group of musical forms, those classed as canonic or fugal. Hence we find

LESSONS OF MUSICAL HISTORY 387

that the first of the three great periods of musical history, the Polyphonic, is chiefly distinguished by intellectual characteristics, because, as I have said, the evolution of form is in the main an intellectual process.

But even the canonic forms were modified by the irrepressible spirit of romanticism. Whenever in the history of music the desire to express one's self has acted upon a man of original mind it has caused a change in forms. The first period of the Netherlands school, for example, was devoted to the formulation of musical science. In the second period came Josquin des Prés, whose desire for pure beauty in music led him to modify the forms left him by Okeghem. In the third period, as we have seen, Willaert and others still further modified forms and introduced the element of tone-painting. In the fourth period we find Lasso again modifying forms and introducing the element of pure emotional expression, which, in so far as unaccompanied church music is concerned, was perfected by his great contemporary, Palestrina. In later periods we find that Haydn laid the foundations of the sonata, Mozart of the concerto and genuine opera, Beethoven changed the whole trend and scope of the symphony, Chopin, Schumann and Liszt remodelled the diction and the technics of the piano, and Wagner produced an absolutely new operatic form. These are only a few instances. This book is made up of the accounts of these and others.

Every original genius in music, then, has something to alter existing forms. Why? Because he could not say exactly what he wished in the forms as he found them. Classicism, in its old sense always resisted just such movements. Original geniuses are not numerous. One makes or changes a form. The mechanical workers (often mistaken for geniuses) take the forms left by the genuises and use them. The impression spreads that the form is the essential thing, and he who does not strictly adhere to it is condemned. An era of formalism usually follows any great improvement made in form by an original mind. This continues till another original mind makes a new departure, which is accomplished always in the face of opposition. This opposition is not wholly wrong, for it must be proved that a man is a genius before it can be admitted that he has a right to offer a new form to the world. It may be that his genius is purely technical, as in the case of Liszt, or wholly spiritual, as in the case of Schumann, but there must be something convincing in the man and his work. A small mind which has nothing to offer cannot justify an alteration of accepted forms.

The contest between classicism and romanticism, now at an end, since classicism simply means devotion to pure beauty of form and matter, is exhibited throughout the three great periods of musical history. The Polyphonic period may be regarded as extending from the beginning of the French school, 1100 A. D., to the death of Bach, 1750. This, as the reader will see, includes the transfer of the technics of polyphonic writing from vocal to instrumental music. The classic period, that in which the great works in the sonata form were produced, extends from the production of Haydn's first symphony, 1754, to the production of Beethoven's "Eroica" symphony in 1804. Then came a transition period, during which the romantic element in music was pushed to the front by the "Eroica" and the fifth, sixth, and seventh of Beethoven's symphonies. In 1821 Weber's "Der Freischütz" was produced, and Schubert's "Der Erl-König" was first sung in public. From that time the romantic school in music has been dominant.

The chief value of the study of musical history to the music lover is the acquisition of a correct point of view, and it is to aid in that acquisition by the reader of this book that I have written these observations upon the characters and purposes of the three great periods. In listening to the music of any composer the hearer should take into account the general tendency, purpose, and scope of musical art of his period and also the particular aims of the composer. No one has a right to say that Mozart failed because he did not achieve what Beethoven did. Mozart accomplished all that could be accomplished with the resources of musical art in his day, and he himself enormously enlarged those resources. That is the achievement of a genius. Every one has a right to say that Donizetti and Bellini failed because they not only did not succeed in accomplishing all that it was possible to accomplish in opera in their time, but deliberately ignored the fundamental principles of the art and also the immense advances in its technic made by Gluck and Mozart. Every one must admit that Verdi has achieved the triumph of a great master in his " Falstaff," for he has utilized everything contributed to operatic art by its leading geniuses, old and new, and yet has produced an entirely original and independent work. In conclusion, therefore, let me call the attention

LESSONS OF MUSICAL HISTORY 391

of the reader to the salient characteristics of the three periods.

The Polyphonic, because of its labors in developing the most rigid of forms, is chiefly notable for its intellectual characteristics. It displays immense mastery of the elementary materials of music and an enormous profundity of thought in purely technical processes. As it advances one sees it gradually developing beauty of style, and finally, from a state in which it is impossible to discover any emotion at all, it advances to one in which there is the purest and most beautiful embodiment of the devotional, contemplative spirit of the religious life of its time. It is the religious life that is withdrawn from the world, not that which is spent among men. For the embodiment of the latter life one must turn to the music of German Protestantism and study the works of Bach. Thus we find that Polyphonic music finds its expressive field in religion, just as did Gothic architecture, to which it so closely corresponds. There is no use of seeking in this music for the note of earthly passion. For that you must go to the opera, and later to the symphony.

The Classic period was the period of pure beauty in instrumental music. It corresponds to the second and third periods of the Netherlands school, and existed for the same reasons, namely, that its formal materials had been developed just far enough to permit its composers to make beautiful effects without aiming at an organized system of expression. In the Classic period we find wonderful symmetry of form, a continual subordination of profound learning to a pleasing style, and a sweetness and serenity of the emotional atmosphere. In Haydn and Mozart we find simple and tuneful subjects and bright, good-natured, and perspicuous treatment. In the sonatas and symphonies of the Classic period one finds no attempt at the expression of anything deeper than sentiment. The note of passion was attempted only in opera, but it was never permitted even there to create a serious disturbance of pure musical beauty.

The Romantic period took its spirit from the romantic movement in German poetry. In it one finds a constant struggle for the definite expression of the profoundest emotions of our nature. Its forms are flexible, its diction the richest attainable, and its conception of beauty based largely on its ideal of truth. It is in this period that music now is, but it does not follow that no contemporaneous composer has a right to offer us a work in the classic form and style. We must accept it as an example of pure musical beauty, and not look for an expressiveness which the composer did not seek to attain. The tendency of composers of absolute music at present is to make less and less use of the strict classic forms. But there are certain fundamental principles of music which they cannot ignore without danger to the art. The music lover who has an understanding of the spirit of musical history will best be able to appreciate their purposes and their achievements, without losing the power to enjoy the less pretentious works of the fathers of modern music.

Index

A capella church music, 79.
A minor, the scale of, 6.
"Abou Hassan," Weber's, 349.
Académie de Musique, the, 295.
"Acis et Galathée," Lulli's, 302.
"Adam and Eve," Theile's, 338.
"Adonis," Perrin's, 295.
Æschylus, 200, 238, 239.
"Æsthetics," Veron's, 384.
"Africaine, L'," Meyerbeer's, 325, 326.
"Agnes von Hohenstaufen," Spontini's, 323.
Agricola, 93.
"Aïda," Verdi's, 282, 284, 285, 288.
"Akebar, Roi de Mogol," Mailly's, 295.
Alaric, 55.
"Alceste," Gluck's, 314, 315.
"Alceste," Lulli's, 302.
Alexandria, Christian communities of, 2.
Allegri, Gregorio, 77; his "Misere," 78.
All Souls' College, 63.
Ambrose, St., 3; his system of chanting, 3, 4, 71, 74.
America, Wagner's works in, 358.
American Academy of the Dramatic Arts, the, in New York, 248.
"Amico fido, L'," Bardi's, 236.
Amsterdam, 49.
Anerio, Felice, 77; his masses, 78.
Anhalt-Koethen, 121.
"Anima e Corpo," Cavaliere's, 148; production of, 149; the first oratorio, 203.
Anti-buffonists, the, 309.
Antioch, 3.
Antiphonal writing, 46.
Antwerp, 40.
Apollo, 200.
Apostles, the, 2.
"Appassionata," Beethoven's, 145.
Arabs, the, 57.
Arcadelt, 39, 75.

Architecture, Doric, 69, 70.
Architecture, Gothic, 70.
Arezzo, Guido d', 19, 86.
Aria, five kinds of, 273.
Aria da capo, the, 263, 265; Scarlatti's development of, 269, 270; Verdi's use of, 282; 287.
Aria form, the, 318, 363, 364.
"Arianna," Monteverde's, 254; 260.
"Ariodant," Méhul's, 322.
Arioso style, the, of Italy, 210, 287, 288, 330, 372, 377.
Aristoxenus, on rhythm, 238.
Armand, St., 14.
"Armide," Gluck's, 315.
"Armide," Lulli's, 302, 303-306.
Arnstadt, 121.
Arpeggios, 105, 107.
Art, the Renaissance in, 69.
"Art of Fugue, The," Bach's, 122.
"Artaserse," Gluck's, 313.
Artusi, 260.
"Ascanio," Saint-Saëns', 332.
"Attaque du Moulin, L'," Bruneau's, 334.
Auber, Daniel François, operas of, 323.
Augsburg, 95.
"Ave Maria," Verdi's, 283.
Avignon, papal court removed to, 24.

B minor, Bach's mass in, 153.
Babcock, Alpheus, 97.
Bacchus, the altar of, 200.
Bach, Carl Philip Emmanuel, on clavichord playing, 108; piano sonatas of, 130, 133, 134; 161; the "father of the sonata," 132; work of, 132-134; his departures from polyphony, 133, 135; 138, 139, 144; symphonies of, 161.
Bach, Johann Sebastian, 90, 91, 93, 98, 100; his "Well-Tempered Clavichord," 100, 122, 139; 106; his use of the thumb, 109; his

396 INDEX

fingering, 109; his style, 109; great compositions of, 115; the fugues of, 120; his life, 120, 121; the most excellent of all models, 121; his works, 121; his organ and clavichord fugues, 122; his mastership of artistic organization, 123; 127; his concertos, 130; his sonatas, 122, 131, 190; orchestra employed by, 152, 153; 188, 189; his chamber music, 190; his settings of the story of Christ's passions, 207, 217, 338; his oratorios, 207; 209, 211, 212; his St. Matthew Passion, 212; his oratorios compared with Handel's, 213, 215, 216, 217; essentially German, 216; his use of the German chorale, 217; criticism of his work, 218, 219; 220, 221, 227, 228, 229, 230, 231, 233, 358, 389, 391.
Baffo, Johannes, the harpsichord builder, 92.
Baini, the biographer of Palestrina, 44.
Ballet, the Italian, introduced to Paris, 291.
"Ballet Comique de la Royne," Beaujoyeux's, 148, 290–294, 296.
Ballet movements, 158.
Ballets, the French, 291, 292, 294, 306, 307, 318.
Baltazarini. See *Beaujoyeux*.
Banchieri, Adriano, on the spinet, 90, 91.
"Barber of Bagdad, The," Cornelius's 356.
"Barber of Seville." See "*Barbiere di Siviglia*."
"Barbiere di Siviglia," Rossini's, 277, 279.
Bardi, Giovanni, Count of Vernio, 236; festival play of, 236.
Baritone, the, 272, 273.
Barromeo, Cardinal, 72.
Bars, 19.
Bass clarinet, the, 155, 156, 157.
Bass lute, the, 148.
Bass trumpet, the, 155.
Bass tuba, the, 155, 156.
Bass viols, 149, 150, 151, 153, 162, 166, 188, 189, 190.
Basses, 272, 273.
"Basso ostinato," a, first example of, 33.
Bassoon, the, 152, 153, 155, 156, 157, 162, 191.
"Bastien et Bastienne," Mozart's, 340.
"Bataille, Le," Jannequin's, 48.
Bavaria, 313.
Bayreuth theatre, the, 148.

Beaujoyeux, Balthasar de, the "Ballet Comique de la Royne" of, 148, 291; 290, 294, 300, 303, 307.
Beaulieu, 291.
Beauty, pure, the advent of, 48, 141; the period in music of, 164.
Bechstein, Frederick W., 93, 97.
Beethoven, Ludwig van, masses of, 80; 95; works of, 111; develops tonecolor, 112; his sonatas, 113, 138; his use of the pedals, 113; 137, 141, 142; life of, 143; his improvements in the sonata form, 143, 144; employs instrumental music for emotional expression, 144; his music divided into three styles, 145; summary of his work, 145, 146; his piano sonatas, 145, 146, 193; his full symphonic orchestra, 153, 163, 167, 168, 170; his symphonies, 170; the work laid out for, 171, 172; his nine symphonies, 172, 175, 176; his technical alterations, 175; significance of his work, 176; his romanticism, 176; 182, 184; his influence of the quartet, 192; his chamber music, 193; his "Rassoumoffsky Quartets," 194; 322, 342, 347, 348, 352; his "Fidelio," 353; his overtures, 353; 358, 387, 389, 390.
"Beethoven and his Nine Symphonies," Grove's, 172.
Beethoven orchestra, the, 153, 164.
Belgium, 34.
Bellini, Vincenzo, operas of, 280, 390.
"Belshazzar," Carissimi's, 204.
Benedictus, the, 8.
Berlin, 97, 337.
Berlioz, Hector, 154; his symphonic writing, 179, 180; 350, 352.
Beverley, 63.
Biber, H. J. F., 129; sonatas of, 139.
Bible, the, 71, 84.
Binchois, 40.
"Bird Cantata," Gombert's, 48.
Bizet, Georges, operas of, 331.
Bohemia, 44, 313.
Boito, Arrigo, 284; his "Mefiitofele," 284, 288; his "Nerone," 288.
Bologna, 105; the home of opera, 253.
Boniface, Saint, 10.
Bonn, 143.
Boschi, the great bass, 273.
Brabant, 45.
Brahms, Johannes, the symphonic writing of, 179; the music of, 182, 184, 185; his chamber music, 197; his "German Requiem," 232; 382.
Brambs, Dr., on "Christ's Passion," 201.

INDEX 397

Brass, the, 156, 187.
Brass choir, the, 156.
Brescia, 150.
Bridge, Dr., 41.
Brissac, Marshal de, 290.
Brittany, the Gregorian chant in, 9.
Broadwood, John, 95, 97.
Brockes, Barthold Heinrich, arranges the text of the Passion, 211.
Bruges, 45.
Brumel, Antoine, 39, 40; a motet by, 43.
Bruneau, Alfred, operas of, 334; influence of Wagner upon, 334.
Brussels, 233.
Buononcini, Giovanni Maria, operas of, 271.
Burger, the "Lenore" of, 180.
Busseto, 281.
Buus, Jacob, the "Ricercari da cantare e sonare," 103.
Byrd, William, 80.

C, the key of, 13.
C, the scale of, 4.
C major, the chord of, 13.
C major, the scale of, 6.
C major, Mozart's symphony in, 164, 166.
C minor sonata, Mozart's, 141.
Cabaletta, the, introduced by Rossini, 278.
Caccini, Giulio, 236; his "Nuove Musiche," 241, 243; 244, 247, 251, 264.
Cadenzas, 279, 326, 327.
Cafarelli, the singer, 271.
Caldara, Antonio, operas of, 271.
Calzabigi, Raniero di, 314.
Cambert, Robert, the composer, 295; his "Pastorale," 295; 296; his recitative, 296-300; 301, 303.
Cambray, 10.
"Camp in Silesia, The," Meyerbeer's, 324.
Canon, the "crab," 41.
Canon, the fundamental principle of, 25; 26, 33, 36; extreme development of, 41; 75, 82.
Canon, the inverted, 42.
Canon by augmentation, the, 42.
Canon by diminution, the, 42.
Canon recte et retro. See *Canon, the "crab."*
Canonic art, 124.
Canonic forms, 386, 387.
Canonic writing, 41.
Canons, "riddle," 42.
"Cantata," meaning of, 103.
Cantatas, church, 338.

Cantus firmus, the, 7, 16, 17, 20, 217; See also *Chant, the fixed*.
"Canzone," Gabrieli's, 104; Frescobaldi's, 104; 148.
Capella, Bianca, 237.
"Capriccio Chromatico," Frescobaldi's, 104.
Carissimi, Giovanni, oratorios of, 204; characteristics of his work, 204, 213; 232, 264.
"Carmen," Bizet's, 331.
"Carnival," Schumann's, 180.
Cassel, 225.
"Castor et Pollox," Rameau's, 309.
Cavaliere, the "Anima e Corpo" of, 148, 203; 236.
"Cavalleria Rusticana," 287.
Cavalli, Francesco, the "Giasone" of, 151; operas of, 263; his style, 263; his melodies; 263, 270, 306, 307.
Cembalo, the, 188.
Cersne, Eberhard, on the "Rules of the Minnesingers," 87; 90.
Cesti, Antonio, develops choral part of the oratorio, 205; 264.
Chanson, the, 58.
Chant, the Ambrosian, 3, 4, 6, 11.
Chant, the church, contrapuntal treatment, 43.
Chant, the fixed, 7, 16, 17, 20, 23, 36. See also *Cantus firmus, the*.
Chant, the Gregorian, 7; its division, 7; in Brittany, 9; general introduction of, 10; 11, 33, 58, 72; 75; 385.
Chant, the liturgical, 217.
Chant, the medieval, 2.
Chant, the Roman, 9, 24.
Chants, Indian, 182.
Charlemagne, 10, 24.
Charles V., of France, 34.
Charles VII., 40.
"Chefs-d'œuvre de l'opéra Français," 296.
Cherubini, Luigi, masses of, 80; operas of, 322, 323.
Choir, the, 3.
Chopin, systematizes the use of pedals, 113; 185, 387.
Choral art, the methods of, 261.
Choral hymn, the Lutheran, 67.
Chorale, the German, 216, 217, 228, 233.
Chord, the, 10, 12, 13.
Chord harmonies, 37, 43, 70, 125.
Chord of the dominant seventh, the, Monteverde's use of, 260.
Chord relations, the fundamental, 46.
Chorus, the, 121.
Chorus, the antiphonal, 79.
Choruses, the old church, 214.

Choruses, oratorio, 214; Handel's, 215; Haydn's, 223; Mendelssohn's, 229.
Choruses, polyphonic, 238.
Christ, 2, 45.
Christian Church, the, chants of, 2.
Christianity, 200.
Christians, the early, in Judea, 2; in Greece, 2; in Rome, 2; hymn of, 2.
Christofori, Bartolomeo, the claims of, 93, 94, 97.
"Christ's Passion," 200, 201.
"Chromatic Fantasia and Fugue," Bach's, 124.
Chromatic harmonies, 104.
"Chromatic Madrigals," Di Rore's, 47.
Chromatics, Lasso's use of, 50.
"Cid, Le," Massenet's, 333.
"Cid, The," Cornelius's, 356.
Cimarosa, Domenico, 276; operas of, 276.
"Cinq-Mars," Gounod's, 329.
"Circe." See "*Ballet Comique de la Royne*."
Citole, the, 85, 86.
Clarinets, 153, 155, 156, 157, 162, 164, 191, 197, 278.
Clarion, the, 149.
Classic period, the, characteristics of, 391, 392.
Classic school, the, Beethoven's symphonies the connecting link between the romantic school and, 176; 177, 342.
Classicism, 178, 319, 380, 381; contest between romanticism and, 382, 389; 388.
Clavichord, the, 85, 87, 88, 89, 90, 92, 101, 103, 105, 108, 121, 122, 132.
Clavichord, the German, 86.
Clavichordists, professional, 102.
Clavicimbal, the, 103.
Clavicymbalum, the, 91.
Clavicytherium, the, 85, 87.
Clavier, the, 122, 168, 189, 190.
Clementi, Muzio, singing style of, 111; his music, 111; his "Gradus ad Parnassum," 111; his rules, 111; 112; his masculine treatment of the piano, 142; his sonatas, 142; 324.
Coda, the, 119.
Cologne, 17.
Cologne, the Elector of, 143.
"Columbe, La," Gounod's, 329.
Columbus, 57.
Comedians, the Roman, 55.
"Compendio del Trattato de' Generi e de' Modi della Musica," Doni's, 241.

Composers, Catholic, 72.
Composers, the classic orchestral, 158.
Composers, ecclesiastical, 22, 23, 54, 70; their scheme of repetition, 117.
Composers, English, disciples of the French, 28.
Composers, the French, school of, in Paris, 24; English composers disciples of, 28; chamber music of, 196; 273; claims of, 290; 310, 327, 332, 334.
Composers, the French court, 292.
Composers, the German, 196; chamber music of, 196; 338.
Composers, the Italian, chamber music of, 196; 220; worthless oratorios of, 221; 275, 289.
Composers, Italian church, 117.
Composers, Italian opera, 317.
Composers, Neapolitan, 302, 303.
Composers, oratorio, 205.
Composers, the scientific, 47.
Composers, violin, early, 127.
Composition, the art of, 36.
Composition, Catholic, schools of, 77.
Composition, modern, basis of, 115.
Composition, monophonic, 243.
Composition, orchestral, modern, 165, 166.
Composition, polyphonic, 22.
Compositions, organ, 101.
Concertos, Bach's, 122, 130, 160; Scarlatti's, 160; Handel's, 160; their influence on the symphony- 161; 168.
Concertos, early instrumental, 160.
Concertos, piano, Liszt's, 179.
Condé, 43.
Condé, the Cathedral of, 44.
Confrèrie de St. Julien des Ménes, triers, the, of Paris, 56.
Congregation of the Fathers of the Oratory at Rome, the, 202.
"Consecration of Tones," Spohr's, 180.
Constantine, Emperor, 3, 67.
Constantinople, overthrown by the Turks, 67.
"Conte Ugolino, Il," Galilei, 240.
Contra-bassoons, 153.
Contra-bass tuba, the, 155.
Contraltos, 273.
Contrapunctus a mente, 25.
Contrapunctus a penna, 25.
Contrapuntal technics, perfection of 39.
Contrapuntal writing, 34, 42.
Contrapuntists, the great French school of, 24, 25, 27, 28, 34.

INDEX

Corelli, Arcangelo, work of, 127; sonatas of, 128, 139; 129; his chamber music, 188; 206.
Cornelius, Peter, music of, 355, 356.
Cornets, 148, 149.
Corsi, Giacomo, 244, 245.
Counterpoint, the art of, 22; described, 24; how it began, 24; completely conquered, 39; made subservient to religious feeling, 40, 48; 46; Lasso a complete master of, 49; 123; perfection of, 166.
Counterpoint, church, golden age of, 38-53, 55, 80, 104; old schools of, 141; devotion of composers to, 235.
Counterpoint, free, 165.
Counterpoint, vocal, 74.
Couperin, François, 109.
Crailsheim, 89.
"Creation, The," Haydn's, 153, 167, 222, 223, 224, 225.
Crema, 263.
Crescembini, on Neri and oratorio, 202-203.
"Cris de Paris," Jannequin's, 48.
Crusades, the, 57.
Cymbals, 155.

D minor, Beethoven's piano sonata in, 145.
Dances, significance of the word, 103; Corelli's, 127, 128, 129; 139, 263.
Dante, the "Inferno" of, 240.
"Daphne," Peri's setting of, 244-246, 290, 336.
"David and Jonathan," Carissimi's, 204.
Delattre, Roland. See *Lasso, Orlando*.
Delphi, 200.
Demeter, the wanderings of, 200.
De Monte. See *Monte, De*.
De Muris. See *Muris, Jean de*.
Descant, the art of, 16, 17, 21, 22.
Descanters, the, 24.
Des Prés, Josquin, 39, 43; his works, 44; his faults, 45; 69, 141, 386, 387.
"Deux Journées, Les," Cherubini's, 322.
Deventer, Holland, 49, 189.
"Dialogo della Musica Antica e Moderna," Galilei's, 240.
Diaphony, the. See *Organum, the*.
"Dictionary of Music," Grove's, 242.
Dies Irae, 9.
Dijon, 10, 308.
Di Lasso. See *Lasso, Orlando*.
"Dinorah," Meyerbeer's, 325.
Diodorus, 3.
Di Rore. See *Rore, Cyprian di*.

"Di tanti palpiti," Gluck's, 321.
"Di tanti regi," Rossini's, 279.
"Don Cæsar de Bazan," Massenet's 333.
"Don Giovanni," Mozart's, 266, 329, 340; essentially Italian, 340; 342, 344.
Doni, Giovanni Battista, on Galilei, 241.
Donizetti, Gaetano, operas of, 280; his style, 280; 390.
"Don Juan," Da Ponte's book, 343, 344.
"Don Juan," Mozart's, 343, 347.
"Don Pasquale," Donizetti's, 280.
Double bass, the, 162.
Double counterpoint, 27, 118, 119, 123.
Double lyre, the, 203.
Drama, the ancient religious, 199, 200, 201, 235, 237.
Drama, the Greek, early days of, 200, religious character of, 200; attempt to revive, 234, 238; 239, 241, 285, 290, 359, 360.
Drama, the liturgical, 201.
Drama, the lyric, 252, 263, 290, 332, 334, 336, 337, 345; Weber's theory of, 351; 357, 359.
Drama, the modern, 199.
Drama per musica, the true, 315, 379.
Drama, the secular, 237.
Dramas, the early Christian, written to offset the influence of the Greek plays, 200, 201; early vulgarity of, 201, 202; Neri's reforms in, 202-203.
Dresden, 209, 337.
Drums, 147, 164.
Dublin, 207.
Dufay, William, work of, 35, 36; his masses, 36; his improvements, 36; 37, 40; 54.
Dulcimer, the, 84, 85, 86, 92.
"Dumka," the, 181.
Duos, 193.
Dutch, the, musical skill of, 38.
Dvorak, Antonin, symphonic writing of, 179; work of, 181, 182; his symphonies, 182; his chamber music, 197: his later writings, 197; his American quartet and quintet, 198.

E-flat major, Mozart's symphony in, 164.
East Flanders, 40.
"Echo et Narcisse," Gluck's, 315.
Edward IV., 62.
Egyptians, the, 84.
Eisenach, 121.
Eisenstadt, 136.

"Eleusinian mysteries," the, 200.
Eleusis, 200.
"Elijah," Mendelssohn's, 226, 229-231; its popularity in England, 232.
"Elisa e Claudio," Mercadante's, 281.
"Elisir d'Amore," Donizetti's, 280.
"Enchiridion Musicæ," 14.
England, Roman singers in, 9; strolling musicians in, 62; her mastery of polyphony, 80; 111, 206; popularity of oratorio in, 232; 266; hostile to Wagner, 358.
English school, the, 80.
"Entführung aus dem Serail, Die," Mozart's, 340, 341.
"Equali," 193.
Erard, Sebastien, 97.
"Erl-König," Schubert's, 389.
"Ernani," Verdi's, 281, 282, 287.
Ernst, Johann, 189.
"Eroica" symphony, Beethoven's 145, 172, 173, 174, 389.
Eschenbach, Wolfram von, 58.
"Esclarmonde," Massenet's, 333.
"Essay on the Troubadours," Ritter's, 57.
Est, Hercules d', Duke of Ferrara, 43.
Esterhazy, Prince, 136; his orchestra, 161.
Esterhazy orchestra, the, 161, 162.
"Etienne Marcel," Saint-Säen's, 332.
"Étoile du Nord, L'," Meyerbeer's, 325.
Euripides, 201, 238, 239.
Europe, addicted to the Italian opera habit, 220.
"Euryanthe," Weber's, 349.
"Eurydice," Rinuccini and Peri's, 149, 245, 246; the first Italian opera, 247; production of, 247; its performance in New York, 248; the orchestra in, 250; peculiarities of the music, 250; 253, 254; in Paris, 294, 295, 315.
"Evolution of the Art of Music," Parry's, 81.
Exposition, the, 118.
Expression, attempts at, 48.
"Eroica," 389.

Faber, Daniel, 89.
"Fable of Arion, The," 236.
"Fall of Lucifer, The," 201.
"Falstaff," Verdi's, 282, 285, 287, 378, 390.
"Famous Composers and their Works," Krehbiel's, 351.
"Fauiska," Cherubini's, 322.
Fantasias, Bach's, 122.

Farinelli, the singer, 271.
"Faust," Goethe's, 288.
"Faust," Gounod's, 329, 330, 331.
"Favorita, La," Donizetti's, 280.
"Ferdinand Cortez," Spontini's, 323.
Ferdinand, the Grand Duke, 236.
Ferrara, Duke of. See *Est, Hercules d'*.
Festival plays, 235, 236, 237, 247, 254, 291, 336.
"Fidelio," Beethoven's, 353, 354.
Fingering, rules for, 105.
Fingering, the Bach system of, 109, 113.
"Finta semplice, La," Mozart's, 340.
First violin, the, 151, 154, 155, 162. 186, 187.
Flageolets, 148.
Flanders, 14, 44, 45.
Flavian, 3.
Florence, 202, 235, 237, 241, 244, 247, 300, 336.
Florentines, the, 248.
Flutes, 2, 148, 149, 152, 153, 155, 156, 157, 162, 163, 189, 190, 193, 203, 250.
"Flying Dutchman, The," Wagner's, 358, 364.
Folk-song, influence of, 36; in Germany, 59; 70, 71, 76, 263, 385.
Folk-tunes, the German, 350.
"Forest Maiden, The." Weber's, 349.
"Fra Diavolo," Auber's, 323.
France, 9, 17, 23; connection between the Roman Church and, 24; 35, 44, 56, 58; quartet-writing in, 190; 246; Italian opera in, 294, 295, 312; love of ballet in, 306; the lyric drama in, 332; hostile to Wagner, 358.
Francesco I., Duke of Tuscany, 237.
Franco, systematizes notation, 17; 19, 20.
Frankish chiefs, the, 55.
Frederick the Great, 93, 133, 189.
"Freischütz, Der," Weber's, 342, 349, 350, 355, 389.
French school, the. See *Contrapuntists*.
French school of opera, the, 275, 303, 333, 389.
Frescobaldi, Girolamo, the ricercari of, 104; his canzone, 104; his chromatic harmonies, 104.
Friederici of Gera. 94.
"From the New World," Dvorak's, 182.
Fugal forms, 386.
Fugue, the, fundamental principle of, 25; definition of, 118; distinguishing part of, 119; advance of, 120; its combination of polyphony with development of a theme, 119, 120; 121.

INDEX

Fugue, the German, 55.
Fugue, the North German, 118.
Fugues, Bach's, 121, 122, 123.
"Furiant," the, 181.

G, the key of, 13.
G, the major scale of, 70.
G, the scale of, 4, 6.
G major, the chord of, 13.
G minor, Mozart's symphony in, 164.
Gabrieli, Andrea, 78; his festival play, 237.
Gabrieli, Giovanni, 78; his work, 79; his orchestra, 79; his influence on instrumental music, 104, 106, 127; 209; his church music, 264.
Galilei, Vincenzo, the "Ugolino" of, 240; 241, 244.
Galileo, the astronomer, 240.
Galliards, the, 128.
Gallo-Belgic school, the, 34, 35; overshadowed by the Netherlands school, 38.
Galuppi, 275.
Gaston, Duke of Orléans, 295.
Gavotte, a, 129.
George I., the Elector, 209.
German Protestantism, the music of, 391.
German Requiem, Brahms', 232.
Germans, the, 90, 129.
Germany, the Roman ritual in, 9; 44, 58; the meistersingers and the minnesingers of, 58, 59; the folk-song in, 59; 60; "imitation" in, 117; 185; the home of chamber music, 189; 206; influence of Italian opera music in, 211; 337; 227, 314; introduction of the opera into, 336; the Christian mythology of, 360.
"Giasone," Cavalli's, 151, 263.
Gibbons, Orlando, 80.
Gibson, Dr., Bishop of London, 207.
"Gieus de Robin et de Marion," La Halle's, 292.
Gizziello, the singer, 271.
Gluck, Christopher Willibald, takes a stand against Italian opera, 221; his operas, 222, 313, 314; 273, 274, 275, 311; early life of, 313; his conversion and his cold reception in Vienna, 314; accepted in Paris as Rameau's successor, 314; his conquest of Piccini, 314, 315; his methods, 315-317; his artistic creed, 317; his use of the aria form, 318; his immediate influence. 320, 321; his successors, 321; his imitators, 321; 322, 324, 328, 330, 334, 352, 357, 378-390.

Goat song, the, 200.
Goethe, 349.
Goldmark, Carl, the "Sakuntala" overture of, 179; his operas, 356.
Gombert, 39, 45; his "Bird Cantata," 48.
Gonzaga, Francesco, 254.
Gore-Ouseley, Sir Frederic A., 119.
Gossec, François Joseph, quartet-writing of, 190.
"Götterdämmerung, Die," Wagner's, 155, 358, 360, 370.
Goudimel, Claude, 39, 45, 50, 74.
Gounod, Charles François, the "Redemption" of, 233; his "Romeo et Juliette," 284; his early life, 328; his operas, 329; his dramatic power, 330; influence of Meyerbeer on, 331; 333, 334.
"Gradus ad Parnassum," Clementi's, 111.
Grand opéra, the, at Paris, 329.
Grandiose style, the, 325.
Greece, 2; Christianity introduced into, 200; 345.
Greek art, 319.
Greek learning, revival in Italy of, 67, 69, 234, 238.
Greek literature, 238.
Greek Lydian mode, the, 70.
Greeks, the, 13, 14, 200, 245, 246, 263, 360.
Gregory, Pope, 7, 8, 9, 10.
Gritti, Andrea, 45.
Grove, Sir George, on "Beethoven and his Nine Symphonies," 172, 175; on Beethoven and the quartet, 193, 194; his "Dictionary of Music," 242.
Guidiccioni, Laura, author of the first oratorio, 203.
Guido, 19.
Guignon, Jean Pierre, "le Roy des Violons," 57.
Guilds, the musical, 60; the work of, 61.
"Guillaume Tell," Rossini's, 277, 279.
"Guiramento, Il," Mercadante's, 281.
Guise, the Chevalier de, 301.
Guitar, the, 149, 207, 250.
"Gunlod," Cornelius," 356.

Hadow, W. A., 184.
Halévy, Jacques François, operas of, 323.
Halle, Germany, 206.
Hallelujah Chorus, Handel's, 152, 157.
Hamburg, 93, 132, 189, 206, 211; a musical centre, 338; its opera, 338, 339.

"Hamlet" overture, Tschaikowsky's, 179.
Hammer action, the, invention of, 92.
Handel, George Frederick, 92, 109, 151; his orchestra, 152; his "Messiah," 152; 157, 207, 212, 215; his concertos, 160; his oratorios, 201, 204, 205, 207; life of, 206; influenced by Italian music, 206, 214; fails as an opera composer, 206; modern oratorio dates from, 207; 211, 212, 213; his "Samson," 213; his oratorios compared with Bach's, 213, 215, 216, 217; his musical scheme, 214; his choruses, 215; 219; his development of the Italian oratorio, 214, 215; 220, 221, 222, 223, 224, 227, 228, 229, 230, 271; his operas, 272; his "Teseo," 273; 313, 339.
Hanover, the Elector of, 206.
"Hans Heiling," Marschner's, 355.
"Harmonie Universelle," Mersenne's, 100.
Harmony, chromatic, 47.
Harmony, diatonic, 47.
Harmony, four-part, 190.
Harmony, production of, 10, 11, 12; the origin of modern, 13; 20, 21, 24, 57; new laws of, 214.
"Harmony of the Spheres, The," 236.
"Harold in Italy," Berlioz's, 180.
Harps, 84, 148, 155.
Harpsichord, the, 87, 88, 90, 91, 92; builders of, 92; 94, 103, 105; first systematic method of playing, 105; 107, 108, 110, 127, 148, 149, 203, 250, 266.
Hasse, 275.
Hawkins, John Isaac, 98.
Hawkins, Sir John, "History of Music," of, 28, 221.
Haydn, Josef, 111; life of, 136, 137; his music, 137; "the father of the symphony and the string quartet," 137, 161; his sonatas, 137; 138; his two principal themes, 139; 140, 141, 142, 143, 145, 153; his "Creation," 153, 167, 222; clearness of his orchestral works, 161; his symphonies, 161, 169; conductor of the Esterhazy orchestra, 162; his attempts in instrumentation, 162; influence of Mozart on, 163; his later work, 167; "The Seasons," 167; 213, 225; transforms the treatment of the orchestra, 168; his quartet writing, 190, 191; his quartets compared with Mozart's, 192; his oratorios, 221, 222; his choruses, 223; his oratorio writing, 224; 387, 389, 392.
Hebrides overture, Mendelssohn's, 226.
Heine, 349.
Helicon, the, 86.
Henderson, W. J., the "Story of Music" of, 249; his "What is Good Music?" 383.
"Henri VIII.," Saint Säens'; 332, 333.
Henry IV., of France, 247.
Hereford Cathedral, 62.
Hermann, the Landgrave, 58.
"Herodiade," Massenet's, 333.
Hesse, Dr., 60.
"History of Music," Hawkins', 28, 221.
"History of Music," Naumann's, 37, 43.
Hobrecht, Jacob, 39, 40; his masses, 40, 43.
"Hodie nobis cœlorum Rex," Nanini's, 77.
Holy Trinity, the, 20.
Horn, the English, 154, 155, 156.
Horns, 153, 155, 162, 191, 278.
Horns, French, 155, 156, 157.
"Hortus Musicus," Reinken's, 189.
"How Excellent," the chorus, 153.
Hucbald, the Organum of, 14; the harmonies of, 15, 16; 18, 20, 35.
"Huguenots, Les," Meyerbeer's, 324; 325, 326, 327, 331.
Hungary, 44.
Hymn-book, the first Lutheran, 71.
Hymns, early, 2; custom of singing, 2; the old anonymous, 8.
Hymns, Latin, 201.
Hymns, Lutheran, 71.

"Idomeneo," Mozart's, 340.
"Imitation," defined, 25; 27, 33, 36, 117.
"Infernal Regions, The," 236.
"Inferno," Dante's, 240.
Instrumental forms, 263.
Instrumental music, modern, 101, 102; a new element in, 106; 110; development of, 116, 189, 194; pure beauty in, 391.
Instrumentation, Haydn's attempts in, 162.
Intermezzi, 236, 259.
"Inventions," Bach's, 122.
Ionic mode, the, 70.
"Iphigénie en Aulide," Racine's, 314, 315.
Isaak, Heinrich, 60.
"Isbruck, ich muss dich lassen," 60.
"Israel in Egypt," Handel's, 207.

Issy, 295.
Italians, the, 129.
Italian school, the, 284; characteristics of, 289.
Italy, 44, 45; becomes the home of modern music, 50; revival of Greek learning in, 67, 234, 238; 94; vocal style in, 117; the oratorio in, 207; the ecclesiastical polyphonic style of, 214; 246, 291; hostile to Wagner, 358.
"Ivanhoe," 355.

Jahn, Otto, biographer of Mozart, 166, 192, 194; on "Don Juan," 344.
Jannequin, Clement, 39, 45; compositions of, 46; his "Cris de Paris," 48; his "Le Bataille," 48.
"Jephthah," Carissimi's, 204.
"Jephthah's Vow," Meyerbeer's, 324.
Jews, the, 2, 212.
John George I., the Elector of Saxony, 336.
John of Forneste, 28.
Jomelli, 221.
Jongleurs, the, 55, 56, 62.
"Joseph," Méhul's, 322.
Josephus, 84.
Josquin. See *Des Prés, Josquin.*
Joyeuse, the Duke de, 291.
"Judas Maccabæus," Handel's, 207.
Judea, 2.
"Judgment of the Hamadryads, The," 236.
"Juive, La," Halévy's, 323.
"Jupiter" symphony, Mozart's, 164.

Keiser, Reinhard, operas of, 339.
Kettle-drums, 153, 162.
Key contrasts, 128.
Keys, the arrangement of the distribution of, 130; Beethoven's freedom with, 143.
Keyboard, the, invention of, 85.
Kinnor, the Hebrew, 84.
Kirkman, the harpsichord builder, 92.
Köstritz, Saxony, 209.
"Kothner," 59.
Krehbiel, H. E., 238; on Weber's theory of the lyric drama, 351; on Weber's genius, 352.
"Kreuzer" sonata, Beethoven's, 145.
Kusser, Johann Sigismund, 338.

La Halle, Adam de, 56; the "Gieus de Robin et de Marion," of, 292.
Landini, Francesco, the first organist, 102.

Laodicea, the Council of, forbids congregational singing, 3.
La Scala Theatre, Milan, 288.
Lasso, Orlando, 40, 49; his Mater, mia cara, 49, 51-53; his works, 49; a complete master of counterpoint, 49; his " Penitential Psalms," 50, 73; his use of chromatics, 50; 51, 73, 80, 120, 387.
"Last Judgment, The," Spohr's, 225.
Last Supper, the, 2.
Lauda Sion, 9.
Laufenberg, Heinrich von, 60.
Lauska, 324.
"Legato," meaning of, 110.
Legend, the, Wagner's use of, 361.
Legendary stories, as subjects for librettos, 359.
"Leges Tabulaturæ," 59.
Legrenzi, Giovanni, 79, 80.
"Lehrcompendium," Zeelandia's, 60.
Leipsic, 121, 134, 339, 340, 357.
Leit motiv, Wagner's, 364, 365.
"Lenore," Burger's poem, 180.
"Lenore," Spohr's, 180.
Leo, 275.
Libretto, the, Weber's idea of, 351.
"Life of Bach, The," Spitta's, 120, 189.
"Limburg Chronicle," the, 59.
"Linda di Chamounix," Donizetti's, 280.
Liszt, Franz, 113; his development of touch, 114; his piano concertos, 179; the inventor of the symphonic poem, 181; his work, 181; 382, 387, 388.
Litany and Responses, Tallys', 80.
Liturgy, the church, 3, 6, 7, 36, 68, 385, 386.
"Lochemer Liederbuch," the, 60.
Logroscino, 275.
"Lohengrin," Wagner's, 267-269, 329, 358, 360.
London, 137, 358.
Lorraine, Christine de, 236.
Lotti, Antonio, works of, 79; operas of, 271.
Louis XI., 40.
Louis XII., of France, 43.
Louis XIII., 294.
Louis XIV., 295, 301.
Louis XV., of France, 57.
"Lucia di Lammermoor," Donizetti's, 280.
"Lucio Silla," Mozart's, 340.
"Lucrezia Borgia," Donizetti's, 280.
Lulli, Giovanni Battista, overtures of, 159; the virtual founder of French grand opera, 300; acquires the

opera patent, 301, 302; his operas, 302; influence of his operas, 302; criticism of his work, 302, 303, 307, 308; his recitative, 306; influence of Monteverde on, 306; Rameau's improvements on the style of, 309-311; 312, 319, 328, 332, 334, 357.
Lully, Jean Baptiste. See *Lulli Giovanni Battista*.
Luscinius, Ottomarus, on the virginal, 91.
Lutes, 147, 148, 188, 250.
Luther, Martin, 44; his music contrasted with that of the Roman Catholic Church, 71.
Lydgate, "Reson and Sensualité" of, 85.
Lyons, 10.
Lyres, 239, 250.

Machaut. See *William of Machaut*.
Madrigals, 39; Di Rore's, 47; 240. Monteverde's, 260.
Maffei, Scipione, 93, 94.
Magdalen College, 63.
Magdeburg, the Cathedral of, 85.
"Mage, Le," Massenet's, 333.
Maggini, Giovanni Paolo, the violin maker, 150, 188.
Magnificat, the, 8.
Mailly, the Abbé, the "Akebar, Roi de Mogol" of, 295.
Mainz, 10.
Major key, the modern, introduction of, 214; 243, 261.
Malvezzi, 236.
Mancinus, Thomas, 209.
Mandolin, the, 92.
Mannheim, 164.
Mannheim band, Mozart's, 164, 165.
"Manon," Massenet's, 333.
Mantua, the home of opera, 253.
Mantua, the Duke of, 254.
Marais, Marin, 308.
Marchand, 308.
Marenzio, 236.
Margherita, Infanta of Savoy, 254.
Maria, the Empress, 78.
Marschner, Heinrich, music of, 355.
Marseilles, 334.
Mass, the, early arrangement of, 8.
Mass, the Marcellus, 72, 73.
"Massaniello," Auber's, 323.
Massenet, Jules Émile Frédéric, operas of, 333, 378.
Masses, Machaut's, 34; Dufay's, 36, 37; Palestrina's, 72; Anerio's, 78; Lotti's, 79; Mozart's, 80; Beethoven's, 80; Cherubini's, 80.
Masters, the Netherlands, 117, 119.

Masters, the Venetian, 122.
Materia musicæ, 385.
Matheson, the "Musikalische Kritik" of, 93.
Matthew, St., 212.
"Matona, mia cara," Lasso's madrigal, 49, 51-53.
"Matrimonio Segreto, Il," Cimarosa's, 276.
Maximilian I., Emperor of the Netherlands, 43.
Mazarin, Cardinal, attempts to revive Italian opera in France, 295, 300.
Measure, dual and triple, 12; the musical, 17, 19.
"Medécin malgré lui, Le," 329.
Médicis, Catherine de, 290.
Medicis, Mary de, 245, 247.
"Mefistofele," Boito's, 284.
Méhul, Étienne Henri, operas of, 322, 323.
Meissen, Heinrich von, 56.
"Meistersinger, Die," Wagner's, 22, 63, 343, 358.
Meistersingers, the, 55; become the musical lawgivers of Germany, 59; the songs of, 59.
Meistersong, the, 60.
Melody, modern, first appearance of, 10; production of, 10; 11, 21.
"Melusine," Mendelssohn's, 180.
Melzi. Prince, 313.
Mendelssohn, Bartholdi Felix, orchestra of, 154; his symphonic writing 179, 180; chamber music of, 196 his "St. Paul," 213, 226, 227, 228 resurrects Bach's St. Matthew Passion, 221, 227; oratorios of, 225 226; his "Songs Without Words," 226; his "Midsummer Night' Dream" overture, 226; his "Hebrides" overture, 180, 226; attracted toward the Protestant oratorio, 227; his "Elijah," 229-231; his choruses, 229; his use of the chorale, 229; his fusion of styles, 230, 232; 352.
Mercadante, Saverio, operas of, 281.
"Merlin," Goldmark's, 356.
Mersenne, Marin, describes the clavicymbalum, 91; his "Harmonie Universelle," 100.
Merulo, Claudio, the "toccata" of, 104, 122; his festival play, 237.
"Messiah, The," Handel's, 152, 207, 212; most popular oratorio in the United States, 215, 232, 223; 272.
Meyerbeer, Jacob, 281, 323; his early work, 324; his operas, 324, 325; his grandiose style, 325, 326;

INDEX 405

his powers of characterization, 327; 330; his influence on Gounod, 331; his influence on Saint-Säens, 333; 334, 356, 358.
Michaelis, Theodore, 296.
"Midsummer Night's Dream" overture, Mendelssohn's, 226.
Milan, 49, 281, 288, 308.
Milton, John, 185.
Minnesingers, the, 55, 56; the era of, 58.
Minnesingers, the German, 56.
Minnesong, the, 58.
Minor key, the modern, introduction of, 214; 243, 261.
Minstrels, the, 55; songs of, 57; 240.
Minuet, the, 138, 139, 144, 168.
Minuet movement, the, 139, 144.
Minuets, Haydn's, 141; Beethoven's, 144.
Miracle plays, the, 56, 201; abuses of, 202; Neri's reforms in, 202-203.
"Mireille," Gounod's, 329.
"Misere," Allegri's, 78.
Mitridate, Re di Ponto," Mozart's, 340.
Mohammed II., 67.
Molière, 301.
Monochord, the, 71, 86, 87, 88, 103.
Monody, Italian, 291, 292.
Monophonic era, the, 81.
Monophonic style, the, 115; development of, 126-146; sonata-form tending towards, 160; 251.
Mons, 49.
Montalto, Cardinal, 246.
Montaud, 333.
Monte, Cardinal dal, 246.
Monte, Philip de, 40, 49.
Montpensier, Mlle. de, 301.
Monteverde, Claudio, development made in the orchestra by, 149; his "Orfeo," 149, 254; significance of his work, 150; his operas, 150; 157; his early work, 253, 254; his "Arianna," 254; his "Tancredi e Clorinda," 259, 262; the Wagner of his time, 260; innovations of, 260; Parry's comments on the work of, 261, 262; 264; his influence on Lulli, 306; 307.
Morley, "Plain and Easy Introduction to Practical Music," 128.
Morzin, Count, 136.
Motets, Brumel's, 43; Willaert's, 48.
Motive, the Walhalla, 377.
Mouton, Jean, 45.
Mozart, Wolfgang Amadeus, masses of, 80; 92, 95, 103; vocal playing of, 110; his operas, 110; 111, 137; life of, 139, 140; criticism of his work, 140; his piano sonatas, 140, 141; his quartets, 140, 192; a master pianist, 141; 142, 143, 145, 153, 162; his influence on Haydn, 163; symphonies of, 164, 167; 169; his Mannheim band, 164, 165; his extraordinary genius, 164, 165; his style, 165; his notable system, 166; influence of the opera upon, 166; transforms the treatment of the orchestra, 168; his chamber music, 191, 192; his part-writing, 192; his quartets compared with Haydn's, 192; 222; his "Don Giovanni," 266; 273, 275; his "Nozze di Figaro," 285; 320, 328, 331; his operas, 340; his German spirit, 341; his "Don Juan," 343-346; a master of form, 347; 358, 387, 390, 392.
"Muette de Portici, La," Auber's, 323.
Mülhausen, 121.
Munich, 49, 337.
Muris, Jean de, on musical instruments, 87, 90.
Music, the three elementary constituents of, 10; relation of poetry to, 316; primary laws of, 386.
Musical art, system of, 380.
Musical learning, diffusion among the people of, 67.
Musical science, formulation of, 387.
Music, ancient, 240.
Music, chamber, defined, 186; origin of, 187; development of, 188, 189; Germany the home of, 189; Bach's, 189, 190; Haydn's, 190, 191; Mozart's, 191, 192; Beethoven's, 193; Schubert's, 196; Schumann's, 196; Mendelssohn's, 196; Spohr's, 196; German, French, and Italian composers in, 196; reasons for retrograding, 196; Brahms', 197; Dvorak's, 197.
Music, church, attempts to form a system in, 3; 19; German, 60; its cultivation in Paris, 24; simplification of, 65; methods in writing, 66; reforms in, 67-74; Roman Catholic, 77; borrows from the opera and the oratorio, 79; 240.
Music, dramatic, attempt to improve the state of, 237; 252.
Music, ecclesiastical, 19, 54.
Music, English cathedral, 80.
Music, Greek, 2, 4, 6, 14, 16, 238.
Music, homophonic, 252.
Musicians, early secular, 55, 61.
Music, Italian, 139; influences Handel's work, 206, 214.

INDEX

Music, modern, early cultivation of, 1; gains independence as an art, 9; its melodic basis established, 10; introduction of harmony into, 12; Italy becomes the home of, 50.
Music, opera, Italian, influence in Germany of, 211.
Music, orchestral, 187.
Music, organ, 102.
Music, passion, the history of, 207, 208, 209; influence of Schütz upon, 209; Sebastiani's, 211; Bach's, 212, 217.
Music, piano, origin of, 101; evolution of, 108; 115.
Music, popular, examples of, 63, 64; 67, 69.
Music, programme, 177; defined, 177, 178.
Music, recitative, 252.
Music, secular, 39; development of, 47; new developments in, 74.
Music, vocal, 106, 108, 116, 234.
"Musikalische Kritik," Matheson's, 93.
"Musurgia," Luscinius', 91
Mysteries, the, 56.
Myth, the, Wagner's use of, 361, 362, 363.
Mythical stories, as subjects for librettos, 359.

Nanini, Giovanni Maria, 75, 77; his "Hodie nobis cœlorum Rex," 77.
Naples, 49, 265.
Naumann, 37, 43.
Nazianzen, St. Gregory, Patriarch of Constantinople, 200.
Neapolitans, the, 302.
Neapolitan School of opera writers, the, 265, 270, 275, 280, 285, 357.
Neri, St. Philip, reforms the early Christian drama, 202-203.
"Nerone," Boito's, 288.
Netherlands, the, 17, 44.
Netherlands school, the great, overshadows the Gallo-Belgic school, 37; periods of, 38-40; formation of its character, 40; 45, 48, 60, 73, 102, 189, 387, 392.
Neumes, the, 17, 18, 19, 383.
New College, 63.
New Haven, 87.
New Testament, the, study of, 68.
"Nibelungen Lied," the, 348.
Nokter, Balbulus, 9.
"Nonne Sanglante, La," Gounod's, 329.
"Norma," Bellini's, 280.
Notation, the earliest form of, 17.

Nottinghamshire, 63.
"Nozze di Figaro," Mozart's, 285, 340, 341, 342.
"Nozze di Tito e di Peleo," Cavalli's, 263.
"Nuove Musiche," Caccini's, 241
Nuremberg, 209.

"Oberon," Weber's, 349.
"Oberto, Conte di San Bonifazio," Verdi's, 281.
Oboes, 148, 152, 153, 155, 156, 157, 162, 164, 191.
Octets, 186, 193.
Odington, Walter, 28.
Okeghem, Johannes, 39, 40, 41, 42, 43, 50, 63, 141, 386, 387.
"Olympie," Spontini's, 323.
"Omme Armée, L'," 36, 45.
Opera, 79, 106, 160; its effect on Mozart, 166; 203; origin of, 234-241; early development of, 243-252; Monteverde's innovations in, 259-262; becomes public and popular, 262; shows a step in advance, 264; three kinds of vocal music in, 265-267; the position of the aria established in, 270: rules for, 273, 274; Weber's definition of, 351.
Opera Buffa, the. See *Opera, comic grand.*
Opera, comic grand, 275, 276, 279, 280.
Opera, pastoral, 291.
Opera, the comic Italian, 236.
Opera, the French, 277; early history of, 290; the real development of, 294-296; Lulli the virtual founder of, 300; Lulli's influence upon, 301-308; Rameau's influence upon, 309-311; Gluck's influence upon, 321.
Opera, the German, 233; early history of, 336-339; development of, 339, 340; the school of, 341; Weber's influence on, 348; enormous influence of Wagner on, 355.
Opera, the Italian, 141; advent of, 148; Europe addicted to the habit of, 220; opposition to, 221, 222; production of the first, 247; Scarlatti's improvements in, 265-269; the laws of, 272; new school of, 286, 287; in France, 294; 295, 312; in Germany, 337; fatal weakness of, 341.
Opera houses, 262.
Opera per Musica, the title, 252.
Opera writers, Italian, 264, 265, 271.
Operas, Gluck's, 222, 313; Monteverde's, 150, 259; Cavalli's, 263; Scarlatti's, 265-269; Rossi's, 271;

INDEX

Caldara's, 271; Lotti's, 271; Buononcini's, 271; Handel's, 272; Cimarosa's, 276; Rossini's, 277; Donizetti's, 280; Bellini's, 280, 281; Mercadante's, 281; Verdi's, 281, 282; Perrin's, 295; Lulli's, 302; Rameau's, 309; Méhul's, 322; Cherubini's, 322; Spontini's, 323; Auber's, 323; Halévy's, 323; Meyerbeer's, 324; Gounod's, 329; Bizet's, 331; Saint-Saëns', 332; Massenet's, 333; Reyer's, 334; Keiser's, 339; Mozart's, 110, 140, 340; Weber's, 349; Beethoven's, 353; Marschner's, 355; Cornelius', 355; Goldmark's, 356; Wagner's, 358.
Operatic declamation, 129.
Operatic finale, Piccini's development of, 275.
Opitz, Martin, 336.
Oratorio, 48, 79; advent of, 148; origin of, 199; influence of Greek plays upon, 200; Neri's influence upon, 202-203; effect of dramatic recitative upon, 203; first performance of, 203; improvements of Carissimi, Stradella, and Cesti in, 204, 205; dates from Handel, 207; its decadence after Handel and Bach, 220; descriptive orchestration in, 224; its popularity in England, 232; improvement in the dramatic recitative and the choral part of, 264.
Oratorio, Passion, 212.
Oratorio, Protestant, Mendelssohn attracted towards, 227, 230.
Oratorios, Handel's, 201, 207, 313; Carissimi's, 204; Scarlatti's, 205; Bach's, 207; Haydn's, 221, 222, 224, 225; Spohr's, 225; German, 232; Italian, 232.
Orchestra, the, 121; evolution of, 147-157; early arrangement of, 147, 148; first organized use of, 148; Monteverde's influence on, 149; plan of the contemporaneous, 156-157; transformed in its treatment by Haydn and Mozart, 168.
Orchestras, continental town, 61; Hungarian, 84.
Orchestration, Wagnerian, 233.
"Orfeo," Gluck's, 314, 317, 318, 319.
"Orfeo," Monteverde's, 149, 337.
Organ, the, 10, 22, 77, 85, 86, 101, 102; first systematic method of playing, 105; 121, 149, 153, 188.
Organists, 101, 102. Venetian school of, 102, 209; Roman school of, 104.
Organ playing, 115.

Organ school, the, of Venice, 102, 209; of Rome, 104.
Organum, the, of Hucbald, 14, 35.
Orléans, 10.
"Orpheus," Schütz's, 337.
"Otello," Rossini's, 277, 278.
"Otello," Verdi's, 282, 283, 284, 285, 286.
Overture, the, Gluck's idea of, 316; advancement of, 353.
"Overture, the Italian," 159, 160.
Overture, the programme, 178.
Overtures, Lulli's, 159; their influence upon the symphony, 161; Weber's, 353; Beethoven's, 353.
"O Welt, ich muss dich lassen," 60.
Oxford, 63.

Paderewski, 114.
Padua, 93.
"Pagliacci," 287.
Paisiello, 221, 275.
Palazzo Bardi, the, 239, 244.
Palestrina, 44, 45, 49; his masses, 72; his development of church polyphony, 74; his career, 74; his style, 75, 76, 77; 78, 80, 120, 328, 338, 387.
Paliarino, an instrument maker, 94.
Pandæan pipe, the, 149, 250.
Papal Chapel, the, 75, 77.
"Papillons," Schumann's, 180.
"Pardon de Ploermel, Le," Meyerbeer's, 325.
Paris, 2, 24, 28, 45, 87, 277; Italian ballet introduced to, 291; 294, 301, 306, 308, 312, 313, 314, 315, 328, 358.
"Paris and Helen," Gluck's, 314.
Paris Grand Opéra, the, 296.
Paris, the University of, becomes the centre of European study, 24; 87.
Parisian symphony, Mozart's, 165.
Parry, Dr. C. H. H., on the "Evolution of the Art of Music," 81; 120, 129, 130; on Beethoven and the symphony, 167, 168, 169; on Stradella and Cesti, 205; 216; his comments on the work of Monteverde, 261, 262; on Gluck, 320; on Meyerbeer, 326; on Mozart, 342; on classicism, 381.
"Parsifal," Wagner's, 358, 360.
Pasquine, Bernado, the works of, 105.
Passacaglia, a, 129.
"Passage-work," 131.
Passion, the, Bach's settings of, 122, 207; Schütz's settings of, 210, 211; Brockes' text of, 211.
Pasticcio, a, 313.

"Pastorale," Cambert's, 295.
Paul, Saint, 2.
Pavanes, the, 128.
Pedal, the "celeste," 97.
Pedalling, 113.
"Penitential Psalms," Lasso's, 50, 73.
Penna, Lorenzo, 105; rules of, 108.
Pergolesi, 275.
Peri, Jacopo, the "Daphne" of, 244, 245; his "Eurydice," 149, 245, 246; his theory of recitative, 247, 248, 249, 250; peculiarities of his music, 250-252; 253, 254, 264, 285, 290, 303, 307, 315, 318, 336, 337, 345, 352, 357; Wagner's theories compared with those of, 359, 361, 377.
Pericles, 319.
Perotin, the "Posui adjutorum" of, 25; 27.
Perrin, Pierre, operas of, 295, 296, 300; 301.
"Persée," Lulli's, 302.
Persephone, the rape of, 200.
Pesaro, 277.
"Peter Schmoll," Weber's, 349.
Philadelphia, 98.
"Philémon et Baucis," Gounod's, 329.
Philip the Fair, 24.
"Phryne," Saint-Säens', 333.
Pianists, professional, 102; their rules, 108.
Piano, the, precursors of, 71; the result of a long development, 83; its fundamental principle, 83; evolution of, 85-98; the Steinert collection, 87; equal temperament in, 98-100; 186, 191, 193, 194; technics of, 388.
Piano, the English, 97, 111.
Piano playing, evolution of, 101-115.
Piano style, the polyphonic, 116-125.
Pianos, Viennese, 96, 97.
"Pianoforte, The," Rimbault's, 93.
"Pianoforte Sonata," the, Shedlock's, 133.
Picardy, 292.
Piccini, 275; his development of the operatic finale, 275; 314, 315.
Piccolo, the, 149, 155.
Piedmont, 290.
Pipers, town, 61.
"Piramo e Tisbe," Gluck's, 313, 315.
Pius IX., Pope, 72.
Pizzicato, the, invention of, 151.
"Plain and Easy Introduction to Practical Music," Morley's, 128.
Plays, Greek, influence upon oratorio of, 199, 200, 201.
Plays, secular, 235.

Plays, the pastoral, 291, 292.
Pliny, the Younger, 2.
Poetry, German, 392.
Poetry, relation of music to, 316.
Poets, Italian, 203.
Polka, the, 20.
"Polyeucte," Gounod's, 329.
Polyphonic era, the, 81.
Polyphonic forms, the, 22, 25, 27; difference between the sonata and, 125.
Polyphonic motet style, the old, 210.
Polyphonic period, the, characteristics of, 387, 389, 391.
Polyphonic playing, 106-108.
Polyphonic style, the, 115, 190.
Polyphonic writing, 44, 73; a new kind of, 112; 117, 124.
Polyphony, church, 74; England's mastery of, 80; 129.
Polyphony, English, 27.
Polyphony, instrumental, 124; comes to an end with Bach, 124; on a new basis, 214.
Polyphony, vocal, 148.
"Pomone," Perrin and Cambert's, 296, 300.
Pompeo," Scarlatti's, 265.
Ponte, Lorenzo da, the "Don Juan" of, 343.
"Posui adjutorum," the, of Perotin, 25.
"Power of Love and Wine, The," Weber's, 349.
"Power of Sound," Spohr's, 180.
Preludes, Bach's, 122, 123.
Printing, invention of, 67; introduction of, 68.
"Prophète, Le," Meyerbeer's, 325.
"Proserpine," Saint-Säens', 332.
Protestant Church, the, 71; in Germany, 217, 218; 228, 229.
Protestantism, the spirit of, 212.
Provence, 292.
Psalms, Hebrew, 2; in the early Church, 3; antiphonal chanting of, 3.
Ptolomæus, Claudius, 86.
Pythagoras, the musical system of, 14; 85.

"Quartet, American," Dvorak's, 198.
Quartet, string, the, Haydn the father of, 137; Monteverde's use of, 150; Scarlatti's use of, 151, 190, 193; the opportunities offered by, 194; 197.
Quartets, Haydn's, 137, 190, 191; Mozart's, 140, 192; 168, 186, 189; Gossec's, 190; complete establishment of, 192; Beethoven and romanticism in, 192-196.

INDEX 409

Quartets, piano, 186, 191, 193, 196, 197.
Quartet writing, Gossec's, 190; Haydn's, 190, 191.
"Queen of Sheba," Goldmark's, 356.
"Quintet, American," Dvorak's, 198.
Quintets, 186, 191.
Quintets, piano, 187, 193, 196, 197.
Quintets, string, 191, 193.
Quintilianus, Aristides, 86.

Racine, 310, 314.
Rameau, Jean Philippe, the French opera composer, 98; his "Traité de l'Harmonie," 100; 308; his theoretical works, 308; his "Hippolyte et Aricie," 309; operas of, 309, 313; his improvements on Lulli's style, 309-311; 312, 319, 321, 328, 330, 332, 334, 352, 357.
Rassoumoffsky, Count, 194.
"Rassoumoffsky Quartets, The," Beethoven's, 194.
Reading, 28.
Recitative, dramatic, invention of, 203; its effect on oratorio, 203; 235, 239, 240; improvement in, 264.
Recitative, the Florentine, 292.
Recitative, French, 313.
Recitative, the Greek, 243.
Recitativo secco, 266, 278, 279.
Recitativo stromentato, 267, 278, 279.
"Redemption," Gounod's, 233.
Reformation, the, 60, 71, 104.
Regal, the, 149.
Regensburg, 10.
"Reine de Saba, La," Gounod's, 329.
Reinken, John Adam, the "Hortus Musicus" of, 189.
Renaissance, the, dawn of, 67, 69, 70.
"Reson and Sensualité," Lydgate's, 85.
Reszke, Jean de, 329.
"Rêve, Le," Bruneau's, 334.
Reyer, Ernest, operas of, 334.
"Rheingold, Das," Wagner's, 358, 368, 377.
Rhine, the, 58.
Rhythm, 10, 11; the appearance of, 16; 21; elementary attraction of pure, 70; Aristoxenus on, 238; Veron on, 384.
Ricercari, Buus', 103; Frescobaldi's, 104.
"Ricercari da cantare e sonare," Buus', 103.
"Ride of the Valkyrs," 154, 260.
"Rienzi," Wagner's, 281, 358.
"Rigoletto," Verdi's, 281, 282.
Rimbault, on "The Pianoforte," 93.

"Rinaldo," Handel's opera, 206.
"Ring des Nibelungen, Der," Wagner's, 358, 360.
Rinuccini, Ottavio, intermezzi of, 236; his work on "Daphne," 244, 245; his "Eurydice," 245, 246, 247, 249, 251; 285, 294, 315, 336.
"Ripieno" instruments, 160.
"Ritorno di Tobia, Il," Haydn's, 221.
Ritter, Dr. F. L., 249.
Ritter, Fanny Raymond, on the Troubadours, 57, 58.
Ritual, the Roman, 9, 10.
"Robert le Diable," Meyerbeer's, 324, 325.
Rohran, Austria, 136.
"Roi de Lahore, Le," Massenet's, 333.
"Roland," Lulli's, 302.
Roman Catholic Church, the, medieval priests of, 1; artistic music of, 1; psalms in, 3; the Sequence in, 8; 16; connection between France and, 24; 49; musicians of, 62; authorized language in, 68; its music contrasted with Luther's, 71, 72; prepares religious dramas, 200; Holy Week in, 208.
Romans, the, 200, 246.
Romanticism, 178, 380, 381; contest between classicism and, 382, 389.
Romanticists, the, 178, 179; new, 356.
Romantic period, the, characteristics of, 392, 393.
Romantic school, the, Beethoven's symphonies the connecting link between the classic school and, 176; 177, 180, 342.
Romantic writers, the, 170.
Rome, 2; singing-schools at, 3; Sistine Chapel at, 43; 45, 49, 51, 55, 67, 68, 71; the pontifical chapel at, 74; school of Catholic composition at, 77; Christianity introduced into, 200; oratorio first performed in, 203, 219; 244.
"Romeo and Juliet," Berlioz's, 180.
"Romeo et Juliette," Gounod's, 284, 329, 330, 331.
Roncole, 281.
Rore, Cyprian di, 39, 45; his "Chromatic Madrigals," 47; 49, 50, 77.
Rossi, Francesco, operas of, 271.
Rossini, Gioachino Antonio, operas of, 277; his abilities, 277; his methods, 277; his improvements, 278; popularity of his operas, 279; his style, 279, 280, 281.
Rousseau, 310.

Rubinstein, 114.
Ruckers, Andreas, the harpsichord builder, 92.
Ruckers, Hans, the harpsichord builder, 92.
Ruckert, 349.
"Rules of the Minnesingers," Cersne's, 87.
Ruta, Girolamo di, 105.

Sablières, the Sieur de, 300.
Sacchini, 221, 275.
St. Bartholomew, the massacre of, 45.
St. Étienne, 333.
"St. Franciscus," Tinel's, 233.
St. Gall, the convent of, 9, 10.
St. Gregory's Cathedral, 62.
St. John Lateran, the Church of, 49.
St. John's College, 63.
St. Mark's, at Venice, 45, 46, 263.
St. Martin's, the Cathedral of, 40.
St. Matthew Passion, Bach's, 212; resurrected by Mendelssohn, 221, 227; 233.
St. Michael Royal, the Church of, 63.
"St. Paul," Mendelssohn's, 213.
St. Peter's, Rome, 75.
Saint-Säens, Camille, operas of, 332; influence of Meyerbeer upon, 333.
"Sakuntala" overture, Goldmark's, 179.
"Salammbô," Reyer's, 334.
Salmon, 291.
Salo, Gasparo di, the first violin maker, 149.
Salzburg, 139.
"Samson," Handel's, 213, 223.
"Samson et Dalila," Saint-Säens', 332, 333.
Sängerkrieg, the great, 58.
Sante, Giovanni Pierluigi. See *Palestrina*.
"Sapho," Gounod's, 329.
"Saul," Handel's, 153, 207.
Scale, the Æolian, 6.
Scale, the Doric, 5.
Scale, the Lydian, 5, 6.
Scale, the Phrygian, 5.
Scale playing, 108.
Scales, ecclesiastical, 235, 243, 261.
Scales, the Greek, 4, 5, 6.
Scales, the Gregorian, 47.
Scales, modern, 6.
Scales, modern major, 4.
Scales, the old church, disappearance of, 214.
Scaliger, 90, 91.
Scarlatti, Alessandro, operatic works of, 107; his use of the string quartet, 151; his "Sinfonia avanti l' Opera," 159; his concertos, 160; his oratorios, 205; his treatment of the aria, 206; his career, 265; the founder of the Neapolitan school, 265; his operas, 265; characteristics of his writing, 265, 266; his improvements in Italian opera, 265-269; his development of the *aria da capo*, 269, 270; 280.
Scarlatti, Domenico, 92, 106; his harpsichord style, 107; 120, 127; sonatas of, 130, 131.
Scherzo, the, 144, 145.
Schiller, 349.
Schink, on "Don Juan," 345, 346.
Schröter, Christopher G., the claims of, 93.
Schubert, Franz, symphonic writing of, 179, 180; orchestra of, 154; chamber music of, 196; 348; his "Erl-König," 389.
Schulz, Christopher, 209.
Schumann, Robert, 113; his original style, 114; his music, 114; orchestra of, 154; 185; his symphonies, 179, 180; chamber music of, 196; 325, 346, 382, 387, 388.
Schütz, Heinrich, the "Seven Last Words" of, 209; his settings of the Passion, 210; writes the first German opera, 336, 337; his "Orpheus," 337.
Sculpture, Greek, 69.
"Seasons, The," Haydn's, 167, 213, 225.
"Seasons, The," Thompson's, 225.
Sebastiani, Giovanni, passion music of, 211.
Second viola, the, 187.
Second violin, the, 151, 155, 162, 186, 187.
Second violoncello, the, 187.
"Semiramide," Rossini's, 277, 278.
Senesino, the singer, 271.
Septets, 186, 193.
Sequence, the, origin of, 8, 9.
"Seraglio, Il," Mozart's, 341.
"Seven Last Words of Christ," Schütz's, 209, 336.
Sextets, 186, 193, 197.
Shedlock, J. S., on "The Piano Sonata," 133.
"Shepherds, The," 201.
Shepherd's pipe, the, 154.
"Siegfried," Wagner's, 358, 370, 372.
"Sigurd," Reyer's, 334.
Silbermann, Gottfried, the claims of, 93, 94; 95.
Simicon, the, 90.
Simius, 90.

INDEX

Simon, Leonard Fitz, the first salaried organist, 63.
Sinay, Belgium, 232.
Sinchard, Henri, 300.
"Sinfonia," the term, 158, 159.
"Sinfonia avanti l' Opera, 159; its development into overture, 159.
Singers, Roman, 9.
Singing, congregational, 67; revival of, 71.
Singing-schools, at Rome, 3, 4.
Singing style, the, advent of, 408.
"Singspiel," the German, 339, 350.
Sistine Chapel, the, at Rome, 43, 75.
Sixtus IV., 43.
Snare-drums, 155.
"Solomon's Judgment," Carissimi's, 204.
Solo singing, introduction of, 106; 121; 239, 340.
Sonata, the development of, 115; its difference from the polyphonic forms, 125; early scheme of, 130; C. P. E. Bach the father of, 132; general plan and purpose of the early, 135, 136; early experiments with, 141.
Sonata, the orchestral, 165.
Sonata form, the modern, 132, 135; Beethoven's improvements in, 142, 143, tending towards the monophonic style, 160; establishment of, 161, 171; 182, 183, 188, 190, 382.
Sonata method, the, 132.
"Sonata," meaning of, 103.
Sonatas, Beethoven's, 113, 138, 145; Bach's, 122; Corelli's, 128, 139; Scarlatti's, 130, 131; Haydn's, 137; Biber's, 139; Mozart's, 140; Clementi's, 142.
Sonatas, chamber, 188.
Sonatas, church, 188.
Sonatas, classic piano, 158.
Sonatas, piano, C. P. E. Bach's, 130, 161; Haydn's, 137; Mozart's, 140, 141; Beethoven's, 145, 146, 193.
Sonatas, violin, 129; Bach's, 131.
"Sonate da Camera," 188; Corelli's, 188.
"Sonate di Chiesa," 188.
Song-forms, 263.
Song-plays, German, 339, 340.
Songs, Roman kithara, 2; popular, 51; Roman lyre, 2; Mozart's, 140; negro, 181; secular, 39, 235.
"Songs Without Words," Mendelssohn's, 226.
"Sonnambula, La," Bellini's, 281.
Sophocles, the "Thamyris" of, 239.

Soprano, the, 270, 271, 273.
Sopranos, male. 271, 272, 273.
Sourdeac, the Marquis de, 300, 301.
Southwell, collegiate churches of, 63.
Spain, 44, 57.
"Spem in alium non habui," Tally's, 80.
Spinet, the Italian, 87, 88, 90, 91, 103.
Spinetti, Giovanni, 90, 91.
Spiritual songs, 2.
Spitta, Dr. Philip, "The Life of Bach," 120, 190.
Spohr, Ludwig, orchestra of, 154; his symphonic writing, 179, 180; chamber music of, 196; oratorios of, 225.
Spontini, Gasparo, operas of, 323.
Square pianos, the first, 94, 95.
Stabat Mater, 9.
Stage, the Italian lyric, dramatic truth restored to, 288.
Staff, the musical, 18, 19.
Steffani, 339.
Stein, Andrew, 95.
Stein, John Andrew, 95, 96.
Stein, Nanette, 95, 96.
Steinert, Mr. Morris, piano collection of, 87, 92.
Stephani, Clemens, passion music of, 209.
Stile parlante, the, 252, 264.
Stile rappresentativo, the, 252.
"Story of Music," Henderson's, 249.
Stradella, Alessandro, the orchestra of, 151; his instinct for choral effect, 205; 264.
"Stratonice," Méhul's, 322.
Streicher, Mrs. See *Stein, Nanette*.
Stretto, the, 119.
Strozzi, Pietro, 236.
"Studies in the Wagnerian Drama," Krehbiel's, 238.
"Suite," a, 128, 189.
Suites, Bach's, 122.
"Sumer is icumen in," 26, 28, 35, 80.
"Surprises d'Amour, Les," Rameau's, 309.
"Surrexit Christus," Gabrieli's, 79.
Susannah, the story of, 48.
Swelinck, Jans Peters, 40, 49, 189.
Sylvester, Pope, founds singing-schools at Rome, 3.
Symphonic band, the modern, 152.
Symphonic poem, the, 178; Liszt the inventor of, 181.
Symphonic writers, the, 179.
Symphonies, Haydn's, 137, 161, 163; C. P. E. Bach's, 161; Mozart's, 164; Schumann's, 179; Spohr's, 179; Schubert's, 180; Mendels-

sohn's, 180; Belioz's, 180; Tschaikowsky's, 181; Dvorak's, 182.
Symphonies, Beethoven's, 145; the highest types of absolute music, 172; the connecting link between the classic and the romantic schools, 176.
Symphonies, English, Haydn's, 137.
Symphony, the, Haydn the father of, 137; definition of, 158; characteristics of, 158; development of, 159, 160; influence of the overture upon, 161; establishment of, 162; its condition when Beethoven began writing, 167, 168.
Symphony, the classical, 161.
"Symphony Pathetique," Tschaikowsky's, 181.

Tallys, Thomas, the father of English cathedral music, 80; his works, 80.
"Tancred," Rossini's, 277.
"Tancredi e Clorinda," Monteverde's, 259, 262.
"Tannhäuser," Wagner's, 58, 154, 306, 358, 360.
Teatro San Cassiano, the, 262.
Technic, difference between piano and organ, 106.
Technics, Chopin, Schumann, and Liszt, 113.
Te Deum, the, 8.
Temperament, equal, 98-100, 107, 124.
"Templar and Jewess," Marschner's, 355.
Tenors, 17, 272, 273.
Tenor tubas, 155.
Tenor viols, 149.
"Teseo," Handel's, 273.
Tetrachord, the, 5.
"Thamyris," Sophocles, 239.
Théâtre Lyrique, the, at Paris, 329.
Theile, Johann, the "Adam and Eve" of, 338.
Theorbo, the, 149.
"Thesée," Lulli's, 302.
Thibaut, King of Navarre, 56, 63.
Thirty Years' War, the, 337.
Thomas School, the, in Leipsic, 121.
Thompson, "The Seasons" of, 225.
Thumb, the, use of, 109.
"Timbre d'Argent, Le," Saint-Saëns', 332.
Time, dual, 19.
Time, triple, 19, 20.
Tinel, Edgar, oratorio of, 232, 233.
"Toccata," the, 104.
Toccatas, organ, Bach's, 122.
Tone art, the, 346; development, 380.
Tone-color, development of, 112, 113.

Tone-coloring, instrumental, Mozart's experiments in, 167, 222.
Tone-painting, development of, 39.
"Total Blindness," Handel's, 213.
Touch, variety of, 113, 114.
Tournay, the mass of, 35.
Tournay Cathedral, the, 35.
Tours, 40.
Tragicomedia, 345.
Tragic writers, Greek, 238.
"Traité de l'Harmonie," Rameau's, 100, 308.
"Tragos ode," the, 200.
Trapini, Sicily, 265.
"Traviata, La," Verdi's, 278, 281.
Tremolo, the, invention of, 151.
Trent, the Council of, 72; orders a reform in church music, 72, 73.
"Tribut de Zamora, Le," Gounod's, 329.
Trinity College, Oxford, 63.
Trios, 139, 168, 186, 191, 193, 196, 197.
"Tristam and Isolde," Wagner's, 154, 358.
"Triumph of Apollo, The," 236.
Trombones, 148, 149, 153, 155, 156, 164, 193.
Troubadours, the, 55, 56; songs of, 57; 62, 240, 292.
"Trovatore, Il," Verdi's, 281, 282.
Trumpets, 149, 153, 155, 156, 162, 164.
Turkey, the Christian scholars of, 67.
Turks, the, 67.
"Tutti" passages, 151.
Tschaikowsky, Peter Ilitisch, symphonies of, 181; his "Symphony Pathetique," 181; his "Hamlet" overture, 179; his symphonic writing, 179; 382.
Tschudi and Kirkman, the harpsichord builders, 92.
Tympani, 153, 155.

Upright piano, the, 98.

"Vampire, The," 355.
Vatican, the, at Rome, 75.
Vaudemont, Mlle. de, 291.
Venetians, the, 104.
Venetian school, the, 77, 78.
Venice, 45, 50, 71; school of Catholic composition at, 77; the home of opera, 253; 259, 263, 344, 357.
Veni Sancte Spiritus, 9.
Verdi, Giuseppe, 277; his "La Traviata," 278; his operas, 281, 282; his three styles, 282; accused of imitating Wagner, 284; his work in "Falstaff," 285, 287; his develop-

INDEX

ment of the arioso style, 287, 288; 331, 332, 378, 390.
Vernio, Count of, 236, 237, 238, 240, 243, 244.
Veron, Eugene, on rhythm, 384.
"Vestale, La," Spontini's, 323.
Victimæ Paschali, 9.
Vienna, 95, 136, 140, 143, 337, 339, 340, 344.
Viols, 147.
Violas di gamba, 148, 149, 150, 151, 153, 162, 186, 187, 189.
Violin, the, 83; its rapid development as a solo instrument, 127; 148, 149; assumes its proper place in the orchestra, 150; 153, 154, 155, 162, 168, 187, 188, 189, 190, 193, 250.
Violins, French, 149.
Violoncellos, 148, 153, 154, 162, 186, 187, 188-193.
"Violons du Roi, Les," 301.
Vincennes, 295.
Vinci, Leonardo da, 69.
Virginal, the, 87, 91.
Vitellozzi, Cardinal, 72.
Vittoria, Tommaso Ludovico da, 77; his works, 77, 78.
Vivaldi, 131.
Vogelweide, Walther von der, 58.
Vogler, 324.
Volkslieder, the old, 59; essential features of, 60.
Voltaire, 310.
Vulgate, the Latin, 68.
Vulpius, Melchior, 209.

Wagner, Richard, music of, 47, 58, 59, 63, 78; 137, 154; orchestra of, 154; 155; 260, 266; his "Lohengrin," 267-269, 329; his "Rienzi," 281, 358; 284, 285; his "Tannhäuser," 306; 314, 320, 325, 331, 332, 333, 334, 335, 342; "Die Meistersinger," 343; 347; Weber the artistic forerunner of, 350, 351; his debt to Weber, 352; on Beethoven's "Fidelio," 353, 354; his enormous influence on German opera, 355, 356; the greatness of his genius, 357; his operas, 358; his system, 358; his theories compared with Peri's, 359; his use of the myth as a subject, 361-363; abandons the old style and creates a new, 361, 362, 364; his *leit motiv*, 364, 365; his motives, 366-368; his works self-explanatory, 371; his recitative, 372; importance of his work, 379; 388.

Waits, the, 62.
"Walküre, Die," Wagner's, 154, 358, 369.
"Walther, Jonathan, passion music of, 209.
"Walther von Stolzing," 59.
Waltz, the, 20.
Wartburg Castle, 58.
Weber, Carl Maria von, 111; his music, 113; his orchestra, 154; "Der Freischütz" of, 342; 349; 346, 347, 348; his influence upon German opera, 348, 349; operas of, 349; the artistic forerunner of Wagner, 350, 351; his definition of opera, 351; his theory of the lyric drama, 351; his genius, 352; his overtures, 353; 355, 356, 378, 389.
Weidenwang, 313.
Weimar, 121, 132; the ducal court of, 189; music at, 189.
Wekerlin, J. B., 296.
Wells Cathedral, 62.
"Well - Tempered Clavichord," Bach's, 100, 122, 139.
"Werther," Massenet's, 333.
Westminster Cathedral, 63.
"What is Good Music?" Henderson's, 383.
Whittington, Dick, 63.
Willaert, Adrian, 39, 45; his work, 46; his monets, 48; 50, 71, 77, 79, 103; his church vocal music, 104, 387.
William of Machaut, 34.
"William Tell." See *Guillaume Tell*.
William the Conqueror, 62.
"Willow" song, Verdi's, 283.
Wind instruments, 151, 153, 155, 162, 166, 193.
Wooden wind instruments, 153, 154, 155, 156, 162, 187.
Worship, Italian system of, 68, 69.
Writers, church, 386.
Würzburg, 10.

Yorkshire, 63.

Zachau of Halle, 206.
Zarlino, 240.
"Zauberflöte, Die," Mozart's, 340, 342, 348.
Zeelandia, H. de, "Lehrcompendium" of, 60.
Zither, the, 85.
"Zoroastre," Rameau's, 309.
Zumpe, Johannes, 95.

www.ingramcontent.com/pod-product-compliance
Lightning Source LLC
Chambersburg PA
CBHW032143010526
44111CB00035B/985